From Beginning to End and Back Again

A Mother's Story about the So-called Death of Her Son

Written by Judith J. Miller

Inspired by "Jay"

Copyright © 2014 Judith Miller
All rights reserved
First Edition

PAGE PUBLISHING, INC.
New York, NY

First originally published by Page Publishing, Inc. 2014

ISBN 978-1-62838-691-2 (pbk)
ISBN 978-1-62838-692-9 (digital)

Printed in the United States of America

Chapter One

Saturday, April 2, 1994, Easter weekend

The weather was good. Conditions were just right for a great day out in the ocean, on the boat, deep-sea fishing. On days like this, we start early. Taking some drinks, sandwiches and two or three people who want to try their hand at some bottom fishing. If everything goes well, they can perhaps pull in a few big grouper; then later they have something to brag about to friends.

On this particular day, Tony (my husband) and I had taken three people out. Mr. Hanemann, a German man; Paul, a real estate agent, both whom we had recently become acquainted with; and Buck, a man employed by my husband's company.

We normally go twenty-five to thirty miles offshore, and then my husband starts looking for ledges on the radar. These underwater rock formations are where Tony always seems to sense big grouper just lying around waiting for a hook and line to drop in front of them.

Everything was going smoothly. The waters were calm and nobody was seasick. With just a few instructions, Mr. Hanemann, Paul, and Buck were reeling in some monstrous-sized grouper. I was even catching a few of these monsters myself, and we jokingly compared the size of each other's catch. (I still think I had the biggest one by the way.)

I normally carry my camera along and take a few comical shots of each angler pulling in the "big one" as they try to remain standing in a rocking boat. When I get some good shots, I give copies to our guests as proof of their catch.

At 12:30 p.m. I glanced at my watch. It looked as if I had some moisture inside, just under the crystal. I immediately put down my pole and went inside the cabin to take the watch off.

This is a special watch, which I did not want to ruin. My son, Jay, and his wife, Christine, gave me this watch about three months earlier as a Christmas gift. They always remembered my attraction and fascination for little hummingbirds when choosing a gift for me. When they found this watch—with a 10-cent Bahamian Hummingbird postage stamp on the face—they knew they were giving me a gift I will always cherish.

I cleaned and polished the watch carefully, looking at the time, thinking to myself, "I should have taken it off before I even picked up a pole." I wrapped it carefully in a towel and put it up, then went back out to fish. I seemed unable to enjoy the fishing as before. All I could think about was the possibility that I may have ruined my watch.

I went back inside, picked up the watch, and to my amazement the moisture was now gone. I thought maybe the face of it had just been smudged with saltwater, but I distinctly remembered the moisture had formed on the underneath side of the crystal, inside the watch. I thought, "Oh well, I don't understand this, but at least it's all right."

As I stood there puzzled over my watch, Paul came in for a sandwich and saw me studying it. I told him what had happened and my reason for being so fond of this watch.

As he ate his sandwich, we talked about my son and daughter-in-law. I told him how they had come to meet in the Bahamas, and that they were married there August 8, 1992. I described how they are living this beautiful, peaceful life together on a little island in the Bahamas. A life that most people say sounds like a fairy tale.

When Paul finished his sandwich, we joined the others to catch more of those patiently awaiting grouper. It seemed like we caught them so fast. One after the other. Before we knew it, we had our limit and it was already time to head back to shore.

I really enjoyed the rest of the afternoon fishing. A deep calm feeling seemed to come over me. The trip back to shore was even more enjoyable than usual. The calmness I felt within myself was incomparable to other calm feelings I had ever experienced.

I thought to myself how nice it would be to just do nothing else but live a life fishing and boating. I daydreamed about going to the Bahamas on the boat; maybe stay there for a few weeks while spending time with Jay and Christine. I envisioned how nice it would be to have plenty of money; to sail to other islands, even take Jay and Christine along if they would like to go.

I even realized how nice it would be to not have to pay high tourist rates for a place to stay while there. How convenient it will be having our own little floating home on the water. If or when they have their first child, my very own grandchild, I could be there near them, maybe even get to baby-sit for them.

Just the past July (1993), Jay told me if they decided to bring a child into this world, they would probably wait another five years. He said that would give them time to spend with each other first, to do some of the things they want to do together. Just the two of them.

When we arrived back at the dock, we cleaned the boat and the fish that each of our guests decided to keep. (Tony usually sells any excess fish to the fish house, which helps cover the fuel expense.) We sent Mr. Hanemann, Paul, and Buck off each with their bag of fish, some memories of a great day on the Atlantic Ocean catching some of the biggest grouper they had ever seen.

Tony asked if I would like to fix something for supper or if I would prefer to go out to eat. Cooking is not one of my favorite pastimes, so I'm sure you know what my answer was.

We went on over to the Steakhouse, with plans to go home and rest for the night. As we ate, we talked about the day. I told Tony how I had felt so peaceful and calm during the afternoon, and about some of my thoughts and dreams.

He started to tell me about a man we know, who owns the property where the fish house is. He once had told Tony of an experience he had while out fishing one night quite some time ago. It seems he saw something come up out of the water, fly up into the sky and just disappear. It frightened the man so much that he has never been out again.

This was a fascinating story to me. I have always been intrigued with strange, unusual things like this. I have even had a few strange things happen to me, which triggered my interest in this story and others like it even more.

We talked about this subject for a few minutes, and I mentioned that I would like to talk to this man about it. We even talked about taking the boat out sometime and anchor someplace for the night. Tony said it's pitch black out there; but I told him that would be fun, and I'd like to do it anyway.

We finished supper and headed home. After our showers, we settled down on the bed to watch some television before going to sleep. It was not long before Tony had difficulty keeping his eyes open. He got comfortable, said "good night," and was out like a light.

I decided to take advantage of this opportunity to watch what I wanted on TV. I found a movie and was watching it, but what I heard and saw seemed to go right over my head—nothing would register. It was as if I was just staring at the set, in a daze. I went out on the porch for a while then came back to try it again, only to have the same problem concentrating on the program.

Finally, I gave up and decided it was simply nice to be relaxed and have some quiet time to myself. That's when the phone rang.

Chapter Two

Tony answered the phone. I listened to pieces of the conversation. I could tell he was talking to Christine. "Here is Judy. I'll put her on so you can talk to her," I heard him say.

I answered the call thinking, "I wonder why Christine is calling and not Jay?"

"Hello," I said.

I heard Christine's voice somberly say, "Judy, it's Christine."

"Hi, how are you?" I asked.

"Judy, I'm afraid I have some really bad news to give you," she said, beginning to cry almost hysterically.

The worst thing I could imagine was she was calling to tell me that she and Jay had a fight or something like that. Maybe they were even breaking up.

When Christine seemed to have her emotions a little more in control, I asked, "What is wrong?"

She replied, "Oh, Judy, I do not know how to tell you this."

I braced myself and bravely demanded, "Christine, tell me straight out. What is it?"

Then came the news that would change my life from this day forward. News so painful that simply the slightest thought of it sends an unbearable pain to the deepest level of my parental heart.

Christine began to tell me about Jay leaving earlier in the day to take a married couple, their two sons, and a friend of their younger son, diving. They had gone to the blue holes at Robinson's Creek. She continued to explain to me that all but one of them, the oldest son, had gone down on the dive.

Christine was told that the boy's mother began to have a problem clearing her ears, so the father brought her up. Jay and the two others continued to go down. After the mother was in the boat, the father started down to have the other three come back up. Apparently he did not have a diving light, and was unable to go down past the level where the surface light was cut off. He saw the lights below and the three beginning to enter one of the caverns but was unsuccessful when attempting to motion for them to come back up.

The father resurfaced and he, his wife, and oldest son waited for the other three to come back up. After so much time had gone by and there was no sign of the others, the man and his wife left the oldest son to watch for the three, and they left in the boat to go summon help.

At this point, Christine began to cry again. I was still trying to stay as calm as I possibly could. I was not yet sure of what she was trying to tell me. Were the boys lost? Could they have come out somewhere else? Maybe they were down there in a pocket of air, waiting to be rescued! When did this happen? Thoughts were running rampant through my mind.

I began to ask some of these questions that were coming to my mind: "What time did they go diving?"

"They left in mid morning, so they probably got down there around 11:30 to dive," Christine said.

Still trying to put the pieces together, I asked, "How much air did they have in their tanks?"

"Probably only enough to last about an hour." Then Christine quietly said, "Oh, Judy, he is gone. Jay is gone! I'm so sorry." She was again crying desperately.

"Whatever has happened Christine, it's not your fault," I assured her.

"He's gone. I know he's gone. I should have told him not to go. I shouldn't have let him go. When he left, he seemed so happy. He came back to give me a kiss and tell me he loves me," she continued.

"Oh, Christine, it's not your fault. It is not your fault," I said trying to comfort her some. "Christine, I'll be there. I'll get the first flight I can get, and I'll be there. I'll call you back and let you know when I'm coming in, but I'll get there, soon as possible."

She said, "We'll wait here for your call."

By this time, my understanding of what she was telling me was that Jay is dead. It felt as if an invisible hand punched through my chest and grabbed my heart, then began to rip and tear it from my body.

Up to this point, I had still been sitting up in the bed before I gave the receiver to Tony to hang up. Now shocked with the realization of what was obviously happening, and the same penetrating into my mind and the recesses of my heart, I doubled over forward in the bed and began to sob relentlessly.

Tony did not know what to make of the conversation. He felt me grip his hand tighter and tighter as the conversation with Christine went on. He began asking, "What is it? What is the matter, Judy? What is it? Honey, what is wrong? What happened?"

I tried to get the breath and composure enough to tell him. Through fits of crying and trying to talk, all I could say was "Jay is lost. He and two other people had gone diving, and they didn't come back up. Divers could not go back in to look for them because the tide was going out, and Christine says he is gone."

"I've got to go, Tony. I've got to get down there. Divers are going down to look for them at high tide tomorrow, and I have to be there. We've just got to find him. I just have to be there to find my son."

Very determined, yet stunned, I jumped out of the bed and started walking around voicing everything I needed to do to get ready to leave. "I need to call Chuck. I have to tell him I won't be at work. I need to call my brother, Alan, my mother and step dad. We've got to call the airport. I've got to pack some things. How much should I pack?"

Speaking to Jay, I was saying, "Jay, do not be afraid. Ask God to help you. I love you. Look for the light. If you are dead Jay, look for the light. Do not be afraid of the light. Go toward the light."

Speaking to myself, I said, "I cannot believe he could be dead. I've got to have faith that he is all right. I've got to trust that God is taking care of him. He's OK. He has to be OK."

Speaking to God I said, "Oh, please, God, take care of Jay. Let him be all right. Please, God, please let him be all right. I'm sorry. I don't mean to tell you what to do. Please help Christine and me. Not my will God, but your will be done."

Then I decided to call my boss, Chuck. "Tony, I've got to call Chuck." I was crying now. "Oh, what do I tell Chuck? How can I tell Chuck?"

As I got over to the phone by the bed, I sat on the floor. I dialed the number, and as it rang, I was thinking, "How am I going to tell everyone what has happened, what am I going to say?" There was no answer at Chuck's house, so I left a message, asking him to call me soon. Then, remembering he had a pager, I dialed that number and entered my number for him to call.

It was not long before he called me back, and I told him the best I could about what was happening. Chuck—always being such a compassionate person—told me not to worry about anything. He said to go ahead and do what I have to do and take as much time as I need.

Next, I called my brother's house. My nephew Blain answered the phone. He said my brother, Alan, and my sister-in-law, Judi, had gone to a movie. I told Blain that something very urgent had come up, and I needed to talk to Alan soon as possible. Blain said he would call the theater and have Alan paged for me.

Again, I start wandering around the house, trying to get my mind together enough to start getting things together. Tony got on the phone with the airlines, making arrangements to get us on the first available flight to the Bahamas.

The reservations were now made. We would leave in the morning at 7:30 a.m. and arrive in Marsh Harbour at 12:30 p.m. I would have left at that very second if only there was a way.

Tony suggested that I needed to go ahead and call my mother. I really found this hard to do because Mother had been struggling with colon cancer for over a year now. I knew this was going to be very hard for her.

I kept thinking of Christmas only three months before. I gave Jay and Christine airline tickets to Kansas so we could all meet there and spent the holiday together. The first Christmas together since we had moved away, and quite possibly the last time we would have together with Mother. Now, could this be? Could it be that this would turn out to be the last Christmas we would ever have been able to spend with Jay?

While I made the call, Tony said he would go over to his mom and sister's house to see if they had any cash. At least enough until we could get to a bank and get some. He left me to pack, wait for Alan's call, and call Mother.

Again, I picked up the phone to make the call. She answered.

"Mother, I have something I have to tell you that is going to be very difficult." Then the best way I could, I explained the situation and what we were planning to do. I told her that I had called for Alan and was waiting for him to call back. I told her that we would stay in touch with them and let them know something as soon as we could find anything out once we arrived in the Bahamas. Same as for me, the real impact came to Mother after we had hung up.

Alan called and was aware that I would not have him called out of a movie unless something serious had happened. Naturally, under the circumstances, he was thinking maybe something had happened to Mother. I told him the heart-breaking news and heard silence for a moment, and then he said, "Oh no, oh, Judy, I'm sorry. Is there anything I can do? Should I get tickets for us to come down?"

I told him of our arrangements and that I did not know that there was anything anyone could do now but pray. He said they would be doing that and told me to call and let them know when we have arrived in Marsh Harbour. I explained that I had called Mother and that she would need some support.

When Tony got back home, I told him that I had spoken to both Mother and Alan. He suggested that we needed to get to bed and get some sleep. I said I was still trying to get things packed and ready to go, and I wasn't sure I could sleep. I was still in such a daze that it was difficult for me to finish one thing before wandering off to start on something else.

Finally, I thought I had it all together and ready. I crawled in bed, and Tony held me close. The phone rang just as we were about relaxed. It was my close friend Cheryl. Chuck had called her to let her know what was happening, and she called to see if I needed someone to talk to. I said that Tony wanted me to get some sleep, and I thought I would be all right for now. I told her I would stay in touch and let everyone know what was happening.

Just as I was beginning to drift off to sleep, I felt as if someone touched the end of the bed, close by my feet. I kept my eyes closed. Even as the thought of it being Jay entered my mind, I kept telling myself, "It can't be true that he is gone. He can't be. I must have faith that he is still alive and all right."

Chapter Three

*I*n the short night I drifted in and out of sleep. Each time I woke up, I would think it was not real but only a dream. Then I would realize it wasn't a dream but indeed something terrible that was actually happening. Each time the same pain would grip me and tear at my heart.

Soon after we went to bed it seemed it was time to get up, yet in another way, it seemed not soon enough. I wanted to be there now. I felt so helpless knowing that we had a long flight ahead of us and couldn't do anything until we got there.

I continued trying to figure out what could have happened and what I could do after arriving in the Bahamas to try to find my son. The thoughts continued to pour through my mind. One right after the other.

We left for the airport early enough to check in and pay for the tickets. "Thank God I remembered at the last minute before going to bed to get Tony's birth certificate. Someone must be guiding me through this, so far," I thought. "They probably wouldn't have let us on the plane without it."

Finally, we were on our way. We had to change planes in Charlotte and again in Fort Lauderdale. Then we would arrive in Marsh Harbour, and Christine and her parents would meet us at the airport and take us over to Hope Town by boat.

On the flight to Fort Lauderdale, I was resting and thinking things out. Suddenly I had a perfect picture in my mind of very peaceful, still, crystal clear water. On the floor, beneath the water in the vision, were tiny little coral colored pebbles. Above the water was a space of air, separating the water from a rock ceiling.

From this vision I felt calmness, very much like the calmness I had felt the day before on the boat. Then a sense of well-being came over me. It was as if Jay was trying to let me know he was all right. Similar to the gentle touch at the end of the bed I had felt and tried to ignore in the night.

I was hoping and wanting to believe that this was telling me Jay was safe. That he was able to find a place down there in the blue hole where there was an air pocket. That he would be waiting to be rescued.

We arrived in Fort Lauderdale, and we had just enough time to go to the rest room and sit briefly before it was time to board the plane for Marsh Harbour.

Again, in the air, I was trying to calm myself and remain as relaxed as possible. I had to fill out the forms for going through customs. Doing anything of that nature seemed like a difficult challenge for me. My brain didn't want to cooperate and give me the information I needed to write on the form. Tony helped me out with his birthday and a few things that I wasn't able to remember.

Finally, we arrived. I felt like I was there to accomplish a very long, hard mission with no time to waste. I reminded myself that everything would work out the way it is meant to work out—for the best. I also decided that no matter what, I would not give up on finding my son, Jay. I was determined to keep my faith and believe that he would be found, and hopefully he would be found alive.

As we entered the terminal and waited our turn to go through customs, I was trying to remember the name of Christine's aunt. It was her cottage where we would be staying. I knew they would ask for the name of where we would be staying and how long we would be staying.

When the customs officer asked, I was blank and sort of stammered and search for some words to say. Tony told the man that we were there to look for my son who has been missing since yesterday in a diving accident. "Yes, I heard about that. I'm sorry," came the reply from the officer. "Please, go on through."

As we got out the door, Terry and Margaret Rose, Christine's parents, were waiting for us. They said Christine was at the car, too upset to come up to the door with them. Margaret Rose began crying and saying how sorry they are that this has happened.

We walked over to the car. Tony and Terry began to load the luggage in the trunk. I put my arms around Christine, and she sobbed and kept saying over and over how sorry she was that she let Jay go off and that this had happened.

In my mind I thought, "It sounds as if everyone has given up hope of finding Jay. Doesn't anyone believe that miracles happen?"

I began asking questions. I had so many questions in my mind about the whole situation. I didn't even understand fully what a blue hole was.

Next, I wanted to know about the other parents. Where were they? And what did they say about what had happened? Christine and her mother said the parents had been there at the airport, but they were leaving as we came in.

"They're what?" I said surprised, "Leaving? The boys haven't been found yet, what do you mean they are leaving? Why?"

Margaret Rose said that she was told that the mother had to be put on tranquilizers and the father had locked himself up in a room away from her and the oldest son. Then they must have just decided to go on back to Virginia to start making funeral arrangements for their son. Perhaps even see the parents of the other boy and tell them what had happened. They seemed a little confused about what was really going on.

"I can't believe they could leave and not wait to hear about their son being found." I repeated again and again to myself and to everyone else. "Why? How could they leave before finding their son?"

Chapter Four

*I*t was a short distance from the airport to the house of another one of Christine's aunts. This was where we would rest for a while and wait for Jay's father, who was to be arriving on a later flight. After he would be picked up, then we would all cross over to Hope Town together.

We were waiting for some news from the Bahamian diving team. Information that was given to Christine and her parents earlier indicated that they should have been able to dive in the blue hole by the time we arrived, searching for Jay and the other two young men, putting an end to this mystery of what happened to them. My mind was set on the continued hope that they were still alive and waiting someplace to be rescued.

The VHF radio was the only connection between the diving team and us. We waited, and finally word came that the other two boys had been found. They were still together in one area of the cavern. Both dead! Jay was not found, and the divers reported that they could not stay down any longer to look for him.

In my mind I was thinking, "Where are you, Jay? Are you someplace waiting to be rescued? Did you find another way out, and are you just waiting for us to find you? We'll find you, son. Don't give up. We'll find you!"

I thought again about the other parents. I felt sad for them now knowing that their sons were found dead. They must have known there was no more hope of finding their son alive. Otherwise, they wouldn't have left the way they did.

I was feeling sad for them, yet I was still confused by their actions. Why didn't they make an effort to talk with us about what had happened. At least, why didn't they tell me about my son and what took place before he was lost. I wondered what he said during the day, and what kind of mood he was in. Was he happy? Did he say anything that could have indicated there was a problem of any kind? What was he like when they saw him last? Questions ran rampant in my mind, and I wanted to have some kind of an understanding of what caused all this.

Terry took us to the boat, and we waited there for him while he went to the airport and pick up Dave. When they arrived, we took off for Hope Town, about thirty minutes away.

Everyone on the boat seemed to be silently thinking of the situation at hand. Each viewing it in their own way. All seemed to be in quiet meditation.

I was thinking how beautiful the water is. The understanding of the love that Jay had acquired for it came to mind. The water is crystal clear, as blue as the sky, even turquoise in places. Just like a giant swimming pool, so clear and magnifying. Starfish on the bottom seem as if they are just below the surface.

Midway to Hope Town, glancing toward the south where the blue hole is located, I thought of my son. All alone there, in the solitude of the area. I felt so helpless. More helpless than I had ever felt in my entire life.

Thoughts of how I could find him ran through my mind. Thoughts of others finding him came as well. Even the thought of him swimming through a long tunnel that connects with the ocean, releasing him on the other side, came into focus in my mind. "He's out there somewhere, and I will find him," I thought.

As we came into the harbor at Hope Town, I glanced in the direction of the little cottage where Jay and Christine have been living. This cottage is one that has been in Christine's family for many years. It's small cozy atmosphere fit the personality that Jay and Christine had developed in their time together. The cottage has weathered many storms.

Its construction is of wood, nailed together from the foundation up, and as solid as any other on the island. Screened windows allow cool breeze to rush through, and wooden shutters seal off the fiercest winds when they blow.

We tied up at the public dock. Quietly but enthusiastically, we unloaded baggage and set off to settle in for the uneasy time ahead, not knowing how long or how short the period would be before Jay could be found.

Tony and I were shown to a cottage next door to Jay and Christine's, owned by Christine's aunt Olive. We would be staying there for the length of time we need to. Dave was taken to the Myerses' home.

Michael and Patte Myers are dear friends of Jay and Christine. It was in the beautiful garden at their house where Jay and Christine were married.

This home would become the meeting place for all of us to gather and hope to receive news of Jay's whereabouts. It became the place to make plans on what to do next. To laugh to cry, to talk about Jay and the many memories we would have of him. It also would become the place where many friends and residents of Hope Town would feed us and care for us, as if we were all a part of their big family.

Chapter Five

As we got settled in to what would be our home for the next several days, we waited for word from the local divers. These courageous men had been out diving, risking their own lives to find and rescue Jay and the other two boys.

We knew that it would be a while before we would hear from them. Since they had located the two boys earlier, they would have to take them by boat to Marsh Harbour. The Bahamian law officials that had been on the rescue with the divers would then take the bodies of the two divers to the airport to be flown to Nassau for autopsies. Later, they would be flown back to the States for funeral services.

Oh, how I continued to hope that my son would not be found this way. I wanted to believe that he would be found alive but maybe shaken. Perhaps cold from being in the water and hungry from being out this long. But he would be alive.

This is what I wanted to believe. Yet, in the back of my mind and in my heart, I knew that whatever would be the result of our search, things would work out the way they are meant to. Hoping for the best was the best I could do at the time. Waiting peacefully and patiently for the answers to come were challenges of great magnitude.

Finally, we got word that the Bahamian divers were in for the day. What came next was that they would not be able to dive the next day to look for Jay. They could not go back down in the blue hole. The dive earlier in the day was all they could handle; it would be too dangerous for them to go back down again.

Immediately, my mind filled with questions. "What could we do to find Jay ourselves? Who could we turn to, to help us? What is this blue hole like anyway? Couldn't there still be something that someone has missed, some way that Jay could have gotten out of there? Maybe they just missed him. If he wasn't there with the other two, then where is he?" I needed some answers.

I wanted to hear it from someone who had actually been in the blue hole. I wanted to know for certain that the other stories I had been hearing were either true or false. A firsthand account of this mysterious underwater deathtrap was all I was willing to take as truth at this time.

I heard that grouper large enough to swallow a man had been seen in blue holes. I was also told that in some places there are several tunnels leading to dead ends, and in other places leading all the way out into the ocean.

Answers, I needed answers. If I could not understand it, how could I come up with any answers, any resolution to the dilemma we were in?

I asked if we could talk to the divers. So a meeting was set up with Dave, owner of Island Marine and one of the three rescue divers. The time for the meeting was set for 10 a.m. the next morning.

Dave would be the only one that felt as if he could talk to us. The other two divers were so upset over the situation that they did not feel they would be able to handle a face-to-face discussion with us about this dreadful ordeal.

They each knew Jay, and it would have been even more difficult for them had they found Jay's body with the others. What they all had been through already, on this Easter Sunday, will linger in their minds for years to come. It was not an easy day for any one of them, by any means. I understood this, and I felt very grateful to them for their efforts.

Now all we could do is wait. Hopefully, other Bahamian divers could be located and could go down at the next high tide. At least that would be the plan for now. We would be notified if anyone could be located.

In between everything else, phones were kept busy contacting family and friends in the States. Each person knowing Jay, Christine, or any of the family members were anxiously awaiting news of some kind. They too were going through preparations for whatever help was needed, depending on what the results would be.

Already, newspaper reporters were calling people on the Island, asking questions and looking for any news they could report on the accident. This put some local people in a very awkward position, especially since many of us were nearby when they would call. All of these wonderful people in the area were emotionally tied to the situation in one way or another. Practically everyone in Hope Town had become acquainted with Jay, many of whom loved him as a good friend.

As we were all tired from such a long day, we headed for our respective homes. Christine and her family were all together at that quaint little love nest that she and Jay have been sharing together. Tony and I now settled into the cottage next door; and Dave, who now had warmed up to the Myerses, was comfortable with his arrangements.

Tony wanted me to be in bed with him. So I prepared for bed and crawled in next to him. He held me close as if he was afraid to let me go. I didn't know for sure if it was for his comfort or for mine that he was holding me so tight. I felt tired and knew I needed rest, so I began to relax myself for sleep. However, as I relaxed and began to drift, I saw something in my mind, something that would bring me to complete wakefulness again.

Just before sleep came, I saw Jay's face. He was looking at me, from behind my closed eyes, with his usual grin on his face. At first, I didn't recognize what was happening, I just continued to drift. Then in my mind I heard, "She's slowly going crazy," and then came the words "flat on the bottom." That was it. Now I snapped back wide awake and knew I could no longer remain in that bed.

I felt certain that Tony was asleep. But the moment I began to move, he tightened his hold on me and asked me not to get up and go out of the bedroom. I said, "I have to! I need to sit up for a while. I'll be all right." I told him as I went out into the living area, pulling the door partway closed behind me.

I sat there in the cool night breeze coming through the open windows and began to cry for my son. As I sat and cried and prayed to God for protection of my son, I felt strength and composure again. I thought of what I had seen and heard in my mind and felt as if it were a message from Jay, somehow telling me that he is all right but concerned for a person he cares for.

Also, I reluctantly took the message about "flat on the bottom" as to be where we could find his body. This was not what I wanted to think of at the time, and I didn't want to think of it as a possibility, so I tried to ignore that I had even heard it.

I said, "I love you, Jay," and thanked God for his protection and guidance through this difficult time. Now I felt as if I could go to sleep.

Chapter Six

Morning came with the soft singing of the birds in the trees all around the cottage. It was as if they too were just awakening for the day. It was just before sunrise, and the light was barely becoming visible. It felt good to me, simply to be lying there listening to the birds. I only wished it was happening while we were there for a visit and not there for this reason. To find my only child, a handsome married grown man—now perhaps dead.

It all still seemed to be like a dream. Not at all real. Something that only could be happening to someone else or in a movie. I couldn't even wish it on anyone else because I couldn't think of anyone else I would ever want this to happen to.

I began to think of the upcoming morning meeting with the diver and all the questions I wanted to ask him, hoping that in getting some of the answers to my questions, I may find some solutions and methods of going about finding Jay.

Staying in bed any longer seemed useless to me. I wanted to get up and be ready. A cup of coffee sounded like a good idea, but where could I get one? I settled on a glass of water from the jug in the refrigerator. That would have to do for now, at least until Patte and Michael were up and around or until Tony and I could walk down to the Hope Town Harbour Lodge. I remembered they had good coffee when we last stayed there at the time of Jay and Christine's wedding.

Just as I got out of bed, Tony woke. He really was resting well, and I didn't want to wake him, but he woke up easily. I reassured him that I was doing fine, just wanted to get a shower and get myself around. With that he spread out on the bed to get a little more sleep.

The closer I came to being ready, the better the coffee sounded. I decided that a quick walk over to Patte and Michael's would perhaps result in that cup of fresh morning brew, maybe even some late news on other divers being located.

Everyone was quiet at the Myerses' house. Only the dog was up and about as I walked around the porch. The garden looked so pretty with all the beautiful tropical flowers in bloom. Some of the flowers didn't actually look as if they belonged on the plants they were blooming on. I discovered later that they didn't. It is one of Michael's daily routines to pick some flowers from one of the many flowering trees and attach them to non-blooming plants, spreading an even array of colorful blooms everywhere in the garden. "How clever to actually think and do something like this," I thought.

When I returned from my walk to the Myerses' house, Tony was about ready to get out. There was activity next door at Jay and Christine's, so I went to see if any of them would like to walk with us to the lodge. Terry, Margaret Rose, and Christine's sister, Anne, were all ready. So we all agreed we would have some breakfast and meet Christine at Patte and Michael's afterward.

The man across from Jay and Christine's cottage had an old dog. When the man would go to work, the dog would hang around the yard or go scouting around Hope Town.

On this particular day, he decided to escort us all the way down the path to the lodge. As we arrived at the steps leading up to the lodge, the dog continued along the path. We laughed as he went on, saying how that was the end of our escort. However, when we had finished having our breakfast and discussing the day ahead, we found him patiently waiting at the bottom of the steps to escort us back up the path to Patte and Michael's house.

Eventually, we were all together in the great room of the Myerses' home, nine of us coming together in hopes of reaching some kind of resolution to this mystery of Jay's condition and location.

I noticed Patte go out the door and soon returned with the diver, Dave Gayle.[1] She introduced him to us, offered him a cup of coffee and a bar stool at the head of our circle. A few casual words were exchanged in the attempt to get everyone comfortable with the topic ahead.

When Dave G. was ready to begin to tell us of the circumstances we were looking at, he began by explaining to us what the blue hole was like on their dive the day before.

"First, let me describe the blue hole to you," Dave G. began. "In this area where this blue hole is located, the water varies in depth. When it is high tide, the water over the entrance may be 10 feet deep. The timing for going in and out of the creek area where the blue hole is located is important because if the water is not deep enough, the boats are unable to get in. There are rock formations to pass through with the boats before even getting on back into the protected area where the blue hole is located.

"Once in the area where the blue hole is, someone needs to be watching for a falling tide so preparations to get back out can be made before the water becomes too shallow." After describing the area around the blue hole, Dave G. told us about the blue hole itself.

"The blue holes are holes that go down beneath the surface in the rock, in this case about seventy-five feet, before reaching a floor or a bottom. From the surface it looks like a dark circle in the water. All the water around the hole looks lighter in color. At the bottom or the floor, the blue hole widens out and divides into tunnels or caverns. It was just inside the first cavern that we were able to locate the two divers yesterday."

---

[1] Dave Gayle will be referred to as Dave G. while Jay's father will has been referred to as just Dave.

At this point I had to ask, "Is there any possibility that there may be air trapped someplace down there, and maybe Jay was able to find it and may be waiting to be rescued?"

"No, it is very unlikely, not the way the rock is. This type of rock is extremely porous. It has lots of holes and bubbles in it. Even the slightest bubble from one of the divers tanks, would work its way up through the rock and be gone in no time at all," Dave G. answered.

"Is there anyway that Jay may have found a tunnel leading out someplace else?" I asked.

"Well, anything is possible, but when a team went in to survey this blue hole several years ago, they were only able to go so far and they had to call the survey off. One of their divers got lost down there, and they never could find him" was Dave G.'s reply. "I guess it could still be a possibility."

"What about lines left by the survey team? Were the other two boys on the lines when you found them?" I proceeded.

"They were off the lines to the side. It looked like they may have been on them and got off somehow. Maybe they got turned around and didn't know which direction they were in," Dave G. concluded.

I proceeded to ask more questions that were already in my mind from before. "Will you be able to dive again to look for Jay when the tide is high?"

Regretfully Dave G. answered, "I'm sorry, but we can not go down again. Yesterday's dive was all one of the divers could take. One of the diver's became ill while down there. With even one diver out, the other two cannot go down. It takes a complete team to make a successful and safe dive. In this case especially, we need all three working together to accomplish this."

I asked, "Have any other divers been located?"

Then came the negative answer I hoped not to hear. "No complete team of divers has been located. With the Easter Holiday and other circumstances, we haven't been able to find anyone yet, not even in Nassau."

At this time, Christine spoke up. She had been sitting and listening with her head halfway down, looking toward the coffee table in front of her until now, "Well, my parents and I were talking about this last night, and since Jay's wish was to be buried at sea when he died, I think maybe we should just go ahead and leave him down there. Since that's where he wanted to be anyway."

As I sat listening to Christine talk, I had the thought that it could be the expense or even the strain of finding Jay that may be influencing her to come to this decision. I concluded that by leaving Jay down there, abiding to his wish, would qualify as an appropriate burial. But in the very heart of me, I knew this was not the thing to do. I had to risk going against the wishes of my son's wife. I knew I would have to speak up.

I quietly said, "I disagree. I'll give up everything I have, if I need to, but I have to find Jay. I can never rest or be at peace knowing he is out there somewhere. I could never go home and relax without thinking that he may be out there waiting somewhere, waiting for us to find him. What if someone else decides to go diving in that hole someday in the future, and they find him? We would all be back here together again, going through this same agony." I proceeded, "We can't leave him down there, we have to find a way or someone who can go down there and find him."

Jay's father spoke up at this time and asked the diver if that could happen, "Could another person diving just happen to find him?"

"Yes, that is a great possibility. If it were my decision, I would like to look for another diving team that can go in there and bring him out." he replied.

"I guess you're right," came Christine's approval. "But where can we find any other divers now? We haven't been able to find anyone else?"

"There has to be someone somewhere. I believe that they will be found if it is meant to be," I said.

The next step was to put a search out for qualified professional divers. Nothing less than a miracle would do at this point. The word was to go out that we needed to find these divers immediately, if not sooner.

Dave G. would be making some calls. Patte would talk to her brother in Florida, and others calls would be made from those calls, hopefully locating the divers that could find Jay.

After Dave G. left the Myerses' home, I expressed my desire to go to the blue hole. I asked if someone would take me along with anyone else desiring to go.

Michael said he would gladly take us in his boat if the weather was cooperative. He said he would get the weather report, and we would go when everything looks right. Then it was decided who wanted to go and who did not.

I was so happy that Christine had decided to go. I really felt that this was an important thing for us to do at this time. I knew it was for me. What I needed was to get a feeling of the area. Right at the exact spot where Jay was last seen.

It was decided that Michael would be taking Dave, Terry, Tony, Christine, and me. Patte picked some flowers for us to take to the site of the blue hole, and when the weather looked fine and the tide was with us, we were off.

As we came closer to the area near the creek, we stopped to see if anyone was at the camp where Jay and his friend Chris Whitten used to spend time diving with some people they knew. Michael wanted to ask anyone that may be there for directions to the blue hole where Jay had been diving.

Sure enough, there was a man there. He offered to ride to the creek with us and help guide us to the blue hole.

When we arrived, everyone was so still you could have heard a pin drop. Had it not been for the gentle purr of the boat engine as we carefully maneuvered our way between the rock formations and worked our way back into the creek, I don't think there would have been any sound at all.

Our gracious new guide directed us right over the top of the blue hole, and Michael threw out the anchor to hold us there. We were sitting right on top of the entrance to the tomb that held my son prisoner. Christine and I walked to the edge of the boat to gaze down into it. We stood there, arms wrapped around each other, looking into the depth of the hole and the area around it.

As we stood there, the boat began to move away from over the top edge of the hole. It swung itself, in the breeze-free water, at least fifteen feet back away from the entrance of the hole below. Christine and I continued to stand looking in the water hugging and holding on to each other. Christine took a flower and tossed it in the water, then handed one to me, and I threw it near hers. Dave joined us in the embrace. We all felt Jay's presence was there. But where?

The entire area was of quiet solitude, beauty, and intense peacefulness. "Never could I have found a more beautiful place to die—if the choice was mine to make—than this place," I thought to myself.

Dave said that he felt Jay is gone. He said he hadn't felt this way before, but now he believes he has gone. I accepted this feeling and agreed, in the respect that I thought that there would be no more need to continue hoping we would find him still alive physically. Spiritually yes, but not in the physical body as we had come to know him as our son.

Tony came over to me and said he thought we should be going now. The anchor was pulled in, and we slowly made our way back out.

We took the kind man that guided us to this place, back to his camp, and he invited us to stay for a cold drink. We scouted around the area, looking at sea shells and native vegetation. He told us a few stories about the area; then we loaded up to head back to Hope Town.

A kind of relief came from visiting the blue hole. I felt as if I could go on now, knowing that it would be enough if only we could find the body of my son.

Back in Hope Town, a special dinner was being prepared for us. Word had come that Jay's friends (Lou Woodward, Chris Norman, and Mitch Davis) were planning to leave for Hope Town. Also, Jay's friend Chris W.,[2] who was already in the Abacos, would be there soon too. I was so glad to hear that news. It was like I was already getting a part of Jay back.

When Chris W. arrived, he said he had been notified by VHF of the accident. He was now planning to stay until everything was resolved, one way or another.

Jay began his adventure in the Bahamas with Chris W. about three years before. During intervals of their trips to the Abacos, Jay and Chris

---

[2] Chris Whitten will be referred to as Chris W. while Chris Norman will be referred to as Chris N.

W. would share an apartment and hang out together in Wilmington. Chris N., Mitch, and Lou would also share in their great adventures. So it seemed only natural that the four of them would be present at this particular time.

Late into the night we waited, still hoping to get word that some divers had been found, but nothing happened. Jay had been missing since April 2, the day after Good Friday, and we still had no idea why he was not found with the other two divers.

Chapter Seven

*M*orning came again. As it had the previous morning, the birds were singing, and the sun was beginning to rise above the crystal clear blue water that surrounds Hope Town.

Just before going to sleep the night before, I sat on the back porch of the cottage, listening to the frogs singing in the cistern beneath the patio. They seemed to be responding to my every thought. When I would think of Jay and my desire to be able to find him, they would begin their deep croak that echoed in my ears.

I looked out across the yard of our cottage to the yard next door and remembered Jay and Christine's wedding reception one year ago this past August. It was held here, just outside the cottage that sits behind Jay and Christine's little home on the island. The water was the outside border of the reception area, making a beautiful, peaceful scene for the event.

"Jay and Christine have been so happy with each other," I thought and I remembered that the top on their wedding cake was two dolphins in a loving embrace, which reminded me of the two of them together as they shared the love and respect of the water. I thought of the cake—carrot cake, my favorite. I wish I could have eaten more. Then the mimosas. This was the first time I had ever tasted a mimosa. Made with orange juice with champagne, they were quite tasty, quenched even the biggest thirst on such a hot summer day in the Bahamas.

On the video of the wedding reception, Jay is pointing to me, saying, "This is Mom." Then I point to him and say, "This is Son." I also had the opportunity to say, "I now have the daughter I always wanted." My dream was to have a son first and then a daughter. Now I have that daughter, Christine. I was so proud of the two of them. My friends probably got tired of hearing about them. They had become my favorite topic as the opportunity presented itself.

Now my thoughts returned to the present. I made myself ready to join Tony in bed. Tonight I felt confident that I would be able to sleep. I had been realizing how important it is to have some quality rest. At least for me it seemed to be the best way to get through another challenging day.

Sleep came shortly after quietly thinking over the sketchily planned day ahead of us. Morning came almost as soon as sleep had a few hours before. I awoke to the sound of some gentle tapping on the front door.

Looking out the bedroom window, I saw Number Nine, Jay and Christine's cat, stretched out with fore paws on the door as if begging to come in. I went around the corner to the door, and as soon as I opened it Number Nine was at my feet, rubbing his body back and forth against my legs. I felt a warm, reassuring feeling from the cat. It seemed as though Number Nine was also comforting me in his own way.

Number Nine was an island cat. He has the looks of a Persian, with long black fur. Like most cats on the island, he had an extra toe on each paw, making his paws look nearly twice as wide as the average cat. Jay had told me that many of the animals on the island were this way, due to breeding amongst themselves. The choice of a mate is limited on the island, so they settle for what nature had offered them.

Chapter Eight

So now it was the beginning of the next day—Tuesday. The day most likely to determine whether or not we would find divers to look for Jay. I thought, "This is it, we either find something out today, or we will have to leave Jay down there in that deep, dark, and cold watery grave after all."

I continued to hope. This time I was hoping for divers to find the body of my son. Not my son in his full physical living condition, but the body. The vehicle that carried my son during his chosen earthly mission.

His body, the one that began as an egg inside my body, blessed by the sperm of his father, and grew to maturation within my womb for nine months. This was a part of me, even if it was Jay's body during his lifetime. It was still a part of me, and I needed to know it would be properly taken care of.

A quick routine was already learned in the time we had been at Hope Town. First, to dress and be ready for the day with some morning coffee with whatever amount of breakfast we could get down. I continued to remind myself that eating and sleeping as normally as possible would be necessary if I were to get through this crisis without becoming ill. This was no time for me to allow myself to become sick.

No noise was heard next door, so Tony and I walked down the path toward the lodge. We missed our friendly guide dog as we began, but not far down the path he joined us. This time a couple of other island dogs followed along. As we neared the lodge, we took the path that led around to the back side of the lodge overlooking the ocean. When we entered through the back door, our friendly guide stopped and watched us go in, then continued with his companions.

Not long after we were there, Christine and her family joined us. I explained to them that we went on because I didn't hear anyone up and around and thought maybe they were still sleeping.

After everyone had finished breakfast, we exited through the same door we had used to enter mainly just to see if the dog would be waiting for us. Sure enough, there he was, ready to walk us back up the familiar path toward the Myerses' house.

When we arrived, Patte was waiting for us with the possibility of some good news about divers. Patte had contacted her brother in Florida and explained our problem. He opened his phone book and saw an ad in the yellow pages for professional divers out of St. Petersburg. The listing was for a place called Sea Hunt. When he called the number, he was greeted by Colleen Marshall. Explaining what the situation was, she said she would get a team put together as soon as possible and get back to him.

I felt like this was it—the miracle I was expecting. Now all we had to do was wait for their reply. So we went back to the cottage and waited.

We pulled out a few lawn chairs in back of the cottage, and Christine's family joined Tony and I in light conversation. I kept thinking that we would hear something any moment. That moment came at 9 a.m. when Patte brought us word that a team of divers was formed. They could leave as soon as they got their equipment loaded and taken to the airport.

The divers would need a chartered jet ready and waiting for them. Colleen said she could locate a jet to get them to the Bahamas if we could call and give a credit card number to cover the jet service. This was done very quickly. As I received the phone number to call, Tony graciously provided me with his credit card. Everything was set up now.

The plan for transporting the divers and their equipment once they got to the island was made. They would be met at the airport in Marsh Harbour by Dave G. Their equipment would be unloaded and taken to the marina, where boats would be waiting to transport them to the blue hole. If all went as planned, they could be there and in the water by 3 p.m.

A feeling of excitement and relief swept through me. The excitement of the news seemed to affect everyone. There was renewed hope that was obviously contagious among all of us involved.

We were told that the divers would need a place to stay for the night. After diving, they would need to rest overnight before being able to fly back to Florida.

We knew that we would be paying a flat fee for the charter and also need to pay an hourly fee for the chartered jet, for however long it was to be on the ground. That seemed very insignificant when considering what the divers would be doing for us. It was planned that the pilots would wait overnight and return with the divers and their equipment the next day.

All the arrangements were made, things were happening, and the divers were on their way to the Abaco Islands. There was nothing else to do now but wait again. "Thank God," I thought to myself. I had learned some patience in my lifetime. It seemed as if God had made me wait lots of different times in my lifetime to help me learn that lesson of patience. I'm not saying I did it perfectly, but perhaps I did better than I would have without the lessons.

Throughout the day, between sitting with each other talking, going for walks, making phone calls to family and friends in the States and doing whatever it takes to bide the time, Patte would contact Island Marine to check on the progress of the entire operation. This word would be spread amongst us like wildfire.

At the time of the dive we all seemed glued to the garden area of Patte and Michael's home, longing for news of Jay's discovery. We weren't certain of the amount of time it would take for us to hear the results; but we continued to wait, talk, and hope.

Finally, word came to us that the divers were unable to locate any sign of Jay after a seventy-minute dive. My heart sank, but new hope was renewed instantly when I heard that the divers were planning to stay for another day. They decided that he had to be there someplace, and that they should go back in the blue hole for further exploration.

Now we would prepare ourselves for another night and another day of waiting, hoping and bracing ourselves for acceptance of whatever the outcome would be. It was beginning to seem like a drama that had no end to it.

The garden at Patte and Michael's became the place of comfort for us. It was closed to news coming in from the outside. It was through their telephone that news went out to loved ones not present and were also waiting to hear what was going on. A circle of chairs on the porch would be where most of us would huddle to talk and strengthen each other.

Chapter Nine

Our evening meal was brought in and served by wonderful, caring friends of Hope Town. On this evening, we had fish that was so delicious. I marveled at how good it was, thinking that it must be the best fish I had ever tasted in my life. We would be sharing lots of fabulous meals while we were here, but this particular one was the most outstanding in my mind.

After I finished my dinner, Margaret Rose asked me if I liked the fish. I explained that I thought it was the best I had ever eaten. That is when she told me that it was fish that Jay had caught just before his disappearance. This explained to me why the fish was so exceptional. It was prepared and seasoned well of course, but there was more to it than the preparation. It had been caught and cleaned by my own son's hands, making it especially good.

We were informed that the divers were in and staying at the lodge. They were extremely tired from their day, so they would not be over to talk to us this evening. Instead, they would get a good night's sleep after some dinner and set out early the next morning for two dives. They were planning to make the first dive in the morning; then after resting for a while and switching gear, they would make a second dive if necessary.

I was disappointed yet concerned and glad at the same time about the divers. Disappointed that I was unable to meet them and talk to them, concerned that they would be all right after such a difficult day, and glad that they were concerned people and willing to give of themselves to such a crucial and dangerous endeavor. I wanted them to do for themselves whatever they needed to do. Putting their own lives at risk is not something to be taken lightly, no matter how much I wanted my son's body to be found.

Along with the arrival of Jay's other three friends—Mitch, Chris N. and Lou—I learned of the decision of my brother, mother and step-father to come the next day as well. They had concluded that they should be there. My brother, Alan, made reservations allowing them to be with us by the latter part of the afternoon. Terry and Michael would meet them and bring them over to Hope Town in Michael's boat.

Plans were now complete—as best as possible anyway—for the following day to come. Step by step, each detail was understood by all. Who was to be picked up when and by whom. We knew what the divers were planning to do as well. Now again, more patience and hope was to be a necessity for each one of us.

When we returned to the cottage for the night, Tony suggested that I call my mother. When we talked, she asked if I wanted her to bring anything with her. I thought about a book I had read in March and how much it had been helping me through this difficult time. I wanted to give Christine a copy of this book called *Embraced by the Light* by Betty J. Eadie.

While visiting with Patte earlier, I told her about this book. I explained how Tony had picked it up in the airport while we waited for our flight to Las Vegas in March. I began to read it, and it was so interesting that I read almost half of the book before the plane arrived, then finished it before we got to Vegas.

She said Michael had been to Nassau a couple of weeks earlier and had also purchased the same book. She was planning to read it as soon as she finished the other one he brought back called *Celestine Prophesy* by James Redfield.

Could this be a coincidence? Or had it been meant to be that this particular book, telling of the near death experience of the author, had been put into our hands to read at such an opportune time? Every detail of this woman's near death experience made the idea of Jay's death seem less frightening.

I saw a report about the author of this book on TV just before Jay's accident. Each person passing through to meet this woman at a book signing reported how they had read the book just prior to or immediately following the death of a loved one. This also seemed to be the case here too.

Mother also said she was bringing Christine some blue jeans, some she had planned to give to her just after Christmas before Jay and Christine left to return to the Bahamas. Tony and I had already returned to North Carolina a couple of days earlier. During the two days prior to Jay and Christine's departure, mother became so ill that she could barely get out of bed. Because of this she was unable to get the jeans for Christine.

She told me how concerned Jay was about her being so sick and how he had stayed up all night just to be sure that she would be all right. He even went out and got medicine for her. Now she would be here with us in the Bahamas to support him, her oldest of four grandchildren.

After a few more phone calls were made to family and friends, and details of what was going on and what was planned were explained, I again joined Tony, who had already retired. In my mind, lying there in bed, I reviewed what had been happening so far and what may or may not be to come.

I thought about my mother asking earlier about funeral arrangements for Jay, before I had accepted that he was surely dead. I had told her I wasn't giving up hope of finding him alive yet.

However, I did tell her of Jay's request of wanting to be buried at sea, and how he had told me of his wishes while visiting me the past July. He had also told Christine that if he died, he wanted to be cremated and have his ashes spread over the waves.

At the time he told me of his choice of burial, he also told me of a time when he saw a ghost. He explained that he had been staying alone at the campsite in the Bahamas where he and his friends had been diving. That is where he saw it. He said that others had seen it before too. "It came right up and wiggled the toes of the wife of one of the men, leaving wet footprints when it moved," he explained seriously.

Another thing he mentioned to me was that he was now able to remember his birth. I didn't fully understand how this could be possible, but then why not? Just because I can't, doesn't mean that he wouldn't be able to remember this.

We also talked about the time when he was a child and he told me he woke up and saw an angel in his room. I asked if he was sure it wasn't me in a white gown that he saw, and he laughed and said, "No, Mom, it wasn't you. Not that you're not an angel, but it wasn't you I saw in my room that night."

Now, a funeral was becoming more of a reality to me. I thought of funeral planning as something sacred, belonging primarily to the wife, especially for Christine since she has been the closest person to Jay for the past couple of years.

Sleep finally came as I let go of all the thoughts. I relaxed in the hope of finding some kind of closure to this episode in the drama we seemed to be living through.

Chapter Ten

Awakening to the sound of Number Nine pawing at the door to get in, I snapped to full wakefulness immediately as I thought of the divers. I wondered if they were up and preparing for the dives ahead. Perhaps they have already left for the blue hole, hoping the weather was favorable for them to get there.

Crawling out of bed, I told Tony I was just going to let Number Nine in. Tony does not share my fondness for cats, but he was cooperating with my compassion for this one. I seemed to feel a bond with this cat and felt in some sense a connection to him. It seemed as if the cat was comforting me in some way, letting me know that everything was all right with Jay.

Being brought up in the Christian faith, I had learned to accept the idea that some people go to heaven, and others may not be so fortunate. Looking at things this way, as I thought of Jay and his life, I believed he would be heaven bound for sure. He wasn't perfect, but he had a good, kind, and gentle heart.

Many times in my life I pondered on the idea of death, what it all means and what happens at death and afterward. There seemed to be so many unanswered questions for me. I felt compelled to research and find answers to my questions, looking everywhere from the Bible to other written material. Recently the compulsion began to lead me to my own heart and mind for the answers.

Now more than ever, the thought of death and its meaning lingered in the recesses of my mind. I truly believe that even though Jay no longer lives in flesh and bone, he is still alive in some way. My intention was to continue to believe this.

Number Nine wandered to the kitchen and seemed to be hanging around the refrigerator, looking at me as if to say, "I'm hungry." Not having any cat food or any kind of food that sounded good for a cat, I decided to pour a little milk in a bowl for him. That appeared to satisfy him for a while.

Since we have been staying in this cottage, I noticed that Tony had not been jumping out of bed at the crack of dawn as he usually does. Normally he is the first to move in the morning, and I just follow along, heading straight to the coffee pot. Here I have been dressing first and then hoping for a cup of coffee from one of the few available eating establishments serving breakfast.

I found Patte to be an excellent source of coffee and began wondering if she could be up putting on a pot. Leaving Tony to rest in bed a while longer, I walked over to Patte's. She was indeed up and starting a fresh pot of her wonderful coffee. Inviting me in and offering me a cup, she said that she had been notified that the divers were on their way to the blue hole for the first dive of the day.

That was the news I was hoping to hear first thing this morning. She and I talked and shared our ideas on several different things. Patte and Michael are two exceptional people. Both full of love and respect for others and for nature. Getting to know them better has improved me in some way and also gave me the understanding of Jay and Christine's fondness of them.

Dave was up and around by this time and joined us in the kitchen. We talked about Jay, the son we brought into the world just slightly over twenty five years ago. We both agreed about how well he had turned out.

The last time I had seen Dave was about nine years earlier. Jay was going through a stage in his teenage years that required his father's support. Everything worked out, and it wasn't necessary for me to contact him after that. I left it up to Jay to stay in touch with his dad. Until now, the time that we would be letting go of our son, there had been no need for contact with each other.

Somehow, I felt sad for Dave. He missed out on a lot of the time I had being able to see Jay grow up. But sometimes things just work out that way, and I could make no good out of wishing things had been different. Now would be the time to look at things as they are, not how they were. Dave had remarried and has two other children. But nonetheless, the loss of his firstborn son would not be any easier for him than for me.

At the bottom of my second or third cup of coffee, I walked back to the cottage. Tony was dressed and lovingly waiting for me. He had been making a few phone calls to keep up with his business and fill his family in on details here.

There was not much we could do except have breakfast, gather around talking with the others at Patte and Michael's, and wait to hear some kind of report from the divers. All of us who have been together during the past few days got to know each other better and developed a bond with each other. We were all sharing a traumatic experience that linked us with one another.

Patte had been doing a few things in the house as we sat in our circle on the back porch overlooking the garden. A few phone calls would come in from time to time, and we would all watch to see if she would come out with news for us.

The divers would be staying in touch by radio with Island Marine. Then word would come by phone to us at the Myerses' home. The call we were waiting for came as expected. We found out that Jay had not been found, again. The second dive would take place as planned after the divers had time to rest and change tanks. One of the divers seemed to have one particular area in mind that he wanted to check on. This would be where they would begin the afternoon dive.

Once we digested the latest report, our little group dispersed. Knowing it would be a while before we would hear anything more, we went our separate ways. Some had lunch, others went for a walk around the island's shops, do laundry, or anything to bide the time until the next report came in or the divers themselves returned, whichever the case may be.

For me, the day seemed to float by. My mind seemed clear, and I didn't think about more than one thing at a time. Partly because of conscious choice and partly because of a feeling that something inside me was acting like a tranquilizer, assisting me to remain calm in the midst of a torrential storm.

The afternoon ebbed away. Then a call came in reporting that the divers were up from the second dive and would be heading back to Hope Town soon. No indication was given as to whether or not they had found Jay's body. My feeling was telling me that they had, but I would wait for a confirmation from them before resting on that feeling.

Before the divers got in, I decided to walk down to the store to pick up a few items. This walk was mainly to help the waiting time go by and to be able to be alone with myself for a little while. I was preparing myself for the divers' visit and preparing myself for their news.

Chapter Eleven

After leaving the store and walking slowly up the path toward Patte and Michael's, I was met by Christine's brother, Louie. He had ridden a bicycle down toward the store to look for me. He said the divers had arrived with a couple of Bahamian officials and were waiting at the Myerses' to talk to the family.

I quickened my pace as Louie rode along beside me. We exchanged very few words as we neared the house. As Louie and I came up on the porch, I saw everyone was getting situated into the familiar circle with the three divers at the head of it. The Bahamian officials were standing off to the side of the porch next to the sidewalk that leads to the front of the house. I was introduced to all of them and then given a seat near Christine and Dave.

Gary Perkins, who was introduced as the lead diver, waited to make sure everyone was there and ready. "I didn't want to start until I knew everyone was here," he began. "We found Jay's body during the second dive."

"Thank God," I whispered.

"After thoroughly searching the first cave yesterday afternoon and finding nothing, we decided to look into the other two caves that branch off in the other direction today," Gary continued. "We followed the plan that seemed to us to be the most likely course any diver would take if they were going to explore the caves. After searching all these possibilities, we could not find anything." Gary paused. "Well, we did find a face mask, but seeing all the growth on it we knew it was one that had been there for a while, not belonging to Jay, but some other diver who had been down there."

"After exhausting all these possibilities, we decided to follow a hunch Al had about a passageway leading off to the right of the cave we had searched first." Al Pertner nodded as Gary explained. "As we searched the first large cave, Al noticed this passageway that branched off toward the right. He had a strong hunch about it, but the opening was rather small, so we decided to stay with our original plan. We thought we could come back to this passageway if we still had some time to spare and if we had not come up with anything in the other two caves."

Proceeding, Gary said, "This was where we found Jay. He looked peaceful, seemed to almost have a smile on his face. Once we had cleared the narrow entrance, we swam right to him. We just knew he had to be there someplace. That's why we decided to look into every possible place he could have gone."

By now, a few questions were being asked of the divers. Gary, Colleen, and Al were very compassionate and clear in their explanations. They were gentle and caring with us when telling us what had taken place down there. Gary explained, "We were not able to bring Jay's body up today. There wasn't enough time left on our tanks, and we didn't want to rush. We ran a line from his body to the surface so we can go back tomorrow and bring him out."

About this time I looked over at Christine, and she was sitting in her chair with her head tilted slightly forward, clasping tightly onto a glass. Her face was expressionless, and the color seemed to have drained out of her face. I asked Christine if she was all right and got no reply or change in her expression. I looked at Colleen, the dive organizer; she seemed to be noticing Christine too. She quickly went over to her and started calling her name, "Christine? Christine? She's going into shock, we need to get her up and start walking her around." She then looked around for a couple of volunteers.

Louie and Chris W. helped her up as Colleen pried the glass out of her right hand. Her steps were staggered as Louie and Chris W. helped her off the porch to walk her out and around, up and down the pathways.

They seemed to be gone for several minutes when I saw Terry and Michael coming up the path with my mother, step-father, and my brother. I hugged them all and began to tell them about the divers' report we had just received, and told them about what was happening this very minute with Christine. Terry headed off to look for her as I led my family around to the back porch.

I introduced my family, and they began talking with people standing around. Patte said that dinner was being brought in and that the divers were going to go shower and change. They would come back later to have dinner and talk with us some more.

My family sat down with Tony and I. We talked about what had been happening during the day and told them more about what the divers had been telling us before they arrived.

I felt so relieved. It seemed as if a big load had been lifted from my shoulders just knowing that the body of my son would soon be returned to us. He was found at last, thank God. Now we can go on with what we have to do next.

Phone calls were being made to family and friends to inform them of the divers' success in finding Jay's body. Dinner was being delivered and made ready for the growing group. Christine was now back and doing much better, talking with us as well as sharing her thoughts and feelings.

Everything seemed calmer now, and everyone seemed to be opening up to each other. It occurred to me that Jay would really be enjoying all this, and I could almost picture him standing back looking over everyone present. So much love and caring support appeared in the midst of such a tragedy. This in itself looked like another miracle to me.

Dinner was now ready to be served. We all filed in and filled a plate to carry to the area we felt most comfortable. The circle around the porch had become my most comfortable spot. Jay's friends, Dave, Christine, Louie, Tony, and I all gathered around to share in the fine meal. The atmosphere was very pleasant, and different stories were being shared about different times and experiences with Jay.

Most of us were nearly finished eating when the divers returned. They were greeted as part of the big happy family were had all become. We all continued to enjoy ourselves and take our turns talking to Gary, Al, and Colleen. When the opportunity arose, I asked Gary if it would be possible for me to ask him a few questions in private. I explained that there were a few things I just felt like I needed to know. I wasn't sure if anyone else felt the same way, but I needed to ask these things for my own benefit.

Patte showed us to the guest room where Dave has been staying. Once in and the door was closed for some privacy, he sat in the chair as I sat on the end of the bed.

"Gary?" I asked, "Since you have seen Jay, and you know what condition his body is in, do you think I could see him when he's brought in? Or do you think it may not be such a good idea? My mother and brother would like to see him too just one last time, but I thought I should ask you about it before we made any decisions."

"If you want to know what I would do, I probably wouldn't want to see him but you will have to make that decision," he said. "Considering how long the body has been down there, there is not as much deterioration as I would have expected. There was one spot on his leg that seemed to be opening up slightly. It could have been from a crawfish. We did see a few of them around down there."

I immediately thought about the scar Jay had on his leg. It had been there since he developed a rather large boil on it a couple of years earlier.

Gary proceeded to say, "It could just be a place that had opened up to allow some of the gases from the body escape, as you know how a body begins to swell after a period of time after death."

"All right, I just had to know for myself. We'll discuss it and decide tonight and get word to you of our decision," I answered.

"Do you have any pictures of Jay that I can look at to compare with how I saw him?" Gary asked me.

I opened the door to call Dave in. He had brought some pictures with him that were taken at his house during the Christmas holiday. I showed Gary the one with Jay in it. He studied the picture for a moment and he said, "Yes, this is how I thought he would look. The blonde hair and size is the same as I saw him."

"Gary, I'm certain that we would like to be there at the marina when you bring Jay in. Even if we decide not to see him, at least I would like to be there," I added as I thanked him for taking the time to talk with me about such a difficult matter.

He said that they would report in about the time they had recovered his body and were about ready to leave the blue hole for Marsh Harbour. These were wonderful words to me. I truly felt it was necessary for me to at least be near his body one last time.

Once out of the room, everyone continued to mingle and talk. For the most part, conversation was light and enjoyable. It wasn't long before the divers decided to call it a night, and return to the lodge to rest up for the difficult task they were to perform for us the next day.

I felt such a warmth and deep gratitude toward Gary, Al, and Colleen. "They must have been sent by God," I thought. "Where else could they have come from?"

Tony and I were planning to pay the divers, but they refused any money. They said that this is something they do as their part in the organization of qualified recovery divers they belong to. Having the training to recover cave diving accident victims, they are available to respond anywhere in the world. All they ask for is the transportation to and from the location, a place to stay, and a few meals while there.

We did find out the name of the organization they dive for: the National Speleological Society, Inc.–Cave Diving Section. Because they would not accept any kind of payment, we decided we would like to make a donation to the organization. Hopefully, it could be used to purchase equipment or help in some small way toward any future rescues they would be called for. This seemed to be a very small token of our appreciation in comparison to what they have contributed.

Knowing we would need to be ready for the next day, we went to the cottage. I explained my conversation with Gary and expressed my desire to go to the harbor to meet the divers as they bring Jay's body in the next day. Tony and my step-dad didn't think that would be such a good idea. I told them that I felt it was necessary for me. Alan and mother expressed their feelings about wanting to be there too. It was now decided that we would get a boat and go as soon as we received word from the rescue group.

Before going to bed, Christine came by and asked to talk with me for a few minutes.

"Judy, do you mind? May I ask what you wanted to talk to the diver about? What did he say?"

My reply was simple, "I just wanted to ask him a few questions about Jay's condition and see what he thought about some of us meeting them when they bring him in. Would you like to go with us? It is your decision, and I would like you to go if you feel you want to go."

I explained how the diver said Jay's body was in better condition than they thought it would be in, that we probably shouldn't view it but simply just go to be close to his body one last time.

After this, Christine said she would probably like to go with us. We hugged, and she said she was sorry that she nearly allowed Jay's body to be left in the blue hole. Now she saw that this was the best thing for us to do and was glad that we had found him and that he is being recovered.

Mother and Russell went on to bed, tired from the long trip from Kansas. Tony also went to bed after being up later than usual. He too was getting worn out from this entire tragedy.

Alan and I sat up and talked for a while. He told me about what he had felt Saturday night after they returned home from the theater. He said he had walked out into the yard to pray for Jay and think about what was happening. While standing there, he said he felt as if Jay's spirit passed through him and then back through him again. After that, he said he had a profound calm feeling come over him. He explained that it was similar to what he had felt in March of '93 when our dad died. I also told Alan about some of the things that I had been experiencing.

Alan pulled a card out of his suitcase and handed it to me. It was from my sister-in-law, Judi Ann. She had written a note inside that brought tears to my eyes when I read it. She wrote how she remembered meeting Jay the first time when he was about four. This was the night she would be introduced to Alan at our house. Jay was the one to greet her. Just out of the tub and stark naked, Jay ran to answer the door. He put his hand out to her and said, "Hi, I'm Jason," introducing himself to his future aunt.

Chapter Twelve

Thursday morning brought another walk to the lodge for breakfast. Our group had grown to nine now. We sat around the patio tables outside to share our morning meal and talked about the things still yet to come. Christine began to tell us some of her ideas for Jay's funeral service.

"Once Jay's body arrives in Nassau, it will be autopsied and then cremated. By Saturday the ashes could be picked up and brought back to Hope Town for the service. If all goes as planned, we could have the service on Sunday morning." She said she thought we could hold the service on the lawn in front of the Abaco Inn and then have several friends of theirs join in a group and paddle out on their surfboards, spread Jay's ashes over the waves, then surf back to shore.

Christine had another friend that plays guitar and sings. She was planning to have her present the music. I thought this sounded wonderful and was proud of her as she told of the special service she was planning in memory of Jay. I could never have picked a better young lady to be my daughter-in-law. My son did very well!

After breakfast, arrangements were made for us to rent a boat from Island Marine. Tony would pick it up, and we would be set for our trip over to Marsh Harbour. This extra boat would be nice to have, especially now that we have more people to get around.

Everything was now ready to go. We waited for the call, and when it came we gathered together to go to the boat. Christine came to me and said that she had decided she was going to stay in Hope Town and not go with us to meet the divers. She said she had things she needed to do and just felt it would be better for her not to go. I reminded her that it was all right, and that each individual must make those type of decisions for themselves. No one person could possibly know what is best for another in this situation.

When the call came that the divers were on their way to Marsh Harbour with the body, we were told to go to the Marina and wait there; they would find us and tell us where the body would be taken off. Mother, Russell, Alan, Tony, and I were now headed across the beautiful clear water to Boat Harbour Marina.

When we arrived Tony stayed in the boat as he let the rest of us out on the dock. He tied up and anchored the boat, then caught up with us as we walked toward the street. We just got there when we saw a white van pull up. We recognized Al riding with a Bahamian man who was driving. They were wearing masks around their necks. This startled me for a moment, but then I understood that this was probably a very sickening task for them to have to perform.

Al told us that we would need to come out of the marina and go up to the ferry dock. That would be the place we could get out and see Jay. They were going to drive back around and wait for us there.

We got back in the boat, and Tony slowly headed in that direction. I moved to the front of the boat to watch ahead for the ferry dock. As we got closer, I could see a boat getting ready to shove off. It was the boat with the divers. They were leaving, and the two Bahamian officials were standing on the dock. I wanted Tony to speed up so we could see the divers before they left, but he said we should let them leave. He was right. They already did what they came there to do, and seeing us again that day could not make things any easier for them.

I stood up in the bow of the boat to watch them leave. They looked our way, and I gave them a wave of thanks. I noticed that they returned the gesture; with that I felt a sense of relief for them having completed their recovery mission.

Margaret Rose had made arrangements for us to have the divers flown back to Florida. First, they would have to spend the night and rest before they would be able to fly. This is a necessary precaution for any diver after making such a dive as they had.

Tony carefully maneuvered the boat up to the dock. The step up onto the dock was a high one. The two remaining men—I remembered as the Bahamian officials from Wednesday evening—tied the lines and helped me up on the dock, then helped Mother. Russell, Alan, and Tony made their way up next.

At the other end of the dock sat the white van. The men walked with us to the van and opened the rear doors. They warned us that the odor could be bad due to the five days the body rested in the blue hole. Mother, Alan, and I weren't concerned about that. We just wanted to be near Jay's body regardless of anything. Russell and Tony lingered midway down the dock as we stood looking through the open rear doors of the van.

Jay's body was wrapped in a tarpaulin. It looked so large and filled the entire length of the back of the van. Without being asked, one of the men explained that Jay still had all of his diving gear on, just as he had been found. I looked toward the front and saw a yellow diving light. He proceeded to explain that this was the light found with Jay. He said the light was still on, but the battery had run down.

We stood there silently and just looked at the tarp-covered body lying there in the van. I began to get a strong feeling that Jay was not in that van but was close to us somehow. Silently I said good-bye to the body and touched the foot of the tarp. Tony and Russell walked closer to us to say we should let the men take the body to the airport now.

I was feeling all right about letting them take the body now. Because I knew Jay was not in that van but was with us in another form. We thanked the men for waiting while allowing us to spend some time there. They closed the doors and put their masks on before they seated themselves in the front of the van. As they pulled away, I thought about their forewarning about the odor. I recalled that all I ever noticed was the smell of sea water, that salty-air smell that you sense as you come near the big blue ocean.

Back in the boat, we decided to return to the marina. By this time we were ready to have some lunch, sit back, and relax for a while. At the restaurant, we were seated at a table overlooking the southern edge of the marina where the docks are filled with mostly yacht-sized boats. In the open air area of the restaurant, we placed our orders then sat quietly with our ice-cold drinks in hand.

I started to notice that feeling of tranquility again. Mother and Alan both said something about how they were feeling such a calmness also. It was a feeling of lightness as if I were floating. I could almost imagine Jay being right there with us at the table. This feeling stayed with me for the rest of the day.

Before leaving for Hope Town, we walked to Little Switzerland, a store near the marina that sells fine perfumes, jewelry, and gift items. We each walked around looking at the beautiful things.

Russell and I were looking at the Silver Swarovski Crystal. I noticed a little clipper ship, like the one Tony and I bought on a trip we had taken the past November. I began to tell Russell about ours and about the revolving solar stand we bought to put it on. "The solar stand is supposed to turn as light reflects on the little panel. Then as light reflects on the crystal, it sends little rainbow colored beams of light out around the room. Ours has never worked right, and we haven't been able to get it to turn," I explained to Russell.

After purchasing some perfume and a few other duty-free items to take back home, we walked to the boat at the marina. The ride back to Hope Town gave me some more time to think back on the relief and gratitude I felt for being able to recover Jay's body. Now we would prepare for the funeral service ahead and then the good-byes that would have to come before the return to our home in North Carolina.

Tony had asked me about whether I thought cremation was the proper thing to do. This had been on my mind quite a bit, so I was planning to stop by Vernon Malone's house in the evening and discuss it with him.

Vernon is a lay preacher at St. James Methodist Church. He and his family live on the corner just down from Jay and Christine's cottage. They have been friends of Christine's family for years. Vernon's family had come to know and love Jay and Christine as part of their family.

Vernon even said some words at their wedding. I remembered them well because hearing the message brought tears to my eyes. "Marriage," Vernon said, "is kind of like the garden we are in. Now and then a few weeds pop up in this garden, Michael and Patte have to continually work at pulling them out to keep the garden nice and free of the weeds. That's kind of how a marriage is. When you see a weed start to grow in a marriage, you just pull it out—nip it in the bud. In this way, the little problems are taken care of before being allowed to grow into big problems, the ones that are more difficult to get rid of."

Hearing the words really made me think of how difficult marriage can be at times. I knew that Jay and Christine were just beginning the process of their marriage, so happy and carefree; but I knew also that there would come a time they would have some rather large challenges. Knowing how difficult these challenges can be, paired with the thought of the two of them having to go through times like that, brought the tears.

As parents, we learn that we can not do the suffering that comes with life for our children. They have to do that for themselves. But often, we find that we are suffering with them. Perhaps one of the greatest lessons we learn from this is one of compassion. We feel the pain with them, but not for them. As I heard someone say describing compassion, "It is the taste of salt in ones mouth as the other sheds the tears."

Back in Hope Town we stopped by Patte and Michael's to check in and let them know we were back. I wanted to tell Christine how we had been feeling and describe the calmness we experienced from the trip to Marsh Harbour.

During the day Michael and Dave had been working to build a park bench out of some driftwood. Michael had some nice large pieces of driftwood he had found and thought it would be nice to build the bench and put a memorial to Jay on it.

They started earlier in the morning and now were no longer in the area where they had been working. Patte said they were carrying the bench to the little hill that overlooks the ocean on one side, and the old cemetery on the other side. This would be the spot the bench would rest, overlooking the ocean, Jay's favorite place, with the cemetery in the background.

When Dave and Michael finished placing the bench and returned, I told Dave about our trip to Marsh Harbour. Then Christine said we would need to start working on the obituary and get it faxed to the newspapers by deadline the next day. She suggested we think of what we would like to say in it and also decide which papers we wanted to put it on. We planned to get together later in the evening and write it out.

I noticed some newspapers lying on a cabinet. Patte saw me looking at them and said that those were some that had stories about the diving accident.[3] I scanned them and quickly noticed a few errors.

Jay's age was given as twenty four instead of twenty five. Also, it was reported that Jay and Christine's families were spending the Easter holiday at Abaco. Terry and Margaret Rose were there for the holiday, but our visit had not been planned. "I wish it had been," I thought.

---

[3] See newspaper articles on pages 62-65

"Maybe then, Jay wouldn't have been taking those other people out and wouldn't have been diving Saturday."

Patte said they would get some extra copies of the articles for me. I wanted some to take home since I was already planning to put together a scrapbook of anything pertaining to Jay I could find.

It took me a little by surprise to see front page headlines in the *Tribune* (Nassau). This made me realize that the news of what had happened here was not just any ordinary story that newspapers hide in the middle of the paper.

Before getting together for our evening meal, everyone seemed to take some time to rest, do some light chores, receive a few visitors bringing food, and make a few more phone calls. Christine's small refrigerator had run out of room, so any extra food brought in was kept at our cottage for all of us to share. Anyone getting hungry for a snack or a meal knew to help themselves.

We all discovered the open door policy to be so warm and friendly on the island. Everyone shared so much with us—their homes, their food, comforting words and lots of support. It impressed me to see so much love and compassion existing here. Something you just don't think is still happening as much these days. My family and I were welcomed with open arms as if we were part of their community. Tears would come when I thought how kind the people were treating us.

While working on the obituary Thursday night, we discovered that it was not an easy one to write. We thought of so many people that should be listed as family members. It started to get very confusing, trying to identify clearly the names and the relationship to Jay. We didn't want to leave anyone out and hurting anyone's feelings, so we struggled with it until we felt we had covered everyone. Finally, we decided to finish it up in the morning, then type and fax it to our chosen newspapers.

1—Death Notices

JASON ALAN HENSLEY
HOPE TOWN, ABACO, BAHAMAS ISLANDS — Jason Alan Hensley, 25, died April 2, 1994, in a Deep Sea Diving accident, near Hope Town. Jason married Christine Kanitsch, Aug. 8, 1992, in Hope Town. She survives, along with his parents, Judith Jane Miller and Tony Miller of Wilmington, N.C.; brothers, Tony Jr., Timmy, and Robert; sister, Christina Miller; and David and Pam Hensley of Pratt, Kansas; brother Heath, and sister, Brenna Hensley; grandparents, Alice and Russell Fox of Great Bend, Kansas, Harley Hensley of Derby, Kansas, Anna Miller of Wilmington, N.C., Don and Gloria Marsh of Pratt, Kansas; great-grandparents, John and Margaret Kachelman of St. John, Kansas.

Following cremation, services were held overlooking Rush Reef, Hope Town, Abaco, Bahamas Islands. Ashes were scattered over the ocean amongst the waves where his spirit loves so much to be, now and forever free. Sunrise service, Sunday, April 10, 7:30 a.m., 1994.

Memorial contributions to be sent to: Bahamas Air and Sea Rescue Assoc., c/o Dave Gale, General Delivery, Hope Town, Abaco, Bahamas.

JASON HENSLEY, 25

FUNERAL services for Jason Alan Hensley, 25, will be held overlooking Rush Reef, Hope Town, Abaco, on Sunday April 10, at 7:30pm.

Jason died April 2nd in a Deep Sea Diving accident, near Hopetown.

He married Christine Kanitsch August 8, 1992 in Hope Town; survivors, include his wife, Christine; parents, Judith Jane Miller and Tony Miller of Wilmington, NC and David and Pam Hensley of Pratt, Kansas; brother, Heath and sister, Brenna Hensley; grandparents, Alice and Russell Fox of Great Bend, Kansas, Harley Hensley of Derby, Kansas, Anna Miller of Wilmington, NC and Gloria Marsh of Pratt, Kansas; great grand parents, John and Margaret Kachelman of St John, Kansas.

Instead of flowers, memorial contributions may be sent to Bahamas Air Sea Rescue Association, c/o Mr Dave Gale, General Delivery, Hope Town, Abaco, Bahamas.

Arrangements by Kemp's Funeral Home Limited, Nassau.

FROM BEGINNING TO END AND BACK AGAIN

An article in the *Tribune* (Nassau), Tuesday, April 5, 1994.

Three American men drowned while diving in blue hole at Abaco

By DIANNE PENN
Tribune Staff Reporter

THE Easter holiday turned tragic when three American men, one of whom was married to a Bahamian, drowned while diving in a blue hole near Hope Town, Abaco.

The incident took place early Saturday afternoon at the blue hole by "Old Robinson's Bight," Little Harbour, a popular area near the Abaco mainland.

The blue hole, which is in a creek, had to be accessed by boat.

Volunteer divers found the bodies of two of the men, who were visiting the island, on Sunday. However a spokesman from BASRA (Bahamas Air Sea Rescue Association) at Hope Town said expert recovery divers will be needed in the search for Jason Hensley.

March Harbour divers Richard Curry and Doug Lorie pulled the two bodies from the blue hole. They were reportedly found in a passage 70 feet down and 100 feet across.

The bodies were flown to Nassau for autopsies. The identities of the two men are not known, though The Tribune was told they were tourists who had rented a house in Abaco last year.

The triple tragedy has stunned the approximately 300-member community at Hope Town.

Mr Hensley — everyone knew him as "Jay" — married the former Christine Kanitsch just prior to Hurricane Andrew in August 1992. Though he has been in the Bahamas for about four years, Mr Hensley had just started working at the Lighthouse Marina in January.

His wife, a watercolour artist who also creates hand-painted t-shirts, is the daughter of Terry and Margaret Rose, Bahamians resident in Palm Beach, Florida. Mr Hensley's father is from Kansas and his mother is from North Carolina.

The popular young couple's main interests were diving and surfing and their families were to spend the Easter holiday at Abaco. Mrs Hensley's parents and her sister arrived at Hope Town Saturday afternoon while her husband's father, mother and step-father came in Sunday.

Ms Patrice Malone, assistant manager at the Abaco Inn, said guests are wondering why her normally cheerful staff aren't smiling. She explained that Mrs Hensley tended bar and did "night supervision" four times a week at the 12-room hotel.

"We were all close to her and Jay," she stated. "They are well known and loved through all of Hope Town."

On Sunday Ms Malone and her staff "pitched in" by taking food from the Abaco Inn to the Hensley house, about three miles away.

"The guests must think it's funny because we're not smiling," she said. Ms Malone noted that three Hope Town businesses — the Abaco Inn, Harbour View Grocery and Harbour's Edge (a bar and restaurant) — are taking up collections to assist the effort, while other residents are offering their homes should the families need to "get away."

"Everybody knew them and everybody loved them," she said.

63

JUDITH MILLER

An article in the *Tribune* (Nassau), Wednesday, April 6, 1994.

Search continues in Abaco for missing blue hole diver

By DIANNE PENN
Tribune Staff Reporter

TWO expert recovery divers from Florida are assisting the Hope Town, Abaco, community in their search for diver Jason Hensley who has been missing since Saturday.

Gary Perkins, lead diver, and Al Pertner, assisted by diver-organiser Coleen Marshall on land, returned to the blue hole this morning where Mr Hensley and two 17-year-old boys from Virginia went missing.

The three divers are from "Sea Hunt," a firm of professional cave divers based in St Petersburg, Florida.

Mr Hensley, 25, and two teenage boys from Virginia, together with two others, had gone to the blue hole at Old Robinson's Bight, Little Harbour, to dive about 10am Saturday.

The Police said the group had left Hope Town on a 22-foot sportsboat and the three young men went into the hole. When they did not surface after an hour, a search was conducted.

The following day the bodies of the teenagers were pulled from the blue hole by Marsh Harbour divers Richard Curry and Doug Lorie. They were identified as Mathew Craig Fidler and Ryan Christopher Smith, both of Virginia Beach.

Yesterday, the expert recovery divers made a complete search — reportedly going as far back as 400 feet into one of the underwater caverns in the blue hole — but nothing was recovered. They spent 70 minutes there, which translated into 103 minutes "underwater time" because they had to surface for decompression.

One of the divers reportedly noted a particular cavern looked "inviting," and that Mr Hensley possibly explored it. They were scheduled to investigate this place today.

On today's search the divers will not surface but instead do two dives and change their tanks underwater. The search should be completed this afternoon.

The tragedy has shown the best attribute of "small-town" life, namely that neighbours care for each other.

"People are still helping out," noted Patty Myers, who has been organising food and clean-up crews.

Hope Town residents have offered free room and board to the Florida divers, who flew in by Lear jet, and to Mr Hensley's family who have come to the island from the United States. They have even set up a collection fund to defray expenses as well as suggesting that donations be made to the local chapter of BASRA (Bahamas Air Sea Rescue Association).

Mr Hensley's wife is the former Christine Kamisch, a local artist. Her parents - Terry and Margaret Rose, Bahamians resident in Palm Beach Florida - and Mr Hensley's father, mother and step-father, had come to Abaco for the Easter holiday.

"These people are like my family," noted Ms Myers.

She said Mrs Hensley is her adopted sister and when she married "Jay," as everyone calls him, nearly two years ago, the ceremony was held in her garden.

"Everyone here is at our beck and call," she said. "They wish they could do more."

64

FROM BEGINNING TO END AND BACK AGAIN

An article in the *Tribune* (Nassau), April 7, 1994.

Missing diver's body recovered from Abaco blue hole

By DIANNE PENN
Tribune Staff Reporter
APR 7 1994

FIVE days after he did not surface from diving in a blue hole near the Abaco mainland, Jason Hensley was found.

The body of the sunburned, bleach-blond 24-year-old surfer was discovered far back in one of the caverns of the blue hole, the same spot where two American teenagers' bodies were found on Sunday.

"The mystery is over," stated a family friend who asked to remain anonymous.

The discovery of Mr Hensley's body ends the triple tragedy that occurred at Abaco over the Easter holiday weekend.

Mr Hensley (everyone called him "Jay"), Mathew Craig Fidler and Ryan Christopher Smith, both 17-year-old tourists from Virginia Beach, Virginia, were drowned while diving Saturday morning.

Accompanied by Mr Fidler's parents, the group left Hope Town around 10am in a 22-foot

See DROWNING, Page 8

Drowning

FROM PAGE 1

sports boat, travelling to the blue hole or "boiling hole" which is located in a creek.

When the three young men did not surface after an hour a search was conducted. It yielded nothing.

The following day Richard Curry and Doug Lorie, divers from Marsh Harbour, Abaco, pulled the teenagers' bodies from the blue hole. They were flown to Nassau for autopsies and identification. Mr Fidlers' parents left Abaco for Virginia that evening.

There had been no sign of Mr Hensley, an American resident at Hope Town.

On Tuesday three divers from Sea Hunt, a firm of professional cave divers from St Petersburg, Florida, were flown in by Lear jet to assist the search.

Lead diver Gary Perkins and Al Pertner, assisted by diver Coleen Marshall acting as "land contact" conducted intensive searches of the caverns inside the blue hole, going as far back as 400 feet and spending 70 minutes underwater.

Mr Perkins and Mr Pertner were again in the water yesterday, diving deeper and farther into the caverns. They had noted a particularly "inviting" cavern which they suspected Mr Hensley had explored, however the young man was found in the same cavern as the teenagers.

Having scoured the blue hole most of Wednesday, they found Mr Hensley's body in the late afternoon. As they were running out of air, the divers marked the spot with rope and returned this morning. They were in the process of retrieving the body from the blue hole at press time.

Mr Hensley and his Bahamian wife, the former Christine Kanitsch, were well known in the 300-member community of picturesque Hope Town. Residents have selflessly assisted the grief-stricken family since the weekend.

Three businesses — the Abaco Inn, Harbour View Grocery and Harbour's Edge (a restaurant and bar) — took up collections to defray expenses incurred by flying in the foreign divers, while other residents have offered their homes and food to out-of-town relatives.

"The guests must think it's funny because we are not smiling," commented Ms Patrice Malone, assistant manager at the 12-room Abaco Inn where Mrs Hensley tends bar and does "night supervision" four times a week.

Several of Mr Hensley's relatives, including his father, David Hensley of Pratt, Kansas; his mother and stepfather, Judy and Tony Miller of Wilmington Beach, North Carolina, and his grandmother and step grandfather, Alice and Russell Fox of Great Bend, Kansas, are now in the Bahamas.

Mrs Hensley is the daughter of Terry and Margaret Rose, Bahamians resident in Palm Beach, Florida, and has numerous relatives from Marsh Harbour and Nassau. The Roses and other family members are also at Hope Town.

Mr and Mrs Hensley were married just prior to Hurricane Andrew in August 1992. Though he had been resident there for about four years, Mr Hensley had just started working at the Lighthouse Marina in January.

A memorial service is scheduled for one of the beaches at White Sound, Abaco, and Mr Hensley's body will be cremated in Nassau.

A friend, who asked to remain anonymous, observed that Mrs Hensley "comes and goes" but that the family can now mourn their loss.

"The mystery is over," they said.

Chapter Thirteen

Meeting first thing Friday morning at Patte and Michael's with our list and draft of the obituary, we went to work. Patte typed, and we proofread it. Then Christine would type and we would proof it again. I had no idea that writing the obituary would turn out to be one of the most difficult tasks of the entire ordeal.

We planned to have the obituary in the Nassau Tribune for the people in the Abacos. Christine's parents live in West Palm Beach, so they wanted it to be in the paper there. In Kansas, where Dave and I both have family, we wanted it to be in the *Pratt Tribune*; the *Hutchinson News*, which covers a broad area of Kansas; the *St. John News*, for where my grandparents live, the *Garden City* paper, for where Jay went to school for almost eight years, the *Great Bend Tribune*, for where Mother and Russell live and where Jay had also attended school. Next would be the *Wilmington Star News* in North Carolina, where Tony and I live, and Jay had also.

We needed to call all the newspapers to find out their procedure for printing obituaries. Each deadline, fax numbers, and cost of printing all needed to be obtained. Fortunately, my oldest stepson's wife, Carolyn Miller, and my friend Cheryl, who both work at the radio station, offered to make these calls. We hoped to fax one copy to the station; from there Carolyn and Cheryl could fax it to the Kansas papers and hand-deliver one to the *Wilmington Star News*.

In the interval, Carolyn and Cheryl would go to my house and look through picture albums in search of a nice picture of Jay that could be used in the *Wilmington Star News*. I had confidence in the two of them to pick out a picture that captured Jay as he was.

After looking through all the pictures, they decided on the one that was pinned to my bulletin board, right under their noses, in my office at the station. It was a shot of Jay in his wetsuit, holding his surfboard next to him. Cheryl just happened to walk into my office and sit down at my desk, and then it hit her. "That's the one!" she said.

We were getting closer to completion. The first deadline was for the Nassau paper. This was first because the time of the service would need to be printed in the Saturday edition so local people could plan to attend the funeral.

The *Wilmington Star News* was next. They requested a death certificate before they would publish the obituary. This required a call to Kemps Funeral Home in Nassau and a signature by Christine. Fortunately, the director of the funeral home knows Christine's family and agreed to fax a copy to us for Christine to sign and fax on. Finally, Carolyn and Cheryl had everything they needed for the *Wilmington Star News*, and my friend Pat offered to hand-deliver it for them.

When the death certificate arrived, I read it and felt surprised and somewhat sickened when I read the cause of death. Not the part that read, "Cause of death: asphyxia due to drowning," but the part that read, "as seen in a severely decomposed body."

This didn't seem to correspond to the description given by the diver. After thinking about this, I concluded that his description of Jay was as he saw him while still in the salty water of the blue hole in full diving gear. Apparently, when his body was removed and by the time it arrived in Nassau, some changes came about in the appearance of his body, especially since the gear had been removed.

During the course of the morning, Margaret Rose decided she wanted to write the obituary for the Palm Beach paper. Mother said she wanted to write her own for the one to go in the St. John and Great Bend papers. Dave decided to get his wife, Pam, to take care of the Pratt paper. All that was left for Carolyn and Cheryl to fax were the *Garden City Tribune* and the *Hutchinson News* in Kansas.

Tony offered to take Mother, Russell, and Alan on a boat ride over to Man-O-War. They left just before we had put the finishing touch on the obituary. I was finally beginning to feel a little relief from the entire rush of the process. Having some time alone at the cottage seemed like a good idea to me. A nap was what I had in mind to help me unwind.

After we were finished with what we had left to do, I walked to the store and then back to the cottage by way of the beach. I stopped to see the place where Dave and Michael placed the bench. The memorial on the back rest read, "We Love You Jay." Sitting down on the bench, looking out over the ocean, I began to cry.

For the first time, I felt whipped. The nagging in my heart had finally taken a hold of me. My eyes were so clouded over from my mascara running that I was beginning to have a difficult time even seeing. The tissues in my purse couldn't keep up with my eyes and nose. I knew it was time to head for the cottage, a short walk away.

Feeling so upset at this time, I thought of how I would like to talk to Cheryl. She has been a dear friend to me and was always able to talk with me and help me see things clearly. She had also been taking care of all my advertising business and helping with the sales staff while I'd been away. This gave me comfort knowing that everything was being well taken care of. I feel that I could trust her with anything.

Strangely enough, Cheryl called just after I got back to the cottage. As soon as she asked how I was doing, everything began to pour out. We talked for a long time, to the point that I began to feel so tired. She suggested I lie down for a while, and we could talk more later.

As I was lying on the bed, a flood of emotions seemed to go through me. Then I heard someone at the door. I looked out and saw it was Dave. He came to return a dish for Patte that came from this cottage. I joined him on the front porch, and we sat down on the steps.

He could see that I had been crying and asked if I was all right. I told him that I thought that everything was beginning to catch up with me now. Up to this time I had been doing pretty good at keeping myself together, but right now it seemed as if I really needed to let go. He said that he felt as if he was starting to get himself together now; getting through the past few days seemed the roughest for him.

I told Dave that I truly believed I had been blessed by being able to have Jay. Even though things did not work out for us in our marriage, it seemed the purpose of our marriage was for me to be able to have Jay.

I've been unable to have other children since Jay was about five years old. After a time of having high blood pressure from taking birth control pills, Dave and I decided not to have any more children. So I had a tubal ligation. Then five years after that, I found out I had early cervical cancer, so a hysterectomy was performed.

The thought now of not having Jay, my only child, was almost unbearable. Also, thinking that I would never be able to have a grandchild of my own hurt terribly deep down in my heart. Dave said he guessed he was pretty lucky to have his two other children, and I told him I was happy that he could have them too.

As Dave stood up to go back to the Myerses', he encouraged me to "hang in there." I thanked him for talking with me, and we agreed that once we can get through the funeral service, things would begin to feel better for everyone.

I couldn't help but think how well Christine seemed to be doing right now, and here I am beginning to fall apart. It was now Christine's turn to be strong and get the service all set up, and she was already doing a tremendous job. The only thing she wasn't sure of yet was what music to have her musician friend do.

Christine was already getting word from several of their friends that were planning to bring their surfboards to the service so they could paddle out with her to spread Jay's ashes. Jay's other friends—Chris W., Lou, Mitch, and Chris N.—would all be there and go out as well.

Chris N. said he didn't think he was going to make it at first. One reason being that he was in school, and the other is his fear of flying. Then as he was just about to go to sleep one night, just after he got the news about Jay, he heard the sound of someone snapping their fingers right up close to his ear. He told me that he even felt the air move, as if someone were actually snapping their fingers right next to his ear. He felt Jay was saying, "Go to the Bahamas," so he told his girlfriend that he was going to go, regardless of his fear of flying.

It has meant so much to me having Jay's friends there. A feeling of closeness came to me from them. Somehow, it was as if I could find a little of Jay in each one of them. They each shared different experiences they had with Jay, and it was fun to hear them tell about the things that stood out most in their minds about him. I thought what fine young men these are and how nice it was that Jay had such good friends as these young men, who traveled all the way to the Bahamas to be with us.

I was beginning to feel better now as Tony returned with my family from their little trip to Man-O-War. Having Tony back helped to give me a more comforting feeling even though they had only been gone for a few hours. My brother and I seemed able to talk openly about Jay's death, which also helped me a lot.

There wasn't much to do for the rest of the day. We had plenty of food provided to be shared between Christine's family, my family, and any one that cared to join us.

Terry and Margaret Rose began cutting up conch and other ingredients to make their favorite conch salad. I had some one time before while visiting the Bahamas, and I really liked it. So I definitely wanted to have some more when it was ready.

In the meantime a few of us got together at Patte and Michael's. We went up on the top of the house where the widow's walk overlooks all of Hope Town and the harbor. A bench built all the way around each side allows a person to sit and have a good view in all directions. The lighthouse sits across the bay from the house.

Beside the lighthouse is Lighthouse Marina, where Jay had been working since he received his work permit in January. Jay was so excited when he got his work permit. Christine's parents had helped him with all the necessary steps in applying for it and getting it passed through. He was very happy with his job and had been doing work as a boat mechanic there since then.

In the morning when he would cross the harbor to the marina, his dog, Lucky, would swim across and join him there. Christine told me this when I mentioned seeing Lucky swimming across in that direction a couple of days before. As soon as she told me, I knew Lucky was probably looking for Jay. Later, Lucky became very protective of Christine and would growl if anyone he didn't know got too close to her.

Christine had been working mostly at night for the Abaco Inn. Lots of those nights Jay would meet her there and escort her home. Between their jobs, they would surf, fish, and dive.

Christine is an artist, so she would also have different projects she was working on. Sometimes Jay would help her with some of the work if it was something he could do.

He always seemed to enjoy telling me about all of the things they had going on and what they were doing. However, shortly before the diving accident, he had told me how difficult it was for the two of them to be working opposite hours. "Oh well, I guess it doesn't leave us anytime to fight," he said as he laughed.

Chris W. came up on the widow's walk about this time to announce that the conch salad was finished. He offered to go back over to Christine's cottage and get me some. When he returned he handed me a Styrofoam bowl full of the wonderful salad. Chris said that Jay had been out diving for conch, and this salad was made from what he brought in. It was the best I had ever eaten, but of course—Jay got it with his own two hands.

I always knew that my son would never go hungry. He was always able to catch or hunt practically anything he wanted to eat. I have to give his dad and his granddad Hensley the credit for helping him to develop this ability. They always enjoyed taking Jay hunting and fishing when he was a child. They taught him to take only what would be eaten and no more.

When Jay and Christine were married, Jay wanted to help me out on the cost of the rehearsal dinner. He went diving for crawfish until he had enough for anyone wanting to have that as their choice of entrees. The Hope Town Harbour Lodge prepared it to perfection, and Jay was so proud when he would see one on someone's plate, mentioning that he caught them.

When my bowl of conch salad was gone, everyone but Chris W. was gone too. So we went over to the cottage to find Mother and Margaret Rose setting out the large selection of food. Everyone grabbed paper plates and found a seat in the backyard or in the living room.

One family that brought food to us also had experienced loosing a loved one while diving in the elusive beauty of the sea. It gave me strength to know that they came through their sorrow and grief. Now they were reaching out to us with understanding beyond compare.

So many tragedies happen to people that we don't seem to notice them or feel their magnitude until it happens to us directly. The understanding of such a tragedy is difficult to comprehend. I now knew what this family must have felt when they experienced their loss. Before, I wouldn't have even come close to knowing the pain they experienced. Real compassion seems to appear out of the midst of such common tragedies as these.

An entirely new education appeared to be presenting itself to me. The education that cannot be learned from books but through living. Not taught by teachers but by experiencing. An education that one thinks they would rather avoid, but when being thrust into it without conscious choice, it may be one of utmost importance in a person's life. As each life eventually leads to death, this education goes with it.

When everyone finished sampling all the different tasty food, the kitchen was returned to its original order. The group dispersed, and each person went on with their own plan.

Michael had flown to Nassau to take care of some business. He was planning to stay overnight and return on the following day (Saturday) with Jay's ashes. His first order of business in Nassau was to go to the mortuary to identify Jay's body. Christine and I would take his boat over to Marsh Harbour and wait at the marina for him when he makes the return trip. From there we would make the crossing back to Hope Town together, carrying the ashes of my son.

While in Nassau, Michael offered to pick up a copy of a book for me. This book, *Bahamian Landscapes—An Introduction to the Geography of the Bahamas* by Neil E. Sealey,[4] had the most accurate description of

---

[4] See description of blue holes on pages 74-77.

the blue holes we could find in Michael and Patte's library. I wanted a copy of this book to take home along with a map Michael had marked for me.

The scale map marks the exact location of the blue hole where Jay died. At the time, this seemed like the only way for me to be close to where Jay is and gain a better understanding of what had happened after returning home.

There wasn't much anyone could do right now. The service would take place on Sunday morning. We would have Jay's ashes the next day.

Description of *blue holes* from *Bahamian Landscapes*.

c) *Blue holes and underground caves* These are features which can only be formed above sea-level (see p. 54). In addition, some of the features connected with them, such as stalactites, are further evidence of an atmospheric origin. Consequently any depth recorded for a blue hole will also be an indication of how low sea-level was at that time. The deepest blue hole known is 111 m (363 feet), so it can be said that sea-level was about this low at some time in the past, probably during the last glaciation.

In recent years attempts have been made to date the blue holes from the ages of the stalagmites and stalactites in them. This is very complicated, because these features will obviously only form after the blue hole has been abandoned by running water. They may also have several layers which grew during different dry (i.e. glacial) periods, and have stopped growing for equally long periods when the blue hole was flooded. One study dated a stalagmite as 150 000 years old. This would suggest that it formed at the end of the third (Illinoian) glacial advance, and that the blue hole, in South Bight, Andros, was formed earlier in that glaciation, or in any of the glacial periods before it.

At present, dating older than 170 000 years is unreliable.

ibs of beach rock have been trimmed to form the walls of e beach just a few metres away.

[1] The Land Resource Study did, in fact, report a 'bottomless' blue hole on Long Island. They concluded that their sounding line had gone right through the blue hole and was falling down the drop-off into the Atlantic Ocean! This would be the case for a blue hole with an exit on the drop-off wall as in Figure 5.16.

[2] Unlike many of the topics discussed in this book, blue holes have been written about quite widely. The authority is Dr George J. Benjamin who wrote 'Diving Into the Blue Holes of Andros', *National Geographic Magazine*, 1970, **II**, No. 360, pp. 347-63. He also made the film 'The Ocean Holes of Andros', *National Geographic Films*, and contributed to a study of blue holes in *Three Adventures* by Jacques I. Cousteau.

[3] Map names can be confusing when they do not agree with geographical descriptions. It should be remembered that the given name may refer to the state at the time the feature was named. Hence a *creek* may now be a *pond*. Also local usage of the names may have been different, such as a creek being used for anything with a tidal flow, or a pond for any form of still water.

The Landscapes and Landforms of The Islands

stone (Figure 5.15).

So, for the rockland, we have a pitted and rocky surface because the water table is always near the surface. But, as the diagrams show (Figure 5.16), when the water table was lower it was possible for much larger holes to form and the largest of these were the blue holes. Today we find them flooded and inactive, but still the most striking of all the Bahamian landforms.

Blue holes All the main islands of The Bahamas have blue holes, but those of Andros are best known. Andros has 178 on land with at least 50 in the sea. Blue holes may also be called *ocean holes* if they appear tidal or otherwise connected with the sea.

For a long time, ideas about the origin of the blue holes were confused, with superstition and myth more acceptable than geological theory to the average islander. Geologists who visited the islands concluded that they could only be very large sinkholes, probably created in the Ice Ages. Similar features were well known in Europe and North America as 'potholes' by cavers, only in this case they were dry, or had streams running into them. Proof that they were indeed created during the Pleistocene Ice Ages lies in the following facts:

a) As sea-level did not drop much more than 122 m (400 ft) in the Ice Ages we would not expect to find any blue holes deeper than that. The deepest known was measured at 110 m (363 ft) near Twin Lakes, Andros, and three others nearby reached 107 m (350 ft).

b) If they were sinkholes they should have connecting tunnels and caverns, with dripstone features in them. Several blue holes have now been discovered with stalagmites, proving without doubt that at one time the hole or cave was empty and penetrated by dripping water. Quite extensive cave

Figure 5.15 The exit from an underground cave system (such as in Figure 5.7). Both figures show caves formed when sea level was higher. Undoubtedly an active system is in operation in the limestone some distance below this abandoned one.

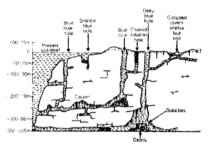

Figure 5.16 An impression of how blue holes might look below ground, and below the sea. Most of the possibilities are illustrated (W.T. = water table). All blue holes connected to the sea will be affected by the tides.

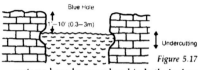

Figure 5.17

systems have been explored in both Andros and Grand Bahama.

c) Wherever dating has been possible the dates have fitted in well with known dates for sea-levels in the Ice Age period.

This knowledge also tells us why we find some blue holes in the sea. During the periods of glaciation, the entire Little, Great and southeastern Bahamas Banks were dry land, and would have been subject to erosion and solution just like the rockland is today. Blue holes would have formed in many areas, but most of them would have been filled in by marine sediments once the rising sea covered them up. In some areas they have stayed open, most notably off the east coast of Andros. This could well be due to the passage of water through them as the tides rise and fall, particularly if there is an outlet into deep water (the Tongue of the Ocean

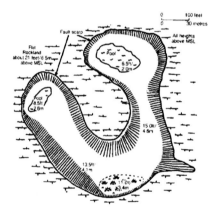

Figure 5.18 Fox Hill ocean hole, N.P. (from plan 6872 1:1200 Lands and Survey Dept.) The ocean hole is large, about 180 m (600 ft) across, but as for the most part it is only 2–3 m (6–8 ft) below the rockland it is dry. There are wet areas backed by cliffs 3 m (10 ft) high or more. The fault scarp can be clearly traced all the way around the hole.

The Landscapes and Landforms of The Islands

in the case of Andros) (see Figure 5.16). Fishermen have often reported whirlpool conditions over blue holes, and avoided them as a result. This is, in fact, a unique feature of Bahamian blue holes. They do exist in other parts of the world, notably in Belize and off the coast of Yucatan in Mexico, in the Gulf of Campeche, where they are known as *cenote*, but none of these places have *tidal* blue holes.

The *shape* and *size* of blue holes is also of interest. Normally they are circular, but some are not. They are most likely to be circular when they have been formed from an opening at the surface, as the numerous little streams running into the hole will tend to concentrate their erosion on any projecting 'headlands'. With the high purity of Bahamian limestones there will also be a tendency for the most efficient shape to form, which in this case will be circular as this will have the shortest wetted perimeter for any size of hole. On a smaller scale there will be little channels cut in the edge of the hole giving it a fretted appearance, and at the water's surface the 'lip' will be undercut (Figure 5.17). The level of water in the blue hole is often affected by the tides, and also by water table levels in the rainy and dry seasons, so the undercut section may be as much as 0.5–1 m (2–3 feet) in depth.

Irregular shapes are more likely in the sea, as on land the absence of large streams today prevents gullies being cut into the side of the hole. In the past, some blue holes undoubtedly did have this feature, and when drowned in the sea it was preserved. Sea water is saturated with calcium carbonate and cannot do any further dissolving, so the shape of the offshore blue holes is probably much the same as when the sea rose to its present level. On land, the irregular shapes were rounded off by rainwater acting on the lip of the hole.

Some blue holes are formed by the collapse of a cavern roof, rather than as an enlarged sinkhole at the surface. The one at Fox Hill in New Providence is of this type, and large amounts of the roof, which apparently fell into a shallow cavern, fill up the generally circular area where the water is present in several shallow ponds at the edges (Figure 5.18).

Most blue holes are quite wide, 50 feet or more across, but some are much bigger such as Church's blue hole near Fresh Creek in Andros which is 134 m (440 ft) across (Figure 5.19). The

The Landscapes and Landforms of The Islands

Figure 5.19 Church's Blue Hole, near Fresh Creek, Andros. This large blue hole is set in typical pine-covered rockland.

Andros holes average about 12 m (40 ft) deep, but some are less than 6 m (20 ft) deep while others reach over 90 m (300 ft). Some well-known blue holes are:

Near Treasure Cay, Abaco	57 m	186 feet
Rock Sound, Eleuthera	43 m	140 feet
Mermaids Pool, New Providence	14 m	45 feet
Church's, Andros	31 m	102 feet

None are 'bottomless'!!

Blue holes have very little life in them, as there is little food available. Leaves and other vegetable matter collect in them and this supports a few small fish. Offshore, blue holes are equally poor producers of food, but are often well populated by all sorts of marine life because of the shelter they provide. Usually the water is clear, and, like a clear sky, absorbs light in such a way as to produce a deep blue colour.

The water in many blue holes is fresh at the surface, but at a certain depth becomes brackish and then saline. The blue hole can be seen as nature's well, with the deeper ones passing through the various layers of the water lens below. The blue hole at James Cistern in Eleuthera has been used as a public well for many years, but all of those in Long Island are salty at the surface.

In the deeper holes there is often a lack of oxygen in the lower layers. Without waves or currents to stir up the water it becomes stagnant, and divers often report a distinctly yellow layer with a high content of hydrogen sulphide at some point below the surface – at about 20–21 m (65–70 ft) in Church's blue hole. Below this level the bacteria (anaerobic) which rot vegetation and other matter generate this gas, a condition which is also found in swamps.[2]

Limestone crusts These are probably present over all the older rock surfaces in The Bahamas, but are, in fact, only seen when the soil has been stripped away.

The crusts are usually white or reddish in colour, and vary in thickness from about 2.5 mm (0.1 ins) to as much as 50–75 mm (2–3 ins). Areas which have been exposed but not otherwise eroded show the crust to be a continuous feature, resembling a blanket draped over the potholed limestone below, and smoothing off the usually rugged rock surface (Figure 5.20). On close inspection the crust appears to be built up of fine layers, and can be described as *laminated*. Above all it is hard, and quite a bit harder than ordinary limestone, and this accounts for its local name of *'flint rock'*. Unlike the limestone below, it is not porous,

Chapter Fourteen

Saturday morning was now here and with the approaching sunrise came a desire in me to go out and sit on the bench. I wanted to see the sun come up over the water and just sit there on that bench soaking up the quiet solitude of the fresh, cool, peaceful Bahamian morning.

Quietly I slipped out the front door, trying not to disturb my brother sleeping on the sofa bed in the living room. He raised up to see who was going out, and I whispered that I was going to the bench for a while.

The sun was just beginning to peek up over the horizon as I sat down on the bench. It moved so quickly and shrunk in size the higher it got. Majestic color beamed out in all directions. The awesome sight filled me with renewed energy. Again, I thought of the magnetism of this area and the way it had drawn Jay from his first sight of it. I was feeling the pull now too.

Thinking of my first trip here while visiting Jay and meeting Christine for the first time, I remembered how I enjoyed it. Jay had everything planned out carefully and we were doing something interesting the entire time. I didn't recognize the true nature of the area and its eloquence then, but it was now very apparent to me.

Sounds of the waking community began to be noticeable. I saw a man a short distance up the beach come out on his porch and take a look around. The birds were chirping, and a couple of dogs were barking somewhere on the island. My thoughts now seemed directed to the activities of the day, such as laundry I planned to get done and the trip with Christine to meet Michael at Marsh Harbour.

Getting up from the bench, I glanced at the inscription on the backrest. "We Love You Jay" really rang true. I had definitely been able to see how many people do love Jay. I ran my finger over each word carved in the wood, pausing on the name "Jay." I felt so proud of him and what he had done with his life. Tears began to well up and roll down my cheeks as I realized just how much he is loved by all who had come to know him.

After returning to the cottage and spending some time talking with Alan, everyone was dressed and ready to go have breakfast. I slipped all the things needing to be laundered in a pillowcase. We would be passing by Suds Ahoy Laundry as we make our way to the lodge, and I thought I could drop the things off and pick them up later.

The laundry wasn't open yet, so I placed my makeshift laundry bag inside the front door. On the way back from breakfast, I would stop and see if I could get it done. As it turned out, the laundry had so much to do that they said it would be the first of the week before they could have it done. Now it seemed I would have to ask Patte if I could wash a couple of loads at her house.

I really was wanting to give her a little break. With all the activities at her house all week, I could see that she was looking tired. But she graciously insisted it was no bother at all for me to do the laundry there. As I started the first load, Patte put on a pot of coffee.

Since Michael had gone to Nassau, Christine stayed overnight with Patte. They had been up late talking and going over final details of the funeral service. We tried to be quiet and not wake Christine, knowing how she would be needing her rest. Dave was still asleep in the guest room.

When Christine got up, she came and sat down with Patte and me on the porch. Gaily she announced, "Judy, I believe I have the music for the service chosen."

"Oh you do? What did you decide on?" I asked.

She went on to explain how late it was before they all wound down and went to bed. "After I got in bed and was going to sleep, I heard this song playing and knew it was the one for the service. I don't know where the music was coming from. Everyone around was already asleep, and it was about 4 a.m. and there weren't any bands playing at the Edge[5] at this late hour." she commented.

"The music seemed very clear, and it was a song called 'I Can See Clearly Now'—do you know that song? You know which one I'm talking about?" she asked as she continued. "Do you think you can find

---

[5] Local people refer to Harbour"s Edge Bar and Restaurant as the Edge. Live music is provided at various times.

that song on a cassette, Patte? It just seemed so ironic that I couldn't decide on the music, and then this song just comes out of nowhere."

We decided that Jay was helping Christine on this, especially after Patte located the tape with the song, and we listened to the words as it played.[6] I don't know how so many goose bumps could pop up on my body; it felt like every inch of me was covered with them as I heard the song.

Christine asked Patte if she could borrow the tape for her friend who would be singing. She called and made arrangements for her friend to meet us at the marina in the afternoon. This very talented lady would learn the song from the tape and be ready for the service by the following morning. "She must be good," I said to Christine.

"She is very good. She plays and entertains in a lot of nice clubs around the Bahamas," Christine stated.

Dave had joined us for coffee as I was continuing with the laundry. He too was pleased with the song and agreed that Jay must be assisting Christine, helping her to get through with the difficult challenge of planning her husband's funeral service.

The morning slipped away as I finished the laundry. I had packed rather hurriedly so we could leave for the Abacos a week earlier. Tomorrow would be the funeral; and my choice of clothing hardly seemed appropriate, but I wasn't concerned about it. I decided to wear my coral colored jeans and the matching jacket I had packed at the last minute.

This would not be the typical type of funeral I was accustomed to, and I'm glad of that. It will have Jay's very own character planned right into it. Laid-back and easy going, amidst the delightful surroundings of the beautiful Abaco landscape. I could never have planned anything more appropriate for him.

---

[6] See lyrics to "I Can See Clearly Now" on page 82.

"I Can See Clearly Now"

Written by Johnny Nash
Reworked by Jimmy Cliff

I can see clearly now the rain is gone,
I can see all obstacles in my way,
Gone are the dark clouds that had me down,
It's gonna be a bright, (bright), bright (bright) sunshiny day.
It's gonna be a bright, (bright), bright (bright) sunshiny day.

Oh yes I can make it is now the pain is gone,
All of the bad feelings have disappeared,
Here is that rainbow I've been praying for,
It's gonna be a bright, (bright), bright (bright) sunshiny day.

Look all around there's nothing but blue skies,
Look straight ahead, there's nothing but blue skies.

I can see clearly now the rain is gone,
I can see all obstacles in my way,
Here is that rainbow I've been praying for,
It's gonna be a bright, (bright), bright (bright) sunshiny day.
It's gonna be a bright, (bright), bright (bright) sunshiny day.
Real, real, real, real, bright, (bright), bright (bright) sunshiny day.
It's gonna be a bright, (bright), bright (bright) sunshiny day.
It's gonna be a bright, (bright), bright (bright) sunshiny day.
It's gonna be a bright, (bright), bright (bright) sunshiny day.
Real, real, real, real, bright, (bright), bright (bright) sunshiny day.

Jay loved to run around in his T-shirt and baggies. His bare feet and his sun-bleached blonde hair had become his trademarks. He seemed to look for the things in life that brought enjoyment and pleasure to himself and those around him. "This," I thought, "is how he should be remembered." Christine's planning carefully allows for exactly that too.

We had time for some lunch at the cottage and a little relaxation before making the boat trip over to Marsh Harbour. Margaret Rose said her two brothers would be coming in from Nassau today and suggested that all of us go to dinner together at the lodge. She said she would call and reserve a large table for about fifteen people, including Patte and Michael, especially because of the hospitality they have shown all of us during the entire past seven days.

The time came for Christine and I to go get the boat. Michael and Patte keep their boat at the dock by one of the villas they rent. They have rental cottages and advertise Hope Town Villas, the name of their business, in several publications. Michael is also a landscaper and does a lot of work out of his office in Nassau. Patte basically handles the rental business.

Christine handled the boat very well. Quietly in my mind, as we raced across the water, I thought about the two of us left alone now. My son, her husband, now passed on, leaving the two of us behind. I wondered if we would be able to stay in touch, or if as time goes by she would go on with her life and forget about me and our connection to each other.

Being alone the rest of her life did not seem likely for such a beautiful person. I also wouldn't want to see her have to be alone, knowing how much it means to me having a close companion and friend, like Tony in my life. Thoughts came and went, and I wondered why I would even be thinking such things at this particular time.

When we slowed down to enter the marina, we saw Christine's friend waiting at the dock. Christine called ahead to tell her we were on our way. She rode over on a bicycle and was still balancing herself on it as we tied the boat up. Christine hopped out of the boat and introduced us. She then began to show her the tape and discuss how she would like to begin the service with the inspired song, and then have the same song close the service.

This particular phase of our trip was now complete. Christine's friend rode off ahead of us on her bicycle, looking very sporty in her shorts and sweat band around her forehead.

Next to the swimming pool at the marina, there is a little bungalow-type bar. Umbrella tables surround the area, inviting visitors in for a cold drink and a shady place to rest. This is the place where Christine and I ended up waiting. We walked around looking to see if Michael had arrived yet but couldn't see him anywhere. We sat on a cement-and-stone wall built along the street for a while. Then thirst from the afternoon heat won out, and we headed for the bungalow.

Island music played on the stereo as Christine chatted with a few local people she knew. She was courteous about introducing me to them as well. The entire scene just seemed so out of character for what was going on inside us yet at the same time felt so relaxing and enjoyable.

After what seemed to be such a long wait—a fairly good breeze started to cool things off a bit—Christine's uncle appeared. Christine began to cry as her uncle put out his arms and wrapped them around her. He is a jolly, happy man and soon had her feeling much better.

Michael waited at the airport for Christine's uncle so they could ride to the marina together and then on to Hope Town in the boat. But first, the uncle offered to buy us all a nice cold drink before leaving.

The wind began to blow, and it looked as if we could get a little afternoon shower. Michael went to get the boat and move it to the dock where they loaded their things. We thought we'd better get going before it got too stormy to make the crossing.

Once everything was loaded in the boat and Christine and I were seated, Michael handed Christine a brown paper bag. She held it close to herself in her lap. I asked, "Are those Jay's ashes?"

"Yes, Judy." she replied.

Michael got the boat out of the marina and pushed the throttle forward. We were well on our way now for a bumpy ride back. All the way back, time after time, I would glance dumbfounded at the brown paper bag resting in Christine's lap next to me.

It didn't seem real that all that was left of my son's body was inside that brown paper bag, like the kind in which you would carry groceries home from the store. I kept reminding myself that Jay is no longer that body now reduced to ashes, but he is spirit with a new kind of body.

Nearing the entrance of the harbor, Michael pulled back on the throttle and carefully maneuvered the boat up to the dock. Christine asked me to hold the bag as she jumped out to tie the boat up. I could feel a rectangular shaped box inside. In my mind, I envisioned a cardboard box about four inches high and twelve inches wide. I barely had any feeling from it all, except a kind of cold, almost detached sort of feeling.

I handed the bag to Christine and crawled out on the dock. Michael said he would take her uncle down to the other end of the harbor and help him carry his things up to the lodge where he had a room reserved.

Christine and I went on up to Patte's, where we were told we needed to go get ready to leave shortly for dinner. Lou and Chris N. had arrived from the States the day before. Chris W. had picked them up at the airport. They were just returning from Marsh Harbour after picking Mitch up from his flight in. We had just enough time to hug each other and share feelings about Jay for a few minutes, and then Christine and I were called to go meet the others, who were waiting for us to go to dinner.

Lou brought some pictures that he took the past November. Right before Thanksgiving, Jay, Chris W., and Lou set out in Lou's sailboat from West Palm Beach bound for Hope Town with only a compass for navigation.

I remembered the time well because I worried from the time Jay called to say they were leaving until I heard from him Thanksgiving Day. In my mind, I imagined all kinds of bad weather and any possible thing that could have gone wrong in the crossing. When Jay called me to let me know they had made it, I was tremendously relieved.

On Thanksgiving morning, as they were coming into the Bahamas, Lou took a picture of Jay. When I saw this picture, I knew it had to be the best picture of Jay I had ever seen. It captured his spirit, his love of life, the love he had for the water. It simply captured Jay! I asked Lou if he could get me a copy of the picture. It was the one picture that really made me feel Jay's warmth and character.[7]

When I got to the cottage, everyone was dressed and ready to go to dinner. Tony said he would wait and walk down with me as soon as I was ready. Christine's family and my family went on ahead to make the reservation time.

At the lodge, when practically everyone was seated around the table—in the same room where we had Jay and Christine's wedding reception—I turned to Tony and began to say, "I wonder where Jay is?" Suddenly it dawned on me what I was about to say, and a feeling struck me that made my insides ache. I couldn't keep myself from crying. Tony gave his napkin to me to dry my eyes as I told him what I had started to say. My brother heard me and said he almost started to say something similar, about Jay not being there yet.

The dinner turned out to be full of conversation, and a toast was made by Christine's uncle to the memory of Jay. I noticed Christine began to get a faraway look in her eyes, and her face looked long. She could not hold back the tears. Apologizing for crying, she said, "It feels so strange being here without Jay." We reassured her that she did not need to apologize for crying. Then Alan and I told her about what happened to us at the table before she got there.

When it was time for the check, we were told that it had already been taken care of. When we questioned trying to find out who to thank, we finally figured out that Christine's two uncles had paid for the entire dinner. I also found out that the oblong boxes I saw him load into the boat at Marsh Harbour were full of long stem red roses. He brought them to be passed out to each person coming to the 7:30 a.m. funeral service.

On the walk back, we all discussed the travel arrangements for the following morning. The Abaco Inn offered to have their van meet the family by the post office near the public dock and drive us to the White Sound area where the Abaco Inn sits on a hill overlooking the sound. We planned to meet there at 6:45 a.m. for the first load to be

---

[7] See photograph on page 3.

taken. Then the van would have time to make another trip to pick up any other people needing a ride.

Vehicles are not too plentiful on the island. Most places are easily reached by a short walk or bicycle. Jay and Christine have their little white Toyota truck on the island, but Christine said it hadn't been running and needed a part. Dave inspected it and saw what it needed, so Chris N. and Lou were called in time to bring the part over with them from the States. I didn't want to leave Christine here with a truck that was not running, especially since she would be going back and forth to work at night again soon, and now alone.

After everything was set for the next morning, we all headed to bed so we could be up and ready to go. Now, the week that had seemed so long and painful was coming toward a closure. In the morning, Jay's family and friends will be gathering to pay their last respects, and then all will go back to their lives again.

Chapter Fifteen

April 10, 1994 Sunday morning came after a night of very light sleep for me. Through the night I felt as if I was asleep, but my mind still seemed to be awake. It was as if my body was sleeping, and at the same time my mind would be picturing the events of the week. I could see pictures in my mind like I was dreaming about something, but it was not like a regular dream. At times I would see a clear picture and at the same time know I was seeing it. Then as I thought about whether I was asleep or awake, the picture in my mind would fade.

At one of the intervals of thinking about whether or not I was asleep, I looked at the time. It was nearly 5:30 a.m. already, nearly time to get up. Thinking about using the bathroom before everyone else needed a turn, I crawled out of bed.

While brushing my teeth, I took notice of that calm feeling within, the one I was beginning to get accustomed to. The same calmness I had felt the previous Saturday on the boat and at the dock, the day Jay's body was brought in. I liked the way it felt but at the same time felt a little guilty that I wasn't feeling more emotional. "After all, my son has died, I'm getting ready to go to his funeral. Isn't everyone supposed to be crying and hysterical at a time like this?" I thought.

I could hear Mother and Russell getting up and around now as I dressed in the bedroom. Tony woke up and asked the time. Then I heard Alan in the front room. Overall, it was pretty quiet as everyone got ready to make the 6:45 a.m. gathering at the van.

All of us were now ready to go with some time to spare. I was glad we didn't have to hurry and rush around on a morning like this. Somehow, everything just seemed so easy. Having Christine plan the service made it almost seem unreal to me, as if it wasn't really happening. I couldn't imagine what it was going to be like or how it would turn out. What she had told me about her plans sounded very nice.

Stepping out the front door of the cottage, I heard Christine's family next door. They began to appear out into the yard, and we all grouped together to walk to the meeting area. Shortly after we arrived and sat down on a bench at the public dock, the van pulled up and the doors were opened. We found our places in the van and rode quietly toward the Abaco Inn.

When we pulled into the area where the service was to be, I saw several people already gathering under the palm trees. Lots of white lawn chairs were set up in the grassy area beside White Sound. Vernon and his wife were standing near some shrubbery in front of the line of chairs. Directly in front of the first row of chairs, I saw a surfboard.

As we each stepped from the van, Christine's uncle handed each one of us a long stem red rose. We walked toward the front row of chairs and stood to the side, waiting for other people to arrive. Tony, Dave, Christine, Terry, and I stood in one little group. A few people walked over to greet us briefly.

Everything was still and peaceful. The only sound I noticed was of distant boats nearing the entrance of the sound then slowing down to make their way up to the dock.

Jay and Christine's dog, Lucky, was lying in the grass near the surfboard I had seen as we arrived. Now closer, I could see that it was Jay's surfboard. Christine had a wreath, made of native flowers and vines, placed on the top of it. I also saw the small gray canvas backpack that Jay used to carry his belongings around in, lying there with the wreath.

People continued to walk up from all directions. One boat came in, followed by another. Surfboards began to line up in the grass near the hill that hides the ocean on the other side. The last vanload of people unloaded, and practically everyone now carried a red rose.

The service was about to begin, so Vernon directed Christine and I to seats in the front row. Tony sat beside me on my left, and to my right was Christine. Dave sat next to her on the other side. Other family members and Jay's friends filled the other seats. The crowd of people gathered around the chairs in sort of a half circle as if to envelope us in love and strength.

I whispered to Christine, "Where are Jay's ashes?"

She whispered back to me, "They are in Jay's backpack. Louie is going to carry them when we paddle out, and I thought that would be the easiest way to carry them."

"That's a nice idea, using Jay's backpack," I said.

Somehow, without noticing, Christine's friend took the spot where we had been standing and began to play her acoustic guitar. Very rhythmically she played the song that seemed to appear out of thin air to Christine. As she began to sing the words, I recognized her professionalism. She is definitely no amateur because she had learned the song overnight and was singing the words as if they were her own.

While listening to the words, a picture came into my mind of Jay soaring toward and entering a bright light. From this I felt a sense of comfort and strength. The thought came to me that this was what Jay wanted to tell us—"I can see clearly now, the rain is gone…"—with the words of this song.

Next, Vernon began to share words of comfort and tell how he and his family had come to know and love Jay. Vernon's son Bryan, Peter Albury, and Scott Patterson had written some things that they too wanted to share.[8] It was very touching to hear in their own words how they felt about Jay and how they viewed his death.

---

[8] See Peter Albury's poem on page 92.

Vernon had selected two songs for us to sing as a group. The music had been copied and passed out.[9] It became difficult for me to sing at this time because I began to think about the remains of my son in the box, zipped up inside the backpack. I couldn't touch him one last time. I would not be able to see his sweet face again.

Christine and I began to cry as we shared the copy of the music being sung. She put her arm around my shoulders, and I held her hand. I didn't know what she was thinking, but I was thinking how it now appeared to be the end of my son, the end of my motherhood, and the end of my chance of ever being a grandmother.

---

[9] See lyrics to songs on pages 93-94.

JUDITH MILLER

Dedicated to Jay

By Peter Albury

Steep we'll drop
and long we'll glide,
and catch it on
the rising tide.

And as we sit
and wait on waves,
we'll think of all
our yesterdays.

The waves we miss,
you can ride,
we'll catch you
on the other side.

O Love That Wilt Not Let Me Go

O Love that will not let me go,
I rest my weary soul in thee;
I give thee back the life I owe,
That in thine ocean depths its flow
May richer, fuller be.
O Light that followest all my way,
I yield my flickering torch to thee;
My heart restores its borrowed ray,
That in thy sunshine's blaze its day
May brighter, fairer be.
O Joy that seekest me through pain,
I cannot close my heart to thee;
I trace the rainbow through the rain,
And feel the promise is not vain
That morn shall tearless be.
O Cross that liftest up my head,
I dare not ask to fly from thee;
I lay in dust life's glory dead,
And from the ground there blossoms red
Life that shall endless be. Amen.

George Matheson, 1842-1906
St. Margaret 88.886.
Albert L Peace, 1844-1912
THE CHRISTIAN LIFE

JUDITH MILLER

I Know Not What the Future Hath

I know not what the future hath
Of marvel or surprise,
Assured alone that life and death
God's mercy underlies.
And if my heart and flesh are weak
To bear an untried pain,
The bruised reed he will not break,
But strengthen and sustain.
And thou, O Lord, by whom are seen
Thy creatures as they be,
Forgive me if too close I lean
My human heart on thee.
And so beside the silent sea I wait the muffled oar;
No harm from him can come to me
On ocean or on shore.
I know not where his islands lift
Their fronded palms in air;
I only know I cannot drift
Beyond his love and care. Amen.

John Greenleaf Whittier, 1807–1892
COOLING CM
Alonzo J. Abbey, 1825–1887
DEATH AND LIFE ETERNAL

At the same time this pain raged in me, I was also thinking of how happy I was for Jay to be free. A varied mixture of thoughts and emotions were going on simultaneously. Something seemingly new to me in my spectrum of experience. I was feeling pain inside for myself while feeling happiness for Jay at the same time.

The service drew to a close with a prayer said in unison. The musician began to strum her guitar with the familiar song. She began to walk toward the hill as she continued to play. Jay's friends and Christine each slipped into their wetsuit, picked up their surfboards, and followed along behind her. Other people followed her up the little sandy road, leading to the hill overlooking Rush Reef. The family members joined in the trek to the top of the hill and several of us walked on down the other side where the beach meets the surf.

Two local men, who had voluntarily come on their own, played Bahamian music once everyone was in place. I sat down on the sandy white beach to watch the organized group of surfers. All together, the eighteen surfers paddled out into the rolling water to a point we where we could barely see them bobbing up and down. They formed a circle and after they said a few words, they scattered Jay's ashes over the waves. Then one by one they rode the waves back to shore.[10]

When I looked behind me, I saw that many people had planted their long-stem rose into the sand and were now turning to leave. I talked to several people I had met on other trips to the Bahamas, and many I was meeting for the first time. Lots of nice things were shared with me about Jay and their experiences with him. It made me feel so happy to hear these things.

Tony came to hurry me up a little due to the fact that the Abaco Inn was ready to serve the family breakfast. Everything was set up and waiting for us. We were all seated at a long table on the patio at the back side of the building. We had a beautiful view overlooking the ocean where the surfers had just been.

Mother wanted to save her red rose to take home. It was beginning to look rather wilted, so our hostess put it in the cooler until we were ready to leave. Then she proceeded with the help of another

---

[10] List of surfers and musicians names on page 99.

young Bahamian woman to bring coffee and freshly squeezed juice for all of us. We were fed our choice of breakfast with toasted homemade bread and jam. Again, I was amazed at the hospitality shown to us by these fine people.

After breakfast, we were taken back to Hope Town's public dock area by van. All of us were now ready to change into cooler clothing as soon as we returned to the cottage. As we opened the door, we saw a large bouquet of gorgeous flowers that had been delivered while we were gone.

I found out that they were brought over from a flower shop in Marsh Harbour since no flower shops are available in Hope Town. The card read, "Employees of WWQQ and HVS Partners," the radio station I am employed by and the owners of the radio station group. "This in itself was a task," I thought "Calling and finding a flower shop that could deliver flowers by water from so many miles away. How very thoughtful of all my coworkers and employers."

After changing, I mentioned to Alan that I would like to have a picture of the bench Michael and Dave built. We decided to walk on over there with his camera. We sat on the bench talking for a while and then took turns taking each other's picture and then of the bench alone.

I had saved my rose to place by the bench. Others must have had the same idea because around the foot of the bench red rose petals were strewn. On the beach, I saw a single long stem red rose sticking up out of the sand. This lone red rose in particular stood out to me, inviting a memorable picture. I asked Alan if he would also get shot of the rose with the blue water of the ocean in the background.

On the walk back, on the other side of the old cemetery, is the ball field. This is where a few vehicles that belong to people who live close by are parked. Vehicles are limited on the island, and the lanes are wide enough for only one small vehicle to drive on.

At the ball field, we ran into Chris W., Lou, Chris N., and Mitch. They were working on Jay and Christine's pickup truck. I decided to hang around with them for awhile as Alan went back to the cottage. Christine was cleaning out the inside and was finding all kinds of things. Jay's tennis shoes, which he rarely ever wore, and an old sword that my dad had given him when he was a child.

Every time I would see something that was Jay's, I would feel compelled to touch it and hold it. I noticed right away how good it made me feel to touch something of his.

It wasn't long before Christine was cranking up the truck, and it was running fine. I was proud of Jay's friends and of their ability and enthusiasm to help Christine out. Not only had Lou and Chris N. picked up the alternator that was needed for the truck but Mitch had also brought one. "No problem," Lou said, "we'll just return one."

Chris N. came in from Georgia, Lou from Maryland, and Mitch from Florida. They each told about their trips and the circumstances surrounding them.

Lou and Chris N. met in Fort Lauderdale and flew in a small airline to Marsh Harbour. Lou explained that he had left home without his passport. He frantically called his mother and had her write a note and fax a copy of his birth certificate and the pages of his passport to the airline after explaining and pleading with them that he had to get to the Bahamas.

The airline agreed to take him with the faxed information. They also offered to call customs in Marsh Harbour to report the circumstances. When they arrived and had their turn going through customs,

Lou explained the situation. The customs officer said, "Oh yes, we know about this and you are clear to go through."

Lou was just beginning to hear the teasing from the others about how he got into the Bahamas with a letter from his mommy. They were now planning to go surfing or snorkeling for the rest of the afternoon.

Tony came out just as they were ready to leave and suggested we walk down to get an ice cream cone. Some of the best ice cream we've ever eaten has been in Hope Town. We had grown especially fond of the rum raisin flavor that Christine got us hooked on the last time we were there.

Names of surfers:

Peter Albury
Tim Albury
Bill Clemens
Peter Cline
Mitch Davis
Ed Early
Jeff Gale
Steve Gale
Christine Kanitsch Hensley
Lou Kanitsch
Chris Norman
Scott Patterson
Andrew Russell
Cooter Schoonmaker
Chris Thompson
Chris Whitten
Lou Woodward
Dave Zabo

Music performed by

Jan Cartwright
Tuson Bob
Herbie

Evening was packing time for our return flight home. Going home didn't seem like something I was ready to do yet, but I knew I had to go home. I felt more comfortable with the idea of Jay being gone simply by being where he loved to be. Now the thought of having to go home and leave this beautiful place behind began to dwell on my mind.

I also felt sad about leaving Christine. I knew most of her family would be leaving soon. Then she would find herself alone in that little cottage without Jay. It made me feel better when I found out her mother and two sisters would be staying for a few more days. Her sister, Kathy, had come at the last minute and had arranged to stay for a few days. Louie was planning to return and spend a week with her after that. But still, the time would come when she would be by herself, especially at night, the time when loneliness can really set in.

This final night in the cottage gave us a chance to have our last gathering and clean up most of the food still left in the refrigerator. We planned to take the leftovers to Christine's. After my family leaves I would sweep the floors and make sure everything is cleaned up for the arrival of Christine's aunt, who would be coming to stay for a while in the cottage we called home the past eight days.

Bedtime came and we each had our things packed, leaving out the clothes for our return trip home. Mother, Russell, and Alan would leave for the airport in the morning, then on to Kansas. Terry, Tony, Chris N., and I would leave on the afternoon flight to West Palm Beach. Terry would be home, Chris would go on to Georgia, and Tony and I back to North Carolina.

Chapter Sixteen

Morning brought with it a little more desire for me to go home. I was still having some mixed feelings about going. I felt a pull from both directions. I knew that I needed to get back home and begin putting things back in order there and also get back to work soon.

I wondered what it would be like going back and seeing all my friends. What would their reactions be toward me, and what would they say? How would I react to them? Going on as I had before didn't seem possible. I felt different somehow, as if I would be leaving a big part of me behind someplace.

After Mother, Russell, and Alan loaded into the boat for their ride over to the Marsh Harbour Airport, Christine joined Tony, and I for breakfast at Captain Jack's Bar and Restaurant at the edge of Hope Town Harbour. They had offered to feed us one night, but we already had more than enough and felt we should decline their offer, thanking them for thinking of us. When Tony went to pay for breakfast, they insisted that it was on them. Another example of the wonderful hospitality we had been shown during the past eight days.

It didn't take long for me to clean the cottage and strip the beds. I rather enjoyed doing it while imagining myself living there enjoying the peaceful nature of the island. Tony and I even discussed the idea of buying some property there and spending some winter months in Hope Town. I think the environment was beginning to grow on him now too.

Time was drawing near to carry our luggage to the public dock. I was with Christine at Patte's house. They asked me to stay there for a little while, saying they would be right back. When they returned, they were carrying a stained glass piece that Patte and Michael had made.

I had admired the beautiful piece hanging in their workshop the second day we were at their house. It is a colorful display of stained glass pieces carefully fitted together, making a delightful hummingbird that hovers over a yellow flower. Christine held it out to me and said it was the gift that Jay had picked out for my upcoming September birthday.

Three days before Jay died, he called me and asked if I was still planning to come see them in September for my birthday. Each time we talked, he teased me by saying that he had already found my birthday gift. He would tell me how nice it is and how much I would like it. Kidding he said, "If you want it, you'll have to come to Hope Town and see us."

The last night we talked, three days before the accident, he said, "You can come sooner if you want to." It seemed as if he had a tone of urgency in his voice, but I remembered thinking at the time that it was because he was feeling a little lonely. Christine was working and he was home by himself. He said he would really like to see me, and I agreed that I would like to see him sooner than September too but didn't think I would be able to make it sooner. I was also thinking of how hot it is in the summer and reminded him about my dislike for such hot, humid weather.

Now I felt bad for saying anything about the heat. I wished I would have told him that I would come sooner. But even a month sooner wouldn't have been soon enough the way things turned out. Then at that point nothing could have kept me away.

Tears filled my eyes as I again admired the stained glass, and I thanked Christine for giving me a gift that will mean more to me than any other. She and Patte wrapped it carefully with foam and cardboard. They even designed a little handle into the package so I could hand carry it as we made our trip home.

It was now time to go meet at the ferry dock. The closer we came to the dock, the harder it was to hold back the tears. It all began to pour out, and Christine began to cry too. We hugged each other for a long time as we stood there.

Margaret Rose said they would like to take a picture of us all together before we leave. Chris W. offered to take it so the family would all be in the shot together. The Hope Town light house was in the background across the harbor, and the neatly wrapped package was clasped tightly in my hand. Next, they took a picture of Tony and I just as the ferryboat was coming into the harbor, and we said our final good-byes.

The ride over in the ferryboat seemed long, and I was in the rear corner next to Tony. I hoped my sunglasses would hide the tears so the other passengers wouldn't be wondering what was the matter with me. When we arrived at the ferry dock, memories of being there the past Thursday afternoon came back. I couldn't help but think of the white van sitting there with Jay's body inside. I probably would have started crying again had it not been for Tony suggesting that we get off.

Christine's cousin from Marsh Harbour was waiting to pick us up and give us a ride to the airport. We still had a few stops to make before we actually got to the airport to check in. Then at the airport we had a short wait before the plane came in.

I went out front to sit on the open-air benches, and one of the Bahamian officials we had met a few days earlier came by and saw me sitting there. He very kindly held out his hand to me and extended his sincere sympathy. I thanked him for that and for all they had done to assist in the rescue of my son.

It was time to board the plane. Chris N. was seated back one row and across the isle. Terry was in the row directly in front of us. I noticed Chris N. had put his headset on and was listening to a CD as we were on our way. I was beginning to feel very relaxed and thought I could easily fall asleep, but I didn't want to miss the last view of the crystal clear blue water below from my window seat.

Without realizing that I had drifted off to sleep, I was awakened by a touch on my chin. It was the gentlest touch I have ever felt. Right on the underneath side of my chin. I felt this touch gently lift my head up from the forward position it had fallen to. I thought to myself as I opened my eyes, "Tony must have noticed my head fall, so he raised it to prevent me from getting a stiff neck." When I turned to look at Tony, he was reading the *USAir* magazine—not even paying attention to me. I asked if he had touched my chin, and he said no.

I told him what I had felt and he said, "It wasn't me, I've just been sitting here minding my own business." I felt a wave of happiness go through me. This time I was certain beyond a doubt that I had been touched by the hand of my son's new spiritual body. I also felt better as if I had renewed energy.

I looked back toward Chris N. to see how he was doing as he looked at me. I told him what I had just experienced. He said he had been listening to the new Pink Floyd (*The Division Bell*) CD he happened to pick up on the way to the Bahamas. He told me about a song that he and Jay's other friends found to be very interesting, especially under the circumstances.[11] He queued the song up and handed me his CD player.

This song gave me such a strange feeling. If was as if I had a common understanding of how Jay's friends felt when they listened to it. In my mind, I could see them together, as friends often are, going through the actions that this song portrays.

As we neared the West Palm Beach airport, we prepared for the landing. I felt sad knowing that we would be saying good-bye to Terry and Chris N. Another phase of this eight-day journey was now coming to an end.

In the airport we got in line to go through customs. I watched others in front of us showing their documents to the agent, but it didn't register with me. When our turn came, the agent asked for our papers, and it dawned on me that I hadn't pulled ours out. The agent was

---

[11] See song lyrics on page 107.

rather gruff as he suggested that we should have already had them out and ready for our turn.

I thought if he only knew what we have been through, he might be a little more understanding. I apologized for holding up the line as we passed on through.

My fumbling caused me to miss saying good-bye to Chris N. He was well on his way toward his concourse to catch his next plane. Terry waited for us, and we walked together to the door where Louie was to pick him up.

Louie returned to West Palm Beach the previous afternoon. He needed to get back and get some things done before returning to Hope Town the following week. Since he was running a little late, Tony and I waited with Terry until Louie arrived. Terry was looking tired and getting anxious when Louie got there. They loaded the luggage in the trunk and each gave me a hug and shook Tony's hand.

Tony and I were now alone, together. We were both ready to complete the trip home. This comfortable haven that I was beginning to long for now, more and more the closer we got.

Home, the place where I could really unwind and be any way I want to be. Cry as much as I want to cry. Sleep as much as I need to sleep. Do nothing at all if I choose to. Talk openly to Jay if I want without being heard by others. I was definitely ready to be in the comfort of my own home, now.

Tony's middle son, Timothy, met us at the airport to take us home. The topic of conversation turned to business. Tony wanted to be updated on what had been going on while we were away. Business was not the choice of conversation I was interested in. It seemed it would be the first of many rude awakenings as we came back into the busy lifestyle. I thought how supportive Tony had been the past several days, and I realized that he would have to turn his attention back to his business. As for me, I was not ready to think about it.

When we got home and had everything in the house, I walked around looking at things. As I entered the "great room," I could see a rainbow reflection moving on the wall and coming from the direction of the foyer. I glanced down the foyer toward the front door, where our showcase sits holding the little crystal clipper ship. To my amazement that little ship was turning around and around on the solar stand.

I called to Tony to come take a look at it. He asked me how I got it to work. I told him I hadn't been able to get it to work and was reminded that he hadn't been able to either. He said, "Well, it's working now!"

Delightful is how I felt when I saw this miraculous development. I recalled telling Russell about the little ship and solar stand on the day that Jay's body was brought in at Marsh Harbour. Now, I felt convinced that Russell was not the only one to hear the story I told him about the crystal ship. In my heart, I knew that Jay had done this for me, and it gave me such a feeling of comfort.

We were very tired from the trip, so it didn't take us long to find our bed and get in it. I had a difficult time going to sleep due to the memories I had about the last night I had been in our bed. The memory of Christine's phone call came to mind. The rush to pack, make phone calls, and the touch I felt near my feet at the end of the bed came to mind. "Oh how I wish I would have opened my eyes and looked to see what I felt touching the bed then," I thought. Finally, I went to sleep.

Poles Apart

Did you know…it was all going to go so wrong for you
And did you see it was all going to be so right for me
Why did we tell you then
You were always the golden boy then
And that you'd never lose that light in your eyes

Hey you…did you ever realize what you'd become
And did you see that it wasn't only me you were
running from
Did you know all the time but it never bothered you anyway
Leading the blind while
I stared out the steel in your eyes

The rain fell slow, down on all the roofs
of uncertainty
I thought of you and the years
and all the sadness fell away from me
And did you know…
I never thought that you'd lose that light in your eyes

Music: Gilmour
Lyric: Gilmour/Samson/Laird-Clowes

Chapter Seventeen

Before I knew it, Tony was getting up to go to work. He told me to stay in bed and rest. He would stop at Dunkin' Donuts to get a cup of coffee, considerately declining my offer to make him some. I was just beginning to sleep well, so I gladly took him up on his offer.

It didn't seem that I had been back asleep long when I heard the door bell. I got up and put my robe on. When I got to the door I saw Sarah, the wife of a man that works for my husband. She hugged me as I opened the door, and she told me how sorry she was about Jay. "I didn't get to know him very well, but he seemed like such a nice young man," she said.

We went in the great room to sit and talk for a while. With her was a book she wanted to loan to me. She explained that it had brought her a lot of comfort when her sister died, and she wanted to share it with me. I thanked her, and we hugged again as she left with tears in her eyes.

Wide awake now, I decided to make some coffee and get dressed. I should probably get the suitcases unpacked and straightened up the house a little. Then I would get on with finding some time to unwind and relax from the stressful days behind me.

Moving slowly around the house, feeling unable to concentrate enough to complete one task before moving on to another, I kept finding myself sidetracked. I couldn't stay away from the foyer. Repeatedly I walked back to look at the ship, checking to see if it was still turning and watching it as it did.

The phone rang in the midst of my morning a few times. The first call came from Barbara, a friend offering to bring us lunch. Then Tony called to see what I wanted to do for lunch. I told him that Barbara was going to deliver some food from Middle of the Island, our favorite little beach restaurant.

This was one of Jay's favorite places to eat too. We used to eat there together every chance we would get. The first time I ate there was when Jay took me there for breakfast about seven years ago. Then when I met Tony, he and I continued to go there often as he had also been accustomed to frequenting the place.

Tony came home for lunch, and Barbara arrived with a box containing more food than we could possibly eat at one time. It tasted so good and it seemed like ages ago since I had indulged myself in their great home-style cooking. It had been less than two weeks since we had been there, but it strangely seemed so long ago.

Barbara sat down as we ate and began to ask what happened and told me how she had heard about Jay's accident. Her mother had died not long ago, and she still felt the pain from that. She also has a son, and in the past we often shared feelings about having our sons. This made it easier for her to understand where I was coming from.

After Barbara and Tony left, I set out to accomplish the things I had started earlier. It wasn't long before Cheryl called and said she was coming to see me. She said she couldn't wait any longer and she would be over in a little while.

When Cheryl arrived, she started crying as she hugged me and said she was glad I was back. She said she brought some things the radio station wanted us to have and went back to her car to bring them in. Our station manager, Chuck, had sent her to Honey Baked Hams, and she brought us a ham, casseroles, rolls and honey mustard.

At least I knew I wouldn't have to go out to eat for a few days or attempt to try to cook. Right now, I didn't feel like stepping out the front door of our house. Our screened-in back porch immediately became my place of refuge. This is the place I took Cheryl so we could sit down and talk.

Cheryl began, "I wish there was something I could do or say to help you, but there isn't anything that anyone can really do to help. I know it isn't going to be easy to get through this"—she paused—"no, I don't know! I can't even imagine what it must be like to lose a child. I don't even want to try to imagine what it must be like."

One of the bonds that Cheryl and I have in common is that we both had only one child. We both named our son Jason, and her Jason seemed to like all the same things my Jason liked at that age. Even though my Jason was several years older than hers, we still considered it to be one of our links to each other. We took an instant liking to each other from the moment we met and have continued to be friends since.

Long-distance phone calls to and from Cheryl while in the Bahamas helped me more than she could ever know. I could never express how much it meant to me to be able to cry and talk freely about Jay. I always felt safe and comfortable talking to Cheryl about anything.

"Some of the others at the station would like to stop by and see you. Is there any particular time that you would like them to come?" Cheryl inquired.

"Well, anytime in the afternoons, I guess. I'm not planning to go anywhere. I just know that I'm not ready to get out yet," I replied. "I don't think anyone would expect you to get out. I think that's why they want to come by here," she answered.

Cheryl decided it was time for her to go and hugged me again at the door as she reminded me, "If you need anything, even if it's just to talk in the middle of the night, call me. All right?"

"OK, I will, thanks," I assured her.

By now, I was feeling so tired that I felt like I had to lie down for a while. Going to bed in the afternoon was really out of character for me, but it was very becoming very inviting, so I succumbed to the invitation.

The next thing I knew, Tony was getting home from work. I jumped off the bed thinking that I didn't want him to catch me sleeping. Laziness was not something I was accustomed to be accused of. Going to bed in the daytime could appear lazy to him, so I thought if I met him as he walked in, he wouldn't know I had been sleeping. But the first thing he asked was what I had been doing. I explained how tired I had become and that I had been resting for a while.

Through the rest of the evening, Tony talked to several different people on the phone. I would hear him tell people in his words what had happened and how I was doing. He would say, "I think she is doing great, I couldn't have done it as well as she has been doing. She's doing really good."

In reality I was beginning to feel awfully devastated, and hearing him say how well I was doing seemed like a lie to me because it didn't ring true with the way I was feeling inside. I didn't know how to tell him this; therefore I would just smile at him when I heard him tell someone that.

Chapter Eighteen

Week two of this terrible ordeal was different than that of the first week. This week I didn't want to get out of bed in the mornings. Quite a change when compared to last week when we were still in the Bahamas. There I couldn't make myself stay in bed and was awake even before the sun rose most days.

This week was filled with floral deliveries, visitors, and phone calls. I felt frail and weak, almost as if I was walking around in a dream state. I ate when it was time to eat because I knew I needed to, not because I wanted to. I wanted to talk about Jay, to anyone who would listen and get the pictures of him out and show them to my visitors.

The newspaper articles, map, and book I brought back with me were also shown when company would come. These things made it easier to give a clearer picture of what had happened. This also took some of the pressure off me having to repeat the long story so many times, although I did try to explain some of the discrepancies in the articles to everyone.

Mother called to see how I was doing and I told her what had been happening since we got home. She began to tell me about the rose she had carried all the way back to Kansas. The wilted rose she had packed in her suitcase—so she could press it when she got home—had opened up and looked as if it had just been picked from the bush.

Christine and I stayed in touch with each other. She would tell me how she was doing, and I would tell her how I was doing. The different things we each experienced were shared with each call.

A friend, who is also one of my clients, called to say she and her husband would like to stop by to see me, so we planned on two o'clock that afternoon. Ginger suggested that she would call first just in case we decided to go out for a while.

When they arrived, I took them to the porch so we could place the lovely plant they brought and sit for a visit. Ginger hesitantly began to tell me of her call before they left to come over. "I don't know if you are aware of the message on your answering machine, but I thought I should say something because you may want to change it now."

"We don't have an answering machine," I replied. "Are you sure you dialed the right number?"

"I was certain that I did," Ginger answered.

"What did the message say?" I asked.

"It said something like 'This is Jay. We're not in right now, but if you'll leave your number, we'll get back to ya.'"

By now Ginger's husband was saying that it must have just been a wrong number and a coincidence that Ginger got a message from another person named Jay.

Not wanting to alarm them with my thoughts, I didn't say how I truly felt it was Jay. However, that was what I had been thinking as she told me what she heard. I didn't know how it could be possible, but somehow Jay was managing to get a message to me.

After visits from several of my coworkers, who brought cards and flowers, my back porch was beginning to look like a greenhouse. It was alive with plants and arrangements. The basket I got out to put cards in began to fill up. Each day the mailman brought a handful of cards to add to my collection. And each day, as I opened and read them, I would cry.

The Bauers, our new next-door neighbors, stopped in to see us one evening. They brought us a cake from Apple Annie's, my favorite bakeshop. Touched by hearing about the death of my son, they wanted to tell me how sorry they were. They explained that they too have a son. Hearing about me losing mine really made them think about how much he meant to them.

Surprised to be meeting new neighbors, I didn't even think to invite them in. I just thanked them for the cake. After they had expressed their concern, they left. It wasn't long after they left that I wondered where my manners had gotten off to—I hadn't even invited them past the front door.

I could see how the experience of losing my son was perhaps in some way a real eye opener to some people, especially the ones who had only one child or only one son.

Peggy, the radio station's business manager, came to see me on Wednesday this first week home. Having an only son, she too could relate to me. She said she could almost feel the pain herself as she had thought of what it would be like to lose her only child.

While we talked, she said that she had come to tell me of an idea that Gisella had. Gisella is one of the HVS Partners, owners of the radio station group. Peggy said Chuck had asked her to talk to me about this, thinking it would easier for her.

This idea came as a big surprise to me. Gisella thought it would be nice for the radio station to sponsor a scholarship fund at the University of North Carolina at Wilmington in Jay's memory. When Peggy told me this, I began to cry. Quickly I assured her that I thought it was a wonderful idea, and I was crying from delight, not sadness. I felt so honored that Gisella would think enough of me and my son to do something like this.

Peggy explained that both owners, Gisella and Tom, would stop by to see me the following Thursday afternoon. Ron, who is the general manager in Salisbury, Maryland, and Chuck, our Wilmington general manager, would bring them.

I felt elated after Peggy left. I could hardly wait to tell Christine about the scholarship fund. When I called to tell her, she was out. Normally I don't like to leave messages on answering machines, but this time was different. When she called me back, she asked what this was I was saying on the message about a scholarship. I then explained the fantastic thing the radio station was going to do, and she thought it was great too.

This prompted a lot of phone calls. I wanted my brother and his family to know about it, and Mother and Russell as well. All agreed that this was such a wonderful thing for Gisella to think of doing, and I would keep them informed about it as plans for a fundraiser were started.

During this week I began to gather every picture I could find of Jay. I looked through them one by one and remembered different things that we had done or talked about, from his birth to his time of death. I decided that I wanted to put all these things together in one place so I could get to them easily when I want to see his face and refresh the memories I have.

I found pictures he made and brought home from school, little treasures he had saved and I put away for him. Baby clothes and his first pair of cowboy boots. A camel costume I made for him for his Sunday school Christmas program. His scout uniform with each badge he earned. Baby teeth that were retrieved from under his pillow after he had gone to sleep. His baby book with a lock of his hair from his first haircut. The Tommee Tippee cup and bowl he ate from and his little silver feeding spoon. Also, the little turquoise and silver baby ring.

I found a few things he had saved that tied his grade school years to the last few years of his life. A crossword puzzle printed on a picture of the Santa Maria. One math paper with a picture of a Spanish galleon, a pirate, and treasure chest. A crayon picture he had drawn of a clipper. One of his papers from his writing class had letters of the alphabet and only two words written on it: "at boat." Then I found a little book he made entitled "Life in the Sea."

Then the real quencher! The October 19, 1977, *Weekly Reader*. This edition had a color picture of a diver wearing a wetsuit, mask, and other dive gear. The diver is touching a large starfish that clings to a coral reef. The short story that went with the picture read:

> What would you do with an old ship or some old tires?
> Some people put them in the ocean.
> Why do people put old things in the ocean?

Sea animals will come to live on the old things.
They'll live on almost anything placed in the ocean.
The fishing gets better near the things.
What do divers find when they go down to check the old things?
They find clams sticking to the sides of the old things.
They see fish swimming around.
They see crabs looking for food.
They see coral growing there.
The old things are homes for many animals.

There was no doubt whatsoever in my mind that Jay was doing what he loved most when he died. His entire life reflected this truth. I felt proud of him for actually doing what he loved to do, doing what he felt drawn to do.

The way he got to the Bahamas in the first place was with Chris W. He and Chris went and ended up diving with a man who had located an old Spanish galleon wreck, sometimes spending one or two weeks at a time camped in a rather secluded area where this old ship was located. They would dive to uncover the pieces to the puzzle that surrounded this mysterious wreck.

Jay was absolutely enthralled with this old shipwreck. He wanted to tell me more about it than he could. He was keeping an oath of silence for the man's discovery, so he said very little about it. It was not until I had the opportunity to meet this man that I found out more.

Yes, Jay definitely had a love and respect for the ocean. He loved the water, the sea life, the recreation it offered, and he loved the mystery that it contains.

Chris W. shared a story with me one night in the Bahamas. He remembered how he, another man, and Jay were sitting on the edge of a boat one evening talking. The man tossed a bottle over the edge, and Jay dove into the water and brought the bottle back up. Chris and the other man sort of scolded him for diving in like that. Chris said it was because of the sharks coming in to feed in the evening hours, and they wanted to warn him. But Jay's reply was "Nobody litters in my ocean."

When we were in Hope Town for Jay and Christine's wedding, Jay and I sat and talked on the beach one afternoon. That is when he told me about the blue holes and his desire to dive in them. He suggested that if I could learn to dive, I could go with him. I have to admit it was intriguing to me as well. Even if it was dangerous—and I cautioned him to be careful if he did dive there—I could understand his desire.

Another interesting thing that came to my attention during this first week home was our desk calendar. This is one of the Heartland Samplers flip-over type. On April 2, the day Jay died, it read:

> Forgetting what is behind and straining toward what is ahead, I press on toward the goal to win the prize for which God has called me heavenward in Christ Jesus.
>
> —Phil. 3:13–14 NIV

> The essence of genius is to know what to overlook.
>
> —William James

On the cover of the calendar is a color drawing of a mallard duck, Jay's favorite wildlife bird. From childhood on, Jay collected anything having to do with mallards. He even saved their little pintails that he found.

With the papers he had saved from high school, I found his hand-written rough draft of his autobiography. Along with this was the typewritten copy that he had turned in to be graded by his English teacher.[12]

Another project that I began to work on this week was to write thank-you notes to friends and relatives that sent flowers and food. I also wanted to write letters to the divers and to the people in the Bahamas that contributed so much of themselves for so many days.

I kept thinking that if I could get these things all done, I would feel better and finally begin to feel rested. But as I would finish one

---

[12] See autobiography in Appendix A.

thing, I would find other things I felt compelled to do. Such as framing favorite pictures of Jay to place around the house; drying and pressing flowers from the flower arrangements, typesetting song lyrics and poems that had special meaning to me regarding Jay, especially "I Can See Clearly Now."

Chapter Nineteen

As the second week rolled over into the third week since Jay's death, I began to think about having to go back to work. I had decided to stay home for another week, realizing that I just didn't have myself together enough to go back yet.

Cheryl was still taking care of my business for me and was beginning to have questions about one thing or another. Some things she would ask me about would have to do with some of my advertising clients. I found it was difficult for me to remember details of what I had been doing at work before Jay's death.

I thought maybe it was because of the two week absence without thinking about work that was probably why I couldn't remember these things. Then Cheryl would shrug it off and say, "That's all right, I'll get it worked out. Don't you worry about a thing."

When Gisella, Tom, Ron and Chuck came to see me, Chuck asked when I thought I could come back. I told him I was thinking of coming back on Monday. He told me to take as much time as I needed. Even if I just wanted to work half days for a while, it would be fine.

"Everything is under control right now, and Cheryl is doing a good job taking care of things for you," he assured me.

Gisella told me some of her ideas about having a fundraiser and getting a nice amount of money together to set up the scholarship fund. She explained that she and Cheryl have been talking about this. Cheryl was setting up a meeting with some people from the university for next week to get things underway.

I was beginning to feel overwhelmed with emotions. Not many people are ever fortunate enough to have a job like I have and work for such outstanding people as these. It was getting difficult for me to hold back my feelings. I wanted to let them know how much I appreciate their efforts and everything they have done for me, but words like these are difficult to find.

During this third week since Jay died, I began to cry over the littlest things. I started going out of the house with Tony some. This felt strange to me. I felt like a stranger in the very place I learned to call my home.

One day I went with Tony to Redix, my favorite shopping place at Wrightsville Beach. They sell great clothes, beach items, and all kinds of fishing and boating equipment. I followed Tony back to the fishing department. While we stood at the counter, I looked up on a shelf and saw some white rubber fishing boots. Just as I remembered the time that Jay bought some boots just like these, a pain shot through me—like a bolt of lightning. Instantly, I was in tears and told Tony I was going out to the truck.

When he came out, he questioned why I was crying. With some difficulty speaking, I told him about glancing up and seeing the boots like Jay had and how that painful feeling hit me.

I wasn't sure he understood why a pair of white rubber fishing boots could set me off like that. But then I wasn't completely sure I knew why it did either.

Another time, Tony drove by an apartment that Jay and Chris W. used to share. As soon as I saw it, I burst into tears again. It seemed as if every memory I had of the time they lived there flashed through my mind in an instant, without even attempting to remember these things.

The little crystal ship in the showcase stopped turning. I noticed it the morning of the twentieth day from Jay's death. It seemed that I had lost Jay all over again. While I had previously felt comfort from the turning ship, now I would have to sacrifice that as well. Before, I could feel the presence of Jay near as I watched the ship. Now it felt cold, as if his presence was no longer around.

I know Tony was beginning to get concerned about my behavior. My crying at the drop of a hat was starting to bother him. He didn't know what to do to help me and was getting frustrated. At times I could hear him talking to people on the phone, telling them that all I do is sit on the porch, smoke cigarettes, and cry. It was becoming obvious that Tony was losing patience with me when he told me, "You've just got to get over it!"

All I could think of was that I had lost my only child, my only chance of ever being able to carry on my own bloodline. My chance of having grandchildren was gone, and I had no one of my own to leave the legacy of my life with.

Sure, I have two nieces and a nephew (Allison, Blain, and Laina), but that is not the same as my own child. I love them and they will become heirs with my brother. But it is simply not the same! After all, Jay had only been gone about three weeks. How could he expect me to just "get over it?"

I felt angry with Tony for saying this to me. Then the more I thought about what he said, confusion began to set in. I was beginning to think that I was not doing things right. After all, what is the right way to grieve over the loss of one's child anyway?

The first day back to work was drawing nearer. I dreaded it so and wished more and more that I could just stay in the comfort zone of my house compiling the memories of my son to leave to—God knows who.

I had started an album of pictures, obituaries, and newspaper articles. Each day I would work on these things, arranging and adding to them and looking into the eyes of my son as he looked out from the pictures. Certain pictures, like the one of Jay wrestling with my dad, would make me smile.

Two of the favorite men in my life were no longer with me. The thoughts of not hearing their voices, seeing their faces, or touching them gave me an empty feeling inside. I would remind myself that I still have Tony, Russell, and Alan. But Jay—Jay!—was no longer with me, and it hurt. It hurt like no words could ever describe. A pain in the very depth of my heart, radiating out through each cell in my body.

Each day, as I would finish working on the album, I would place everything on the coffee table in the great room. When Tony would get home, I would attempt to sit and watch TV with him. It wouldn't be long and I would end up back on the porch.

Watching TV seemed ridiculous. Tony would act disinterested, so I wouldn't try to talk to him about Jay and the death. He appeared to be tired of hearing about it. "Perhaps this was an easier way for him to deal with his emotions," I thought. So I would head back out on the porch to sit and allow my mind to wander.

Chapter Twenty

When Monday morning came, I carefully prepared myself to go to work. Hoping to look nice and not give the impression of how I was actually feeling inside, I took extra care to dress well and apply the proper amount of makeup. Taking one last look at myself in the mirror, as tears began to well up in my eyes, I thought that I didn't look like a mother suffering from grief. My preparation had been successful.

This was to be my first real understanding of "one can never know what kind of problems a person has just by looking at them." The double thought of not wanting to give the impression that I was grieving and at the same time wanting to grieve, was baffling.

At work my coworkers all greeted me with hugs and encouraging words. I was welcomed back and felt comfortable not having so much put back on me right at first. Several times I found myself talking about Jay and the accident.

The first days back to work usually ended early. By early afternoon I felt exhausted. It felt like all the energy had been zapped from my body. Since I had been given the opportunity to work partial days, I wrapped things up and went home early to rest.

I started to see just how easy it was for me to lie down for a while and quickly drift off to sleep. It didn't take long for me to get over feeling guilty for resting during the day. I felt so much better for doing it. My mind even improved in clarity after waking from the sleep.

One afternoon, I woke up and started to work on the album. I was adding some pictures that I had developed from some old negatives. I found the negatives in my cedar chest, while looking for items belonging to Jay. These were pictures taken during Jay's childhood. When Dave and I divorced, he kept the photo albums. I had very few pictures of Jay as a child, so when I found the package of negatives, I felt I had found a treasure.

While putting the things back on the coffee table, I thought, "What a nice compilation I have of Jay's life, from the birth to death. I stood there looking at the things and touching them. In my mind I heard a quiet, soft voice say, "You should write a book."

Without much thought of where this voice was coming from, I replied, "Me? Write a book? I don't know how to write a book. All I've ever written are poems, song lyrics, and commercials. How could I ever write a book? Oh, I don't know about that!" Then I thought how silly it would look to Tony if he walked in and saw me talking to myself. I soon had my mind off of the subject.

The day that Gisella and I were to meet with the ladies from UNCW turned out to be very promising. We met Margaret Taylor Robison and Elaine Penn in the conference room. Gisella asked if I could tell them a little about Jay after she explained what she would like to do in Jay's memory.

I told them how Jay loved the ocean and the life it has and his concern to protect it. Then I explained how he met Christine and they were married. I shared with them the picture of Jay on the sailboat as well as how he died.

I could see that these two ladies were touched by hearing the story. Elaine especially seemed to savor each word. They asked a few questions and began to explain the types of funds that could be set up.

Gisella wanted to set up a fund that would continually recognize outstanding students in the oceanic department year after year. They explained that a named endowment fund would do that. It could be started with fifteen thousand dollars.

Another thing they told us about was the documentary the university had been working on called "River Run—Down the Cape Fear to the Sea," a study of the Cape Fear River's water quality and issues that affect its future. Upon completion, it would be aired on the public access channels, made available to schools and anyone else with an interest in it.

Gisella got this look in her eyes and asked, "Do you think we could have a memorial to Jay added at the end of the documentary? We could make a donation to help in the cost of the production. Let's say of about one thousand dollars."

Margaret and Elaine looked at each other and Margaret said, "We don't see why not, but we would need to get it cleared and get back to you."

Another meeting was planned for the following week. In the meantime, they would contact us as soon as they had clearance on the documentary.

Before the day was over, we had the approval. They said they would need something written to put at the end of the documentary where the credits are shown. There was also the possibility of having Jay's picture added too. But that would depend on how far along the editing was.

The picture that Lou took of Jay on the sailboat would have to be overnighted to make it in time. I called for Lou, and he and I began to work out a plan to get a copy of the picture.

As it turned out, the editing was too far along to be able to use the picture. It would have been to costly to have to go back in and rework the film, so the memorial I wrote was tagged to the end.[13]

---

13   See memorial on page 130.

DIGEST

University Bond Issue Passes

UNCW students can expect some relief for overcrowded science labs and classrooms. On Nov. 2, North Carolinians passed a $310 million bond issue to build improvements to North Carolina's state universities. Within the package was a $18.5 million science building for UNCW and $992,000 to enlarge and renovate UNCW's Bear Hall. The measure passed statewide with 53 percent of the vote — 63 percent in New Hanover County.

"The bond issue result shows the confidence the greater community has in the university," said Chancellor James R. Leutze. "North Carolinians have always been visionary thinkers when it comes to the value of higher education."

UNCW, in partnership with the other universities in the UNC system, mounted an intensive effort to inform the public about the need for the university improvements on the Nov. 2 ballot.

The chancellor thanked all those in the university community who worked hard on behalf of the bond issue, and expressed appreciation to the media for its fair coverage.

The new science building and improvements to Bear Hall will help to house rapidly growing programs in chemistry, physics, biology and earth sciences.

UNCW is among the fastest growing campuses in the University of North Carolina system. In recent years, classroom and laboratory space has not kept pace with enrollments, which have swelled by 25 percent in the last five years.

— *Mary Ellen Polson*

UNCW Plans Documentary on the Cape Fear River

It is made up of more than 6,189 miles of stream and passes through nearly a third of North Carolina's counties. From its beginnings in Moncure, N.C., to its mouth near Bald Head Island, the Cape Fear River shapes the cities and towns that line its banks.

Wilmington relies on the Cape Fear for drinking water. Industries and municipalities dispose waste into it. Pleasure boaters use it for recreation. As important as the river is to the livelihood of North Carolina, what do we really know about its condition? Not much, say researchers at UNCW.

That's why the university wants to develop a program to study the river's water quality and issues that will affect its future.

"Right now, there's no statewide monitoring system for the river," said Project Director Elaine Penn. "We want to serve as an information source so that future decisions about the Cape Fear can be made based on scientific fact." The university will serve as a valuable resource to state and local governments and the industries that line the river.

The university's first step is the upcoming production of an hour-long documentary that will air on public television stations across the state, and possibly nationwide, next spring.

Frank Chapman (foreground) observes as Mary Moser and Chancellor James Leutze wrestle some white water along the Cape Fear.

Written by Philip Gerard, director of professional and creative writing at UNCW, the program will explore the river's history, with visits to historic sites like Brunswick Town and Moore's Creek, and take a look at efforts now under way to preserve the river and the things that can be done to maintain it for generations to come.

Chancellor Jim Leutze and a hearty crew of university staff members, researchers, videographers and several reporters spent three days last spring traveling down the river by canoe and then power boat. The group completed initial filming of the documentary, collected water samples, and studied areas of discharge along the river's banks.

"The documentary isn't an exposé," said Penn. "Instead, we hope to educate people about the river so that we can all take responsibility for its future."

— *Carolyn Busse*

At least now I had the picture, the one that captured Jay at his finest. In a boat on the water. Where he loved to be. I had several copies made to send to friends and relatives. It was the best current picture, perfect for everyone to remember Jay by.

A couple of weeks later I received a call from a man identifying himself as Terry Tomalin, outdoors writer for the *St. Petersburg Times* in Florida. He said that he was doing a story about the cave divers and their efforts in rescuing cave diving victims. His plan was to focus on Jay's rescue.[14]

Gary and Al had given him my phone number from the letter I had written. They suggested that he contact me and include some of my thoughts on the story.

During the interview, Terry asked if I had a picture of Jay that he could use in the article. I answered, "Boy do I have a picture. Just the right one." He promised to send me a copy of the paper as soon as it was printed.

Ecstatic with the idea of an article being published in the *St. Petersburg Times*, I called to tell Christine. I guess I was hoping that she would be as excited as I was. I had been careful to make sure that I told the reporter about Christine and the other people in the Bahamas. I explained how much they had done for us and how Christine led the surfers in the disposition of Jay's ashes.

When I received the copy of the article, I found that Jay's name was spelled wrong. Christine and the others had not even been mentioned. I felt terrible about this and wanted to call her to tell her what had happened.

By the time I was able to reach her, she had already seen a copy of the article that had been faxed to Vernon. I felt disappointment coming from her voice, but she said she understood how those things can happen. She said the paper was just looking for a story they could sensationalize.

---

[14] See St. Petersburg Times story on page 128-129.

Below is the article that published in the *St. Petersburg Times*.

St. Petersburg

Deep dive, grim find

Two Largo cave divers went to the Bahamas to search for a diving victim. His life was the water, his mother said, and the water took his life.

By TERRY TOMALIN
Times Staff Writer

The telephone was ringing when Coleen Marshall opened her dive shop that Tuesday morning.

"We were their last hope," she said. "They had nowhere else to turn."

Three young men had died scuba diving in a cave in the Bahamas. Divers quickly recovered two bodies, but now, three days later, the third had yet to be found.

The caller, a friend of the missing man's family, found Sea Hunt in the yellow pages.

"Our advertisement mentions cave diving," explained Gary Perkins, who co-owns the Largo dive shop. "I guess that's why he came to us."

The victim's family was willing to pay, the caller said. How much would it cost?

Nothing, Perkins replied.

"Who could accept money for something like that. We had the training. How could we say no."

• • •

Locals call it the "Blue Hole."

Times photo - BRIAN BAER

DIVING ELITE: Al Pertner, above, helped recover the body of Jayson Hensley, left, who was lost in an underwater cave several days earlier.

From the surface, you'd never know it was there. Saltwater caves appear inviting to divers in search of lobster or grouper.

They enter, swim a few feet, and wonder, should I go on? Most back out. But a few, overconfident or, perhaps, simply naive, resist the natural urge to stay in the safety of daylight. They kick toward the darkness, and die.

Matthew Fidler and Ryan Smith, 17-year-olds from Virginia Beach, Va., didn't have much scuba diving experience. Smith had learned to dive only a few weeks before.

The third diver that day was their friend Jayson Hensley. He had led other divers on tours of the ocean cave before. Hensley wasn't a trained cave diver but was comfortable in the water. He loved to surf, fish and sail.

"He knew the water," said his mother, Judy Miller. "It was as if he were born in it."

Divers had found Fidler and Smith together, 100 feet from the cave's entrance. What they found was gruesome. They didn't want to go back down into the cave to look for Hensley.

"It was too much for them," Miller said. "One of them got sick. They just couldn't do it again."

But the North Carolina woman couldn't bear the thought of her only child, alone, in that cold, dark coffin of the sea.

"I couldn't leave him down there," she said. "If I had to sacrifice everything, spend all my money, whatever, I'd do it. I had to get my son back."

• • •

Florida has about 500 certified cave divers, and about 50 of them are trained to recover cave diving accident victims. Law enforcement maintains a list of trained recovery divers who will respond anywhere in the world.

Al Pertner and Gary Perkins' names are on that list. But Judy Miller had a friend who acquired their services the old-fashioned way — the telephone book. It was three days after Easter.

"We didn't have much time to get ready," Perkins said. "We got the call and a few hours later we were on a jet to the Bahamas."

The plane set down at 1:30 p.m. They told the pilot to wait.

"We didn't think it would take that long," he said. "We were wrong."

The long boat ride to the accident site gave both men time to think. Rolling across turquoise seas, they passed dozens of beautiful coral reefs.

"Why dive in a cave when you have all these wonderful reefs," Pertner said. "It is hard to understand."

At 4:30, after an 18-mile boat ride, they reached the dive site. They strapped on their gear and descended about 75 feet to the cave.

Their electric lights glistened off white walls as they moved slowly across the sand bottom. A passageway led off to the right, and Pertner paused to look.

"Something hit me ... like I got punched in the face," he said. "I knew he was in there."

But the rescue divers stuck to their game plan. They traveled deep into the cave, trailing a safety line to guide them out.

"That's the natural course ... when somebody panics, they swim toward the clear water," Pertner said. "And that is usually deeper into the cave."

But the cave was empty.

• • •

When Pertner and Perkins came back without the body, Miller began to panic. Please don't give up, she thought, please don't leave my boy down there.

Pertner and Perkins stayed the night. They did what rescue workers shouldn't do.

"We ate dinner with them, looked at photographs of the boy and shared stories," Pertner said. "I wish we hadn't. It's hard enough to do something like this without becoming part of the family's sorrow."

Neither man slept that night. Pertner paced the room. He's in that cave, he thought to himself, he's in that cave.

Perkins went over the possibilities. Maybe he went into another cave. Maybe he surfaced and was swept out to sea.

Dawn brought no answers, just another long boat ride and an empty cave at the bottom of Blue Hole.

The first and second dives of the day were discouraging. Adjacent caves produced nothing.

They were running out of time; they had been too deep for too long. They could squeeze in one more dive.

Let's try the first tunnel again, Pertner told Perkins. *I've got a hunch. I know he's down there.*

It took time to get through the narrow passageway. They were running low on air. Then Pertner saw a fin mark in the sand.

"It was one of those 'belly in the silt, tank on the roof' kind of openings," Pertner said. "But once I was in, I knew exactly

FROM BEGINNING TO END AND BACK AGAIN

Times

where he was. I couldn't see in all the silt, but I swam right to him."

They tied a guide line to his body and swam back to the surface.

■ ■ ■

The local police asked the divers to tell the family.

"As we came in back to the dock, the whole family was there waiting," Pertner said. "We could see them through the window."

The divers sat in the living room because Hensley's mother had gone to the store.

"It was only 10 minutes, but it seemed like 10 hours," Perkins said. "Everybody quiet, just sitting there looking at us."

When Mrs. Miller returned, Perkins broke the news.

We found him.

Another sleepless night, followed by another long boat ride. Recovering a 5-day-old body is grim work.

"You can't help but leave a little piece of yourself down in that cave," Pertner said. "It is something you never forget."

They brought Jayson Hensley to the dock in a body bag. His mother wanted one last look, but Pertner advised against it.

"I remember pulling away from the thing. She just waved softly. That was all the thanks I'd ever need."

"Those men were special," Mrs. Miller said of Pertner and Perkins. "I know how hard it was for them. They helped me, how much I can never say. Now, finally, I can move on."

Hensley's body was flown to Nassau for an autopsy. A few months before, he had then returned to the sea.

"He was environmentally conscious and believed that our future was tied to the ocean," she said. "His life was the water."

On a warm morning, Hensley's surfing buddies paddled his ashes out beyond the break. They scattered his remains, then, one by one, rode waves back to the beach.

Times photo — RICARDO FERRO
TOOLS OF THE TRADE: Scuba divers Gary Perkins, left, and Al Pertner show the equipment they use on recovery missions deep inside underwater caves.

39 River Run Jim Leutz and students from UNC-Wilmington journey down Cape Fear river, assessing its envionmental and cultural value.

"River Run—Down the Cape Fear to the Sea"
A production of the University of North Carolina at Wilmington,
NC State and UNC Television. Copyright 1994

Below is the memorial tag shown at the close of this film.

In loving memory of Jason Alan "Jay" Hensley. His belief that the future of our planet depends on the preservation and research of the Earth's bodies of water will live on forever in the hearts and minds of his family and friends.

FROM BEGINNING TO END AND BACK AGAIN

Center for Marine Science Research
The University of North Carolina at Wilmington

7205 Wrightsville Avenue
Wilmington, North Carolina 28403
910-256-3721

Revised 5-20-94

THE CAPE FEAR RIVER PROGRAM

The Cape Fear River Basin is a valuable natural resource important to North Carolina and especially to the southeast region of the state. The river is currently being used for industry, transportation, recreation, as a public water supply, and for aesthetic enjoyment. The water quality of the Cape Fear River must be managed in order to ensure that the river continues to serve as a valuable resource.

The **mission** of the Cape Fear River Program is to develop an understanding of processes which control and influence the Cape Fear River and to provide a mechanism for information exchange and public education. The initial area of concern will be the lower Cape Fear River Basin. Specific **objectives** are:

A. Develop, implement, and manage a basin-wide coordinated physical, chemical, and biological water quality monitoring program. Point, non-point, and naturally occurring sources will be considered in developing the monitering plan.

B. Interact with regulatory agencies, academic institutions, local industries, and other groups to determine additional studies and analysis needed to develop an effective and successful management plan. Initiate the studies, and assist in securing funding to conduct the research.

C. Develop scientific information to provide environmental education about the basin targeting point and non-point source contributors and produce reports to identify changes or trends.

D. Develop, consolidate, and maintain a data base on the Cape Fear River Basin including historical and current data and make data available to public and private requestors including regulatory agencies.

Teaching • Research • Service
A constituent institution of The University of North Carolina — C. D. Spangler, Jr., President
an equal opportunity employer

JUDITH MILLER

Center for Marine Science Research
The University of North Carolina at Wilmington

7205 Wrightsville Avenue
Wilmington, North Carolina 28403
910-256-3721

STATEMENT OF PURPOSE

The Center for Marine Science Research at the University of North Carolina at Wilmington is dedicated to providing an environment that fosters a multidisciplinary approach to questions in basic marine research. The mission of the Center is to promote scientific and applied research in the fields of oceanography, coastal and wetland studies, marine biomedical and environmental physiology, and marine biotechnology and aquaculture. The Center fosters research programs of the highest quality and thereby enhances the educational experience in marine science provided by The University of North Carolina at Wilmington for both undergraduate and graduate students in marine science.

1. OCEANOGRAPHY

The objective of the Oceanographic Research Program is to promote study of the marine environment from the continental shelf to the open ocean. Research emphasis focuses on continental shelf and slope processes with interdisciplinary approaches (biological, chemical, physical, and geological oceanography). The program currently encompasses three primary areas of research activity: an inshore component concerned with the integration of the estuaries and the near shore continental shelf particularly the effects of coastal development on, water quality, recruitment, nursery ground degradation, and groundwater quality; a mid-shelf component primarily concerned with "resource issues", especially living marine resources, habitat requirements, production and its forcing functions, and recruitment; and an offshore component heavily influenced by a major ocean current, the Gulf Stream.

RESEARCH PROGRAMS

The Center for Marine Science Research is the host organization for the NOAA sponsored National Undersea Research Center for the southeastern United States. Based upon competitive proposals NURC annually supports fisheries management, ocean floor processes, and other research projects from the Gulf of Maine to the Gulf of Mexico.

2. MARINE BIOMEDICAL AND ENVIRONMENTAL PHYSIOLOGY

The objective of the Marine Biomedical and Environmental Program is to promote basic research that will enhance the understanding of human physiology such that it may have an impact on the diagnosis, prevention, treatment, and rehabilitation of human diseases. Research encompasses the fields of biomineralization, genetics, comparative physiology, neurobiology, anatomy, membrane transport physiology, and the physiology of extreme environments. Since basic physiological phenomena can sometimes be best investigated using marine and freshwater vertebrates and invertebrates as model systems, the basic research activities involve the study of organisms in the marine, estuarine, freshwater, terrestrial and extra-terrestrial; and they include investigations of acclimatory and adaptational processes as diverse as the organisms and habitats.

3. BARRIER AND ESTUARINE SYSTEMS

The objective of the Barrier and Estuarine Systems Program is to promote study of the complex interrelationships between barriers, adjacent estuaries, and ocean waters and to evaluate impacts of human activities on these systems. The program encompasses three areas of study: ecology and living resources, nutrient cycling and chemical studies, and physical processes. Research efforts include studies of the many aspects of organismic biology within the region including identification, collection and mapping. Specific studies include life history and ecology of microorganisms, birds, sea turtles, invertebrates, fish and plants. Chemical studies include determination of mixing patterns of fresh and salt water, rainwater chemistry and nutrient fluxes. Physical processes research explore barrier island migration and sedimentology of the near shore and deeper continental shelf.

4. MARINE BIOTECHNOLOGY PROGRAM

The objective of the Marine Biotechnology Program is the application of biotechnology to select and improve marine and aquatic organisms for use in environmental technologies, as sources of natural products, and as economic or industrial resources. Research emphasis include attempts to modify cytogenetic and cloning procedures to develop commercially useful seaweed isolates for mariculture, factors affecting calcification and molting in crabs, natural genetic exchange between marine bacteria in polluted environments, the use of marine bacteria as sensors of the level of pollution, and benthic microalgal and zooplankton studies. Other studies examine marine organisms for traits which have potential for commercial exploitation.

RESEARCH FACILITIES

The Center's primary facilities are located on a four-acre tract near the Intracoastal Waterway at Wrightsville Beach. Encompassing 16,000 square feet these facilities house fourteen research laboratories, various science and administrative offices, a video equipment/editing room, a fully equipped machine tool shop, an aquatic specimens holding room, a seminar/conference room and a USDA licensed animal facility. Additional laboratory space is available for research requiring constant flow-through seawater.

Teaching • Research • Service
A constituent institution of The University of North Carolina — C. D. Spangler, Jr., President
an equal opportunity employer

FROM BEGINNING TO END AND BACK AGAIN

The Center maintains seven research vessels ranging in size from thirteen to twenty-four feet and specialized equipment including a Superphantom Remotely Operated Vehicle, a low temperature aquarium room, an atomic absorption spectrophotometer, and an extensive microscopy capability including transmission electron, inverted, phase-contrast, and confocal tandem scanning.

ACADEMIC PROGRAMS

The University of North Carolina at Wilmington offers Bachelor's degrees in biology, geology and chemistry. Graduate students in marine biology may select one of three tracts which include general marine biology, coastal studies, or biological oceanography.

OCEANOGRAPHY: Program Coordinator - Joan D. Willey, Ph.D., Professor. acid rain, seawater chemistry; Lawrence B. Cahoon, Ph.D., Assoc. Prof., benthic microalgae; Ileana E. Clavijo, Ph.D., Asst. Prof., fisheries biology; William J. Cleary, Ph.D., Professor, deep sea sedimentation; James A. Dockal, Ph.D. Asst. Prof., deep sea sedimentation; Alan Hulbert, Ph.D., Assoc. Prof., productivity of natural reefs; Robert J. Kieber, Ph.D., Asst. Prof., chemistry of natural waters; Richard A. Laws, Ph.D., Asst. Prof., ancient diatoms and coccolithophores; David G. Lindquist, Ph.D., Professor, artificial reefs, fish attraction devices (FADS); Martin Posey, Ph.D., Asst. Prof., estuarine ecology.

RESEARCH STAFF

MARINE BIOMEDICAL AND ENVIRONMENTAL PHYSIOLOGY: Program Coordinator - Richard M. Dillaman, Ph.D., Professor, cell structure and function; Timothy A. Ballard, Ph.D., Asst. Prof., development of connective tissues; Robert D. Roer, Ph.D., Professor, mechanisms of calcium deposition; David B. Roye, Ph.D., Professor, crustacean neural biology; Sybil K. Burgess, Ph.D., Assoc. Prof., biocalcification; Thomas H. Shafer, Ph.D., Asst. Prof., molecular biology of development; Mark Gay, Research Technician II, analyzing muscular elements in bone during simulated weightlessness.

BARRIER AND ESTUARINE SYSTEMS: Program Coordinator - Martin H. Posey, Ph.D., estuarine ecology; James F. Parnell, Ph.D., Professor, ecology and nesting of waterfowl; Joan D. Willey, Ph.D., Professor, acid rain, seawater chemistry; William J. Cleary, Ph.D., Professor, deep sea sedimentation; Lawrence B. Cahoon, Ph.D., Assoc. Prof., benthic microalgae; Robert J. Kieber, Ph.D., Asst. Prof., chemistry of natural waters; Richard A. Laws, Ph.D., Asst. Prof., ancient diatoms and coccolithophores; David G. Lindquist, Ph.D., Professor, fish ecology and behavior; Paul E. Hosier, Ph.D., Professor, marshland and vegetation mapping; S. Bart Jones, Ph.D., Asst. Prof., electrochemical speciation of chromium and natural waters; Paul A. Thayer, Ph.D., Professor, suspended sediment transport, tracer studies; William D. Webster, Ph.D., Asst. Prof., Loggerhead sea turtles; Joan D. Willey, Ph.D., Professor, acid rain, seawater chemistry.

MARINE BIOTECHNOLOGY PROGRAM: Program Coordinator - Kimon T. Bird, Ph.D., Assoc. Prof., phycology, aquaculture; Donald F. Kapraun, Ph.D., Professor, mariculture, cytogenetics; Anne Kendrick, M.S., Asst. Prof., an evaluation of antibiotic effectiveness; James F. Merritt, Ph.D., Director - CMSR, cytogenetics of marine and aquatic organisms; Joseph R. Pawlik, Ph.D., Asst. Prof., invertebrate zoology, marine natural products; Daniel B. Plyler, Ph.D., Professor, plant physiology; Pamela Seaton, Ph.D., Asst. Prof., chemistry and activity of algal natural products; Ronald K. Sizemore, Ph.D., Assoc. Prof., environmental microbiological genetics; Julie A Dutcher, M.S., Research Technician III, algal genome characterization, DNA hybridization.

CONTACT PERSON:

Dr. James F. Merritt
Center for Marine Science Research
7205 Wrightsville Avenue
Wilmington, North Carolina 28403
(919) 256-3721

The University of North Carolina at Wilmington is committed to equality of educational opportunity and does not discriminate against applicants, students, or employees based on race, color, national origin, religion, sex, age, or handicap.

Member of the Southern Association of Marine Laboratories (SAML)

Chapter Twenty-One

      Plans were coming along for the Jay Hensley Endowment for Marine Studies, the name chosen for the fund. The entire staff at the radio station was on the lookout for donations for a silent and a live auction. A place to have the dinner-auction-dance fundraiser was located, and invitation lists were made.

Elaine from the university turned out to be an excellent source of help. Her family is made up of highly talented individuals. Elaine herself has rare musical talent. The group that her family has was chosen to perform the music for the fundraiser. Elaine herself would be singing, and she would present a song called "Jay."

Not long after our initial contact, Elaine called to tell me she had a gift for me. When she arrived for our planning meeting, she carried her guitar. When the conference room door was closed, she said she had written a song for me. She picked up her guitar and began to sing the most beautiful song.[15]

---

[15]   Song lyrics printed on pages 136-137.

I found it difficult to believe that a person I had only been acquainted with for such a short time would do something as special as this for me. I was told that she had also written a theme song for the documentary. She definitely could be a star if she chose to be. Elaine is that talented.

So much was happening in my life since Jay's death. I marveled at the way people were affected by hearing the story. Each time I would remember the voice telling me, "You should write a book," I would laugh to myself and think, "I don't know how to write a book."

Still feeling torn up inside and beginning to realize I needed some help dealing with it, my friend (Pat) gave me the name of a support group called Compassionate Friends. I asked Tony if he would go with me to the group, and he obliged. I hoped this could help me and at the same time help him understand me better.

JUDITH MILLER

"Jay"

Music and lyrics written by Elaine Penn

When you were only one or two, I'd bend down and tie your shoes.
I was there to dry your eyes, And watch you grow another size.
Little feet playing in the sand, Then you grew up to be a man.
But tell me who could ever know, That one
day I would have to let you go.

Now I'm afraid as time goes by, Each pass-
ing year, When I stop crying,
The memories might be erased, It will be hard to see your face.
Then the other day inside my mail, I opened up a miracle,
I smiled and cried, And then I laughed,
You were smiling at me from a photograph.
You were where you loved—in a boat by the sea.
I was barely hanging on you see,
But now I'm holding on to the picture-perfect memory.

Sometimes it's hard to get through life,
Thinking of you and your new wife.
If she's the girl that you described, I know
she's feeling lonesome inside.
I always thought we'd have tomorrow, But
you were only mine to borrow.
At least I know you're not alone,
'Cause son I'm sure you've finally made it home.

FROM BEGINNING TO END AND BACK AGAIN

I was afraid as time went by, Each passing year when I stopped crying.
The memories might be erased, It would be hard to see your face.
Then the other day inside my mail, I opened up a miracle.
I smiled and cried, And then I laughed,
You were smiling at me from a photograph.
You were where you loved—in a boat by the sea.
I was barely hanging on you see.
But now I'm holding on to the picture-perfect memory.

At the first meeting, each person took their turn telling the name of their child and how they died. When it came to me, I broke down and began to cry. Someone in the group passed the box of tissues to me as I proceeded to explain that I was having a problem getting over the experience as Tony thinks I should be. It didn't take long for a few people in the group to begin to explain to him how it feels, and how it is not something that a parent can just get over.

I could tell that Tony was not liking this very much. He took his turn before me and had explained that he was there for me. He never mentioned to the group that he too had lost a newborn baby, his first born. So they had no idea that he knew this experience, and he didn't bother telling them either.

After that first meeting, Tony went with me one more time and was totally silent. When his time to speak came, he passed. He was just there for me after all.

I went to a few more meetings and checked out a few books and tapes. This helped me for a while, but I was feeling the need for something more. Tony was pulling me from one side, and my insides were nagging that I needed to do something.

I began to read books and I listened to tapes. I found lots of books written by doctors telling of other people's experience with death. From the death of a child to accounts of near-death experiences. The information was soaked up as fast as I could read it. But I felt I wanted more—much more. I had an insatiable appetite for as much information as I could find time to look for and absorb.

My mind was filling up with all kinds of questions about death that I did not understand. I was beginning to have dreams with Jay in them. What could these mean? I also hurt when I would think about Jay's dying experience. Did he suffer? Where is he now? What do I need to do?

Nearing the end of June, almost three months after Jay died, I was feeling like a total wreck. My mind didn't seem to work the same way it had before. At work I was having difficulty focusing on anything. It just didn't seem as important to me. My memory appeared to have taken a long vacation, leaving me behind looking very conspicuous.

Tony and I sold a piece of property to a couple I knew casually. At the closing, I introduced myself and reminded the lady that I had met her several years before. I thought she looked at me rather strangely but figured it was because she didn't remember the meeting. As I was lying down to rest later that afternoon, a scene of me sitting at a round table with a group of people flashed into my mind. Suddenly, I now remembered that I had shared a table with these people at a banquet only four months earlier.

Embarrassment set in. I wanted to call and explain myself to them. I tried calling a few times, but each time they were out. At this point, I thought I would let it go. Someday I will bump into them again and can laugh about my absent mindedness.

This absent mindedness was no laughing matter to me at this time. I could imagine it becoming that way, but now it was a serious issue with me. At work I was beginning to feel incapable. When even the most familiar name would escape me, I would cry. I felt frightened by what was happening, and I was not one that was prone to fear. "There is not room for fear and faith to reside in me at the same time," I reminded myself.

It got to the place that I longed to get through the workday. Then upon returning home I would head straight for the porch or to bed as soon as I could. Many nights Tony would come in the bedroom and find me crying under the covers. At this time, I could see why he would get concerned about my sanity. After all, I was too.

My physical condition was beginning to feel out of order. I was so tired and felt like I could barely muster up the energy to go to work, much less face the employees that I had a responsibility to. By now, to others Jay's death seemed like any other memory, but to me it was as if I was living it over and over—every day, each hour.

Even Christine was doing well with going on about her life. She was working and socializing again. I could tell that she was concerned about me for having so much difficulty, but she was attempting to understand.

After the first Mother's Day, I received a letter from her saying, "I realize now how difficult Mother's Day must have been for you. No, maybe I don't." She went on to say, "You are my mother and I carry the love Jay had for you, with you and shared together, always."

I appreciated her concern for me, and I was happy that she was able to pick up the pieces and go on. But still, I did wonder if she had really worked everything out or if she was simply sweeping it under the rug. So the concern was actually reciprocal.

I know, no two people will ever be able to deal with and experience something like this in the same way. Christine would have to do what she needed to do, the same as I would. This freedom with each other would be needed if we were to both recover, I believed. It would not be easy—this I knew for sure.

One evening as I cried in bed, I thought of Pat—the friend that suggested Compassionate Friends to me. She had told me a long time ago about a lady she knew that was psychic. Suddenly, I somehow knew that I needed to talk to this woman.

When I called Pat to ask her for the name and phone number of this woman, she said she was just thinking about me. Not only that, but she had been questioning herself about whether or not to suggest her psychic friend as a source of help.

The last time she had told me about her, I was not too interested in hearing about psychic anything. It had become my belief over the past several years that this was an unacceptable notion for a Christian to even consider. Not to mention what my husband and other friends and relatives would say if they find out I'm going to see a psychic counselor.

After Pat and I talked about the coincidence of my calling and the information I was asking for, I hung up. Now I held the receiver in my hand as I gave myself the courage to make the call that I was feeling compelled to make.

When I had Sammye on the phone, I explained that Pat had referred her to me and that I wanted to schedule an appointment with her. She said she could see me the next day, and to bring about ten written questions I want to ask and a blank cassette tape to record the session on.

I felt a sense of relief for simply just having made the appointment. I even felt like getting out of bed and joining Tony at the TV. As I thought of the questions I wanted to ask, I wrote them down. The thought of how to tell Tony where I was going the next day came to mind. I decided to wait until morning for that answer.

Chapter Twenty-Two

When I woke up the following morning, I had my answer. I came to the conclusion that the best thing was to just tell Chuck that I had an appointment to talk to a counselor and would need to leave early. As for Tony, I would tell him the same thing and see if we could meet for an early lunch before my appointment.

I had a two-and-a-half-hour drive each way to see this lady. The appointment time would allow me to be back home by the end of my normal work day.

When I got to work, Pat asked me if I had talked to Sammye. I told her my plan, and she reassured me that she thought I would really like her and wished me the best.

I felt a little nervous anticipation during the morning and through lunch with Tony. Knowing that I had plenty of time to find the address Sammye had given made me feel better.

The two-and-a-half-hour drive helped me to get my thoughts together better. I wanted to be sure my mind was clear and that I remember everything I had been bothered with. After all, I didn't think people would be able to put up with my recent behavior for another three months.

While I drove, I thought about Sammye's deep voice and wondered what she would look like. I even thought about whether she and her home would look like pictures or films I'd seen about gypsy fortune tellers.

I had a little difficulty finding the address and had to call for directions. Time wise, I was all right, but after making a complete circle of the city, thinking I was lost, I was a little on edge. My normal one-hour-sized bladder had now been stretched to nearly the three-hour exploding size.

Driving up to Sammye's house I checked my watch. I made it right on the nose. She answered the door, and I saw a beautiful white-haired lady, maybe in her late fifties. We introduced ourselves, and she led me to her reading room. After I put my handbag down, I asked if it would be all right for me to use her restroom, explaining that I had already gone past my limit.

Needless to say, I was impressed. Her lovely brick home sits on a tree-shaded corner lot. It is quiet and peaceful, from the front porch, throughout the house. With one quick glance inside the front door, I could see we shared a common appreciation for oriental decor. A basket of seashells decorated her bathroom, and an open window allowed the afternoon breeze to gently move the curtains of her reading room.

I already knew I liked her. It was just the next hour that I was anxious about. This too was gone in the length of time it took for her to get me through the introduction into our session.[16]

Many of my questions were answered before I had been prompted to ask them. She said many things that corresponded with feelings or thoughts I already had yet questioned myself about. How could I know these things? I had not read about them in the books, and no one else had given me the information that I knew of.

Any doubts or fears that I had before the session about her as a psychic were gone. We hugged as I prepared to leave, and she insisted that I call on her anytime if I feel a need to do so. She also put together

---

[16] See transcription of session in Appendix C.

some data about her background to send with me. Teaching classes and doing radio and TV broadcasts are part of her work.

One stop for a large ice tea and use of the restroom, and I was headed home. I wasn't even out of town yet as I put the cassette in. Hearing the message the second and third time on the way opened up even more of an understanding of what she had said.

Sammye made an impression on me when she said that I needed to see my doctor. She was convinced from what she said that I would end up in the hospital if I didn't take some time off and pamper myself some. The stress had been working on me so much that she had picked up on it and knew it was important for me to take care of myself.

I knew in my heart that she was right. My body was telling me that it needed my care. It was important to do as she suggested and follow through on her suggestion.

The next thing I planned to do the very next day was to call my doctor and make an appointment to see him as soon as possible. I was a little frightened of the thought of telling Tony that I needed to get away by myself for a while, but I knew that it was important if I were to get myself back together again.

I decided to wait and talk to him after I had a chance to see my doctor. Telling him that a psychic counselor suggested that I needed to get away would possibly push him to believe that I had indeed flipped my lid.

One thing that seemed to surface after my session with Sammye was something that had happened about a month before Jay died. As this memory began to come forth and present itself to me, I knew that I had to have some time to work on this. Just the thought of this experience threw me into a tailspin.

Approximately one month before Jay's death, between Valentine's week and mid-March, I had a vision or a premonition. Actually, I plainly and simply came to *know* that something was going to happen to Jay.

In the past few years, everything seemed to be going right in my life. For the most part I was happy. I was blessed with a wonderful son and daughter-in-law, and for the first time in my life everything seemed to be going the way I always thought I wanted it to. I had met Tony a few years earlier, thanks to Jay. He seemed to be the perfect mate for me, and we have been good for each other. Not to say we haven't had our problems. You know the kind of things that usually create marital problems—children, money, etc.

It appears we have been able to get through those things and have been enjoying our lives together. But something still did not seem right.

One night after Tony had gone to sleep early, as he usually does, I felt drawn to go out on the porch and pray. I even went beyond the porch and out the door into the backyard. Tears and emotions overcame me. Soon I was on my knees asking, "What else is there for me in this life? There has to be something else. This can't be all there is to an entire lifetime."

"Yes, I have my family, my son, my husband, a nice car and home, a good job and plenty of money now. But could this be all life is about?" I didn't think so! I felt I needed more. I had gone the Christian route, the attempted suicide route, the twelve-step-program route, and many others in between.

I have been blessed with all the comforts of this life, and I worked hard to get where I am. "But what is missing? What is it I'm supposed to accomplish on this earth? I must have a mission, a purpose that I am to fulfill. Please, tell me what it is or let me leave this place if this is all there is for me.

"I would like to leave here, but I promised years ago that if you didn't take me when I attempted suicide, then I would know that you had something special that you want me to do here. I promised I would never try to take my life again. But please, I'm tired and I want to come home," I prayed. "Yet how can I leave? I know how it would hurt Jay so very much, and I don't want to hurt him, Tony, or my other family and friends. I just ask for your will, God, not mine to be done."

A few days later, on another night, as Tony and I went to bed I was beginning to relax just enough to fall asleep. I began to have a strong feeling move through me that something was going to happen to Jay. I was not completely asleep but in that stage of deep relaxation that comes just before sleep.

I know it was not like a dream that a person has in sleep. It was more like a burst of knowledge that permeated every cell in my body.

Kind of like an instant knowing of something happening without being told or taught about it. I just knew!

When I realized what it was that was being revealed to me, then it came to the conscious level in my mind, I sat straight up in bed. I felt stunned and numb. I began to cry as I realized what I had just come to know about.

Tony turned over and asked me what was wrong. I tried to explain to him that I knew something was going to happen to Jay. Explaining something like this to him was very difficult. It felt morbid even saying the words to him. He tried to reassure me that everything was all right, but I knew different.

I couldn't go to sleep, so I got up and went out on the porch to sit and think about this experience. As I sat on the porch, I thought of how precious my son is to me and how I always told him he was like a gift from God.

Since I could not have any other children, and he was my only child, I often reminded him to be careful with whatever he chose to do. I did not want to loose my precious son. Now it seemed as if I was being forewarned or prepared for just that. The very thing that I never wanted to happen.

I went back to bed and put it out of my mind. I did not remember this happening until this time. As I remembered, it disturbed me tremendously. I couldn't understand why this had happened. I somehow felt afraid that I may have caused Jay's death by having this precognition.

Chapter Twenty-Three

The following morning I made a call to my doctor. This is a man that is hard to get an appointment with right away. He has a full schedule all the time. Sometimes it takes one or two months to schedule an appointment.

When I had the appointment secretary on the phone, I explained that I was having difficulty dealing with problems resulting from my son's death. She said she would see what she could do and would call me right back.

Her call came soon afterward. She had a time for me to be at his office in the afternoon. I felt a little nervous thinking that I was seeing my doctor so he could tell me I needed time off to deal with my emotions. For some reason, I felt like I owed my sanity to a job and my husband. If I left work again, I would leave them in a bind, and my husband would have to take care of things by himself for a while.

Nonetheless, I was convinced that this was exactly what I was to do. How could I be of any use to anyone if I continued in the manner that I had been. Also, I didn't want to ruin the image I had worked to build over the past years in my career. I knew that in the long run,

I would end up looking incapable of doing my job; therefore being demoted or, even worse, fired.

Not being able to do my job properly was never something that I would consider to be my style. I had developed myself into a responsible, reliable, organized company person. The job I held brought with it plenty of stress and responsibility. More stress in my life at this time would only do me more harm than good.

Through my mind the entire day was the thought, "If I can just hold myself together long enough to make that appointment, tell my husband I need to get away, then find a place to go, then I'll be all right."

At the doctor's office, as I sat there waiting for him to see me in the examination room, I felt a swelling of emotions begin to rise within me. I sat there holding them in and trying not to cry. When the doctor came in and looked at me, he asked, "How are you doing? I understand you're having some difficulty dealing with your son's death."

As I began to explain how I had been feeling, the emotions began to flood out of me. I tried to tell him that I had thought of myself as a strong person, able to conquer any challenge and face any kind of stress. But this time I can't seem to get myself together. I don't think I can keep up the way I used to and continue to work the way I have in the past. "I'm just tired—really tired. I feel like I'm letting a lot of people down now."

He wrote a note on a prescription pad, tore it off, and gave it to me. It read, "Ms. Miller should be excused from work from 6/29/94 through 7/7/94 for medical reasons. Contact me if details are needed."

Next he explained that he himself had never really experienced a death of a close family member and could not fully understand the impact. But his mother-in-law had lost her husband and had difficulty dealing with it. She had found it helpful talking to Dr. Patterson, who seems to be very good at helping people get through issues like this.

He went on to say that he would like for me to see this man. He thought the sooner the better would be advisable, even in the next day or two if I could get an appointment. He even offered to put a call in, referring me to this doctor.

One other thing he thought would be helpful, he suggested, was a prescription for an antidepressant called Zoloft, explaining to me that these have a new formula, very safe and non–habit forming.

He gave me some samples to take with me until I could get the prescription filled. I didn't think that this was what I needed to help me. What I needed was to get lots of rest and have plenty of quiet time to myself.

When I got home, I called Chuck to explain that my doctor had recommended some time off. Again, he reminded me that I should take the time I needed and they would take care of things. Now I had to tell Tony.

Before Tony got home, I looked up this Dr. Patterson in the phone book. I saw his listing was under psychiatrists. He is to diagnose and treat me for a mental disorder? Then I became even more confused. "Have I become deranged or something? Could I be crazy?"

Here I just thought that I was going through the grief process; now I'm being referred to a psychiatrist by one of the top doctor's in Wilmington. With credentials like his, there must be something wrong with me.

Yet deep down I felt that my help would come from peace and quiet. Time away from everything and everybody, allowing myself to sort through the past three months undisturbed.

I don't think Tony took me seriously when I told him of the doctor's recommendation to take some time off, go see Dr. Patterson, and take antidepressants. He still seemed to expect me to pick up the pieces and go on, full force, as he knew me to do as always before.

The biggest thing for him to swallow was that I wanted to go away *without him* for a few days. He gave me a look of suspicion as I told him that I wanted to do it by myself and felt that I needed to be alone for a while.

I went on to call Dr. Patterson's office, all the time thinking that I could see him in the next day or two. Then on Saturday I could leave for a few days, knowing that I was doing what my doctor advised me to do and what my insides were advising me to do.

This man's appointment secretary was cold and unobliging as I explained that my doctor was referring me to her doctor. I even explained that my doctor suggested that I see him as soon as possible—this week even.

She said the soonest she could get me in would be toward the end of the following week or it would have to be the week after that. I knew I couldn't stay around feeling the way I do, waiting a week to see a man I didn't think I needed to see in the first place. I told her, "Put me down for week after next," thinking that by then I may just decide to cancel.

I wondered what a person that was actually suicidal would do if they urgently needed to see this doctor. Suicidal was not the condition I was in, although it appeared that my doctor may be thinking I was. At least that's the impression I had from the way he was urging me to see the psychiatrist so quickly.

Tony and I did not discuss my plan to get away during the rest of the evening. I think that he thought I would just change my mind about the whole thing and stay at home. But I knew differently. Now had to be the time that I took for myself—to be with myself. After all I have a life too, and I need to begin caring for it.

Some jealousy had begun to arise in me. Tony has four children, three sons and a daughter, and his life revolves around his business and his three sons that are in his business. He has always taken good care of them and their needs. Now I had needs of my own. Especially to deal with the death of my only child and get my life back on track.

I felt guilty for feeling jealous of Tony's relationship he has with his grown children. In no way would I ever want to see him go through having to lose any one of them. It hurts too bad, and I just couldn't stand the thought of him having to suffer like this. I knew that I needed to get rid of this feeling of jealousy. It would only harm me, and it is not their fault that I have been suffering from my loss.

Writing out my problems was something I had learned from Al-Anon several years before. I discovered that when I take an inventory of all the good and the bad things going on with me, turn it sincerely over to God, then destroy the remains, it would be taken and developed into good things in my life.

Taking my laptop was my first priority on the list of things I would take on my sabbatical. Next, I would gather all the books I wanted to read and take my camera to take any pictures of beauty that captured my eye. The place that came to mind that I had always wanted to see was the Outer Banks.

Jay and Christine had gone to Hatteras Island in the fall of '93. They asked if I would like to go, but with Tony and work I declined. (Being the responsible person I am, how could I go off and play with my son and daughter-in-law just because they are visiting?)

I remembered Jay telling me how wonderful their trip was to this place. He said the drive up reminded him a little of Kansas in the summer. There were large fields of crops, including wheat, and farm homes along the way. He hadn't seen this in other areas of North Carolina, and neither had I. Wide-open spaces are few and far between in this state.

Other friends have told me about their peaceful getaways to the Outer Banks. From my youth, I could remember hearing stories and watching TV documentaries about the little horses that roam wild in this area. They are thought to have been left there by early Spaniard ships. I used to dream of traveling from Kansas to North Carolina to adopt one of these horses. Now I was hoping I would just be able to see one.

Chapter Twenty-Four

*M*aking reservations someplace quiet presented a problem to me. How would I know where to stay when I do not know of any particular place? The travel agency I advertise for could help perhaps," I said to myself.

Calling the lady that I already knew proved to be helpful, and her first suggestion was in a little place called Duck.

"I like the name of that one, Duck. Could you give me a phone number of a place to stay there?" I asked.

She came up with a few numbers of places available, and I started making calls. I found out from the first place in Duck that they were totally booked, and so were the other places there. Reminding me that this was the fourth of July weekend—I had completely forgotten that—he suggested that I may want to try a place called Castaways on Hatteras Island.

When the lady at Castaways answered my call, I asked if she had anything available. She said she had a cancellation through Tuesday the fifth. I could have that room until Tuesday, and by that time they would have something else open if I wanted to stay longer. I asked her if this was a quiet place where I could get some badly needed rest. Her reply was that it is a very quiet place for me to do just that.

"Wow! This has really fallen into place so easy. I hope I'm doing the right thing. I believe I am doing the right thing," I thought. The fear of standing up for myself and doing something that I wanted to do for myself could appear somewhat selfish to Tony and his family. But now was not the time for me to be worried about that too.

As I began to gather a few things together for the trip, I decided to take all the pictures and other things I had been compiling. The collection had grown to the point of needing two large albums to hold everything. I wanted to get the compilation in some kind of order. It seemed important to me to have things arranged by the order they happened.

I planned to organize one album with documentation of Jay's childhood up to the point of his first trip to the Bahamas. The second album would hold everything from the past four years up to now and could include any new additions.

In the afternoon I spent some time talking to Cheryl and Gisella on the phone going over what I needed to do. Both were very understanding and supportive. When I mentioned the idea of the antidepressants the doctor had prescribed, they both agreed that maybe I should take them. "Perhaps they will help you get through this a little easier," Gisella suggested.

After thinking it all over for a while, I decided I would try one and see how it made me feel. It didn't seem to take long before I was feeling kind of floaty and numb, almost as if all my feelings were gone completely, and I didn't like that.

I knew it was necessary for me to feel my feelings, not mask them with pills. This would be the only way for me if I were to be able to deal with the feelings at all. Even if the feelings were uncomfortable, I have to feel them to be able to work on them.

I spent about two-thirds of my life hiding my feelings and not dealing with them. This was definitely not the time for me to begin the process all over again. I decided that I would not take any more of those pills. One was plenty for me—I needed no further proof.

One more day at home and I would be on my way to the Outer Banks. It didn't seem real—I was actually going to go through with this plan. Not only the trip ahead of me, but everything—everything in my life was beginning to feel like a dream.

All the arrangements for my trip were made. I went to the bank and got some cash. A few stops to buy some extra books, film, and run a couple of "responsibility-type" errands, and I would be ready to leave in the morning.

I was now set and ready to do the actual packing. By the time I had finished, the trunk of my car was practically full. Getting up there and settled into the room for quiet seclusion was what I was looking for. I didn't want to have to go out looking for things that I may need. So I was going prepared with anything that came to mind. If there was a chance I thought I would need a particular item, I put it in the trunk.

All that was left to do was get up in the morning, get dressed, and drive. I even got a map and planned the route to take. I was beginning to feel excited about taking this trip. A strong belief grew in me and reassured me that I would face myself in that room and resolve many of the issues going on in my life at this time.

Talking with Tony when he gets home from work was another thing I needed to be prepared for. It was not easy for me to tell him that I still intended to go away. He looked deeply concerned about me going away as I told him what I wanted and felt I needed to do. He asked, "Where would you go? And where would you stay?" He even suggested that if I could wait a little while, he and I could go someplace together.

Explaining my desire to get off alone someplace was somewhat difficult for him to understand. But I did my best to assure him that I would be all right.

When I told him that I had found a place at Avon on Hatteras Island, he just asked how much it was going cost me and where was I getting the money to go. I explained that I had enough money to do this and that everything else, meaning bills, had been taken care of.

Chapter Twenty-Five

*M*orning came, the morning to leave for my rest. Between sleeping and waking, I became aware of a song running through my mind. It was a song called "Independence Day" by Martina McBride. This song played over and over as I continued to lie in bed half asleep.

I remembered a thought I had shortly after returning home from the Bahamas as I sat at the table on the porch. "You have your freedom now." I questioned myself about this thought and said to myself, "Having my son has to be better than having my freedom." Then I wondered why in the world would such a thought have even come into my mind like that. Another thing I hadn't remembered until the session with Sammye.

Then my eyes popped open when I heard this gentle voice inside my head say, "I am not as one." Eyes wide open, I lay there thinking about what I heard. What could that mean? Where did it come from? Could it have been Jay? All of a sudden I was filled with questions. I became even more anxious to get up and get on the road. I could hardly wait to be alone, having a feeling that I would be hearing more.

Tony got up and was getting ready to go leave to do a few hours of work. I told him that I would probably be leaving in a little while. "You're still going, huh?" he asked.

"Tony, it's not as much that I want to go away, but that I need to do this" was my reply.

After we said good-bye, he left looking rather solemn. I felt sad for him. I knew he had to be worried about me; and I was sorry that this was something he had to go through with me, but it just is.

Once dressed with coffee in hand, I looked the house over for anything I might have missed. I was on my way. Before I got completely out of Wilmington, I could see the rain cloud open up and pour its heavenly water upon the area behind me.

The weather was looking rather dreary, and rain appeared to be on the way. I love rain. I don't mind driving in it unless it becomes so intense that I can't see. On this morning, that didn't happen. The rain stayed behind me until I had driven completely out of the system. Then it became clear and sunny.

I continued to drive, only stopping for my bladder's sake and the chance to refill my coffee. The scenery was different from what I had left behind earlier in the morning. Jay was right—the farmland did look quite a bit like Kansas. The area became more beautiful as I came closer to my destination. It is unspoiled in many areas, with an undeveloped beach still intact. No wonder Jay said it was awesome to see.

Today marks three months from the day Jay died. I couldn't help but feel a little sad, thinking that things would probably begin to get a little less eventful now. Especially after what Sammye had said about what usually happens at the time of death. But maybe I misunderstood, and it's around the third to sixth month that they begin to get a little more active again.

I listened to the tape again as I drove. Yes, I was wrong. It is the third to sixth month period that he could begin trying to contact me from wherever he is. This made me begin to feel excited about the next few months ahead. I was wondering how this could happen and what would happen. I even thought of how people would probably think of me as being crazy to even consider such things.

By now I didn't care as much how people thought of me. Just as long as I knew that I was doing the right thing for me and my conscience. Other than that, whose business is it anyway to be passing judgment on the way I conduct my life as long as I'm not hurting anyone? "How could this possibly hurt anyone else? It could just turn out to help someone, someday, somehow."

I began to realize that I should be nearing the area where I was told Castaways would be located. Looking to my left, I passed a large building set back off the road. In front was a large grassy area, and both sides of the building were vacant. The first thing I had noticed was a small horse tied up near a little playground in front. I wondered if that could be one of those horses I had become so interested in.

Driving on further, looking for numbers on street signs, I saw that I had passed the number I was looking for. When I turned around and headed back in the direction I had just come from, I saw the sign. Castaways. It was right out in front of the place where the horse stood grazing on the grass. I guess I had been so busy looking at the horse that I missed the sign the first time by it.

Pulling in and driving toward the lobby door, I noticed the restaurant sign. It had a colorful picture of a parrot and the name Blue Parrot. Already I was thinking, "This is perfect! There are very few cars around, the horse is out front, and the restaurant is named after another one of my favorite things—birds!"

When checking in, I got the idea that this was a family-operated business. Local people, native to the area was the idea I had. They were quiet and polite as they prepared everything for me. The older woman, I presumed to be the owner and operator, looked at me in a compassionate way. I thought that she must have been the lady I talked to on the phone and explained that I needed a quiet place where I could get lots of rest.

In the room I found a little refrigerator and sink and a balcony that looked over the vast ocean. Very little else could be seen from the balcony except beach and sea oats. Best of all, it was wonderfully quiet.

My plan was to check out the restaurant, carry things to the room, and go from there. Whatever I felt like doing at the time would be what I would do. No schedules, no deadlines, and no one to call me. "How could I have done better?" I was feeling satisfied.

After a few trips carrying things up, I headed for the restaurant. I was the only one in there and looked over the menu. The menu had several specialty dishes that were Caribbean style. I made my selection from one of those, thinking of the Bahamas. On the wall were some great pictures of waves. "Jay would have liked these, especially if he could have ridden them on his surfboard," I thought.

When my meal arrived, I asked the cheerful waitress, "Who took all the pictures of the ocean and the waves?" She said her brother had taken them a few years ago.

"Aren't they good?" Later I saw a man I presumed was her brother. I was stunned to see how much he resembled Jimmy Buffett. Another one of Jay's pleasures in life was listening to Buffett's music.

This is all really amazing to me, and to top it off, the food was excellent. The chef had learned to make these dishes when he lived away from the island. He decorated the plate with garnishments as if it were a work of art. Something like you would get on a top-notch cruise ship.

I thought how nice it would be to have him come to Wilmington to prepare the food for the fundraiser. Gisella and I had been discussing different types of food that could be served, and this would fit in perfectly. The only problem would be the expense, and that was something we needed to look out for. We want to raise more money than we spend.

Walking back toward my room past the indoor pool, I noticed a few people with children. I wondered what some would think, seeing a woman hanging out here alone on a holiday weekend. This happened to be the first time I can ever remember doing something like this. I have to admit it felt a little strange.

Now settled into the room for the rest of the evening, I picked out the first book I decided to read. I began with *Reunions*, by Raymond Moody.

One interesting thing I read soon into the book was "apparitions of the deceased don't look exactly as they did before they died.

Strangely—or perhaps not so—they look younger and less stressed in their apparitional state, but still they are recognizable as who they are."

Another thing that caught my attention was "our faster pace of life has the effect of discouraging people from enjoying the delights of altered states of awareness, many of which require you to slow down and think differently from the way you have become accustomed to."

This had definitely been my lifestyle in the past twenty-five years. I seemed to be noticing how it had affected me, even before Jay's death. Constant heartburn and the need to take stomach pills every day had become a way of life for me in the past two years.

The book went on to say, "Dreams, for instance are held by many thinkers as classic examples of something unreal." I got the understanding that dreams do, after all, have deeper meaning. Something I had always believed to be true but was afraid to talk much about. You know how mainstream religion frowns on that stuff. "They are a means of exploring true reality more effectively," according to Moody.

One other section that I had underlined for future reference—if I should ever end up writing the book as suggested to me—was "Visionary encounters with departed loved ones are not frightening. On the contrary, they tend to be positive experiences that give people hope and a sense that the departed is comfortable, happy, and still with them spiritually."

I thought this book was interesting, and it did answer some of the questions I had been contemplating pertaining to the death experience. However, some aspects of the book were difficult for me to grasp.

It discussed certain methods to provoke visionary encounters with departed loved ones. These appeared to be unnecessary steps to bring the encounter into fruition. "Why couldn't it be possible without going through the process described?" I wondered. "Why wouldn't it just happen if it is meant to be?"

Chapter Twenty-Six

After staying up until 12:30 a.m. the previous night reading, I slept until 9 a.m. this morning. I was drawn to open the curtains and take a long look out over that beautiful Atlantic sitting just outside the window. The thought of Jay's ashes being spread out over this big body of water came to mind.

A portion of another song kept running through my head again. This song "Every Once in a While," made popular by a country group called Black Hawk says, "He said, 'I wonder if she ever still thinks about me?' She said, 'Every once in a while…every once in a while.'"

When I went in the restroom to go through my usual morning routine of brushing my teeth, I saw bruises on my shoulders. A bluish colored bruise was on my left shoulder, and both shoulders had reddish looking lines. The lines looked like they were made by the straps of my gown being pulled into my shoulders, I thought as I studied them.

I spent the next few hours going through the picture albums and arranging them in the order I had planned. At one point I became so overcome with emotion that I began to cry. Speaking out loud I asked, "How can I have so much joy and yet so much sorrow at the same time?" The joy came from seeing Jay in the pictures and remembering the times we had together. The sorrow was coming from the separation from him.

Around 1 p.m. I realized another song going through my mind. I asked myself, "Why this one?" I have no idea right now. This was a song I had not heard in years. "Pennies from Heaven" went over and over in my mind, and I was even singing it aloud. I felt good, and with it came comfort. It seemed that music, being something of great importance to me, was the means of communication for now.

After working with the albums most of the day, I thought I would get ready and go out for a while. I spotted a grocery store down the road and wanted to get some fruit, bottled water, and coffee. Room service was not available here, but a microwave in the room would at least allow me to make some coffee. I stopped at the Blue Parrot for a nice meal and was back in the room by 6 p.m.

My second book was ready for me, and I was ready to delve into it. I read all of the other one and was excited to begin the one entitled

To Touch the Light. Kevin D. Randle wrote this book about people who have had the near-death experience.

I didn't know how much the near-death experience could relate to the actual death experience and the grief. But I was willing to read as much as I could, hoping to find more peace from the haunting questions that persisted in me.

After reading several near-death experiences as reported by Mr. Randle, I came to chapter 8. He refers to *The Tibetan Book of the Dead* and how it provides those who were dying with a map for how to do it properly, with skill and grace. It provides instruction on what will happen to those who die and provides comfort for those left behind.

He continued to say, "There is discussion of a being of pure light, which the dying individual is counseled to approach with feeling of compassion and love. And, there is discussion that there may be others around the one dying, in a state similar to that being experienced."

I wondered how a person could be in a state similar to that of a dying person. The title *Tibetan Book of the Dead* sounded a little frightening to me. I wasn't sure I could even walk into a bookstore and buy a book that sounded like this. I could almost picture the look a bookstore clerks face would have as they viewed the title.

Mr. Randle shared something that a Native American told him that did strike my interest. He said, "The other side is an area that can be accessed to provide data for those on this side." He related this to information retrieval in the computer world.

The computer is something I can relate to. I have been fascinated with the ability of being able to store great amounts of information on such a small device. It made sense to me that if we can do that with a computer, then why shouldn't it be possible for data pertaining to a person's life be stored—in some manner similar to this—someplace?

Another aspect of this book that left me with more questions to contemplate was the section referring to reincarnation. The author reports that the near-death experience and reincarnation both incorporate something, maybe the soul, surviving death. The consciousness is carried to the other side. "Perhaps, there is a personal identity that is carried from this side to the other," one of the near-death experiencers, Tom Dolembo, said.

"This all seems very intriguing to me, but reincarnation? Oh, I don't know about that." This was a subject that I took interest in nearly twenty years ago and dumped because I became afraid of it. I heard several TV preachers say it was of the devil, and so I became cautious. I did not want to allow that character in my house.

One thing that I did question was the possibility that reincarnation had been edited out of the King James Version of the Bible because it did not fit into the Christian doctrine of that time. Mr. Randle's book relays this message, and I have read and heard the same report elsewhere.

I began to think that I didn't want to take any one person's word on this. For me, I would have to come to know it to be truth for myself. I could understand reincarnation as a means to allow us to grow. Today's problems experienced could also be the result of a trauma or event in a past life.

This made sense to me. I see its possibility when comparing it to the problems that are a result of behavior in this life. I know that if I were to go out and rob a bank today, the next few years of my life would be drastically altered by that act in a negative way. Likewise, if I were to plant seeds of goodness today, the future would reflect that as well.

"Could there be a parallel here? Isn't it possible that this life is a parallel to a previous life?" I questioned. This would take a little more thought and investigation on my part before I could understand the true nature of this issue.

I called Tony and Christine in the evening. Describing the place to Tony prompted him to warn me to keep my door locked. He seemed a little more talkative than he had before I left, which made me feel better.

When I got Christine on the phone and told her where I was, she said, "Oh man! I wish I could jump on a jet and fly up there to be with you." She shares the love Jay had for this area and was looking forward to her trip up to see me in September. She was also planning to spend a few days with friends on Haterras Island at this time.

Before I left home, I knew one of the things I needed to face was anger. I still wasn't sure how long I was going to stay here, but I did know that I had to deal with the anger. "Today just isn't the day," I convinced myself.

Chapter Twenty-Seven

Upon awakening today, Independence Day, I immediately thought about the anger issue that had been on my mind. Today would be the day to face it. Independence Day coincidentally seemed to be the appropriate day to do exactly that. I noticed the song "Independence Day" began running through my mind again.

Lying in the darkened room, I drifted back into sleep. A while later I was awakened by the ringing of the telephone. Startled into wakefulness, I fumbled around for the phone. When I picked up the receiver, I heard the sound of someone hang up.

Remembering that I hadn't given out the phone number, I surmised, "Someone must've called my room by mistake. Or it could have been meant to get me started on the project I've succeeded to put off so far."

This was possibly the little kick in the rear I needed. Especially since I have always been good at putting off dealing with anger in the past. Several years ago I had to learn to express my anger appropriately.

It was an emotion that I had great difficulty showing. I had learned that it wasn't nice to get mad, so I began to hide it and mask it with other emotions.

This particular time in my life, or any other time for that matter, could not be the time for me to regress to such detrimental negligence of myself. I prepared the computer and was ready to begin writing about my anger. But first I put the finishing touches on the albums. "Could this have been another delay I was trying to create for myself?" I wondered.

"Maybe working on the albums was another delay," I considered as I closed the albums and allowed myself to begin to feel the anger. "OK, this is it, it's time to start," I said as I took a deep breath and headed to the table where my computer was waiting.

When I put my fingers on the keyboard of the computer, they began to move around the keys. Anger began to spill out on the screen as I wrote. "Who was I angry with? What was I angry about? Why do I feel angry?" were all questions I began to pose to myself. "What circumstances led up to the anger? Is it justified? Did it come from feeling hurt? Is it real?"

Next I read all the material that I had written about my anger. I analyzed it and looked for any I had left out. I decided I needed to search for the reason why I had allowed myself to get this way.

I discovered that I was angry for several different reasons. All the reasons seemed to lead to other emotions or feelings. Jealousy, envy, hurt, pride, helplessness, despair, and hopelessness to name a few.

After spending most of the day working on this anger, I came to the end of it. I had cried, argued, and even caught myself trying to rationalize the anger. By the time I had finished, a desire had grown to full intention of ridding myself of it and work harder to keep it cleaned out.

The final phase of this anger-banishing procedure was to turn it over to God and let it go. I prayed and asked God to help me turn loose of the garbage I had accumulated. As I took one last glance through the pages, one by one I deleted them and watched the anger disappear from the screen.

I thanked God for helping me get through this and felt lighter for having done so. Hunger became the dominant prompting I felt now. It was almost 5 p.m. and time to have a nice meal.

While I was having my dinner, I began to feel more like going home. I did have a few mixed feelings about leaving already, but I made the decision to go. I realized that I was beginning to miss Tony.

After dinner I took a drive to see the Hatteras Lighthouse and take a few pictures. I planned to start loading my car with things I wouldn't be needing this last night. Then I had plans to sit out on the balcony with the ocean view in front of me as I read.

On the way to the lighthouse I passed an area of water loaded with colorful catamarans. On the way back I stopped to take some pictures. The sails were so colorful and beautiful. All colors of the rainbow were represented in this display. They darted off in one direction and returned in the other, twirling and swirling in the salty water. "These would turn out to be better shots than the lighthouse," I thought.

After loading the car, I got my next book and headed for the balcony. I noticed a bank of clouds building in the sky. I found it difficult to concentrate on reading; my attention was continually drawn back to the clouds.

I remembered how as a child I would sit and look at the clouds for long periods. I would study them and find shapes of things in the fluffy white and gray formations, and then watch them until they developed into something different. I began to think how this was what I was doing in my life now. I am watching things turn from one form and develop into a different form gradually.

Documenting the experiences of each day had become important to me. At the bookstore I found a blank book, with seashells on the cover, and started recording the things I was beginning to hear, see, feel, and dream.

Jay had suggested that I begin to keep a journal about two years before. He had been given a book to write things pertaining to his life in, and he found it to be something of great importance. When I found the book, I bought it and began writing, starting with the day I met with Sammye.

Inside the first page of my journal I made a note of a word that I remembered waking up with in my mind one night. The word came to me on August 9, 1994, and had no specific meaning to me. Actually, I didn't even know what the word meant and had to go to my dictionary. I had written the word on my calendar, thinking that it was odd to have it come to me in the way it did.

My *Webster's II New Riverside Dictionary* defines the word "anomaly" as a "1. departure from the normal form, order, or rule" or "2. something irregular or abnormal."

The word seemed to fit the things that were going on in my life the past months. "But where did it come from? And why would I wake up in the middle of the night reciting it over and over so I wouldn't forget it?" I questioned. I just knew there had to be some special reason for this word coming to me.

Taking my attention again and again from the book to the clouds, I kept noticing little flashes of light. Far to my right I watched a light move, glowing through the clouds until it was in the clouds directly in front of me. Then I began to see the clouds light up with flashes of light coming from behind. The entire panoramic view in front of me, covered with clouds, would glow when this light flashed.

I thought, "How interesting the lightning is up here." It was lighting up the clouds in the same place repeatedly. I wondered what else could be out there; maybe it was the same type of thing Tony told me the man at the fish house had seen.

This display of flashing light continued for at least fifteen minutes. Then it got dimmer until it quit completely. The sun had set on the other side of the building, and it was dark.

When it was too dark to read, I went inside to call Tony. I wanted to let him know that I had decided to leave the next morning. "Are you better now?" he inquired.

"I feel better, but I would like to have some time to talk about some things when I get home," I replied.

I made myself comfortable on the bed and began to read. Realizing another song was merrily playing in my mind, I made a note of it in my journal. "I'm Looking Over a Four Leaf Clover," another song that I had not heard in years, kept repeating in my mind.

It got my attention and made me think of what Sammye had told me. She said to watch for something about flowers, my yard, or something in my yard that Jay wants me to watch for. I knew I had never seen any four-leaf clover—or any clover at all for that matter—growing in or around our yard. I wondered, "What in the world could this mean?"

I gave up on reading and turned out the light. The little tune must have sung me to sleep.

Chapter Twenty-Eight

Upon awakening, I reached for my journal and a pen. I had a dream that I wanted to write about.

Two woman that I know—one from the past and the other from the present, both owner/managers of exclusive dress shops—were in the dream. I was riding in a pickup truck with a man who had beaten another man. He stuffed the body behind the seat of the truck. When we got to our destination, he took the body out into a field. I was sad and afraid for the injured man. I knew that the driver of the truck was going to finish him off as he was taken away. I went looking for him to help him. I found him alive and different from the way I had seen him before.

This dream did not make any sense to me, but I wrote about it anyway, deciding that perhaps later it would. "Maybe if I could find a book on dreams, I could begin to understand some of them," I planned.

While I was getting ready to abandon my little retreat, I recognized another song running through my mind and out through my mouth. This one was a newer song called "Bubba Shot the Jukebox Last Night," recorded by Mark Chestnut. It goes on to say, "Said it plays a sad song, it isn't right. Went outside to get his forty-five. Bubba shot the jukebox last night."

Well maybe, just maybe, the dream and the song were meant to tell me that I don't need to be sad about Jay. That he is all right and lives in another form somewhere else. Maybe the dream was even telling me I was one way and now I too am in a state of becoming different.

I didn't know why I came to this conclusion. It just became apparent to me that this was what it meant. But I still questioned myself about it.

By 9 a.m. I was on the road. The morning was beautiful and sunny. I felt so good as I drove along the island, seeing water on both sides at times. Coffee sounded good, but I decided to wait and stop someplace after I crossed the bridge that connects the island to the mainland.

On the way home I listened to Vince Gill's new tape. I was very impressed with the song "Go Rest High on that Mountain," which he had written about his brother. Vince's brother Bobby died in March of '93. I had just returned from Kansas that same week. My dad died, and we had his funeral just two days earlier.

I listened to the tape all the way through twice. I cried as I heard this one particular song. I felt for Vince and his family. I knew the sorrow they were going through over the loss of a son and a brother.

I remembered I had another tape I had not listened to yet. These were remakes of Bob Wills songs. I slipped the tape in and said, "This one is for you, Dad!"

Dad was a big fan of Bob Wills and the Texas Playboys. We often would listen to his music in the years before. It was fun driving along listening, singing, and picturing Dad getting into the music he liked.

He was a pretty good dancer too. I remembered a time before he got so sick. We went to hear a band play at the Cowboy Casino in Hutchinson, where he lived. I knew he got a kick out of dancing with me as some of his old friends watched, probably wondering who the young woman was that Wayne was spinning around the dance floor.

I didn't care now what they thought. I was happy that Dad and I had this last opportunity to go out and spend some time together. It was the last time that I saw my Dad behave closest to the way I had always known him. After that, he went downhill gradually until he died. He had acquired stomach cancer and Parkinson's disease.

Now I realized how much I missed him and saw that I hadn't really grieved as much over his death as I have with Jay. I was truly happy for him to be able to leave. He had been suffering so much, and it was painful to see him—a big strong man now reduced to a dependent bedridden nursing home patient, and only 63 years old.

"If I can be happy for Dad being able to leave, why is it so hard to be as happy for Jay?" I voiced aloud. I believe they are both in a better place. Maybe its because I want to be there with them, more than I wished for them to be still here with me.

"Yes, that's it. I want to be able to go be where they are. I wonder what it is I'm supposed to do here, what is it that I am to finish before it is my time to go?" I quizzed the space in the car around me.

I came to the understanding with myself that I was going to do whatever it takes to fulfill my purpose on this earth. It is time to slow my life down and begin to enjoy it. "Stop and smell the roses" came to mind with greater meaning.

With the conclusion of my trip came a better understanding of myself and the desires in my heart. I now knew what I needed to do first. It was time for me to shed some of the pressure I have with my job. This could mean a drastic change in the lifestyle Tony and I had become accustomed to. But I need to do this—I must do this.

When I got home, I put my things away and went out to the porch to water the plants. I was watering the small dogwood tree, a gift from Sandy and her daughter Kristie. What I saw—and that took me totally by surprise—was a full growth of clover. It was growing at the base of the tree. "I'm Looking Over a Four Leaf Clover?" I hadn't seen any four-leaf clover growing in the pot, but I had the idea that something was going on here.

I was ready to greet Tony when he came in at 5:30. Things were a little quiet at first. Very little was said about my time away.

At bedtime I invited Tony into conversation about our lives. I explained to him how my life seemed to be taking a turn, and I was planning to make some changes. I went on to tell him that I would like to quit working so much, maybe even write a book.

He listened attentively and commented, "You know we'll probably have to sell our house, don't you? I don't bring home enough money to cover the bills." I heard what he was saying and knew he was concerned about the amount of money I would be giving up when I put my new plan into effect.

I didn't know what would happen when I speak with Chuck. I simply knew that at this point in my life it was necessary for me to lighten up. This meant resigning from my position as general sales manager at the radio station. It would not be easy, but it was clear that I must do it.

A lot of my decision was based on getting rid of a lot of stress in my life, spending more time getting myself in better condition. I felt I had worked too hard in my job to continue as I had since Jay's death. I wanted to bow out gracefully without leaving too many mistakes for someone else to have to straighten out. My ability to think and act as I had before had changed. The enjoyment I had for the work before seemed to be gone now.

Tony acted as if he understood as I explained how I felt. But I wasn't certain he really did. The exact financial impact would not be known until after I had a chance to speak with Chuck. This would determine what he would be willing to do, what he would work out with me.

I felt better by being able to have Tony's attention while discussing my situation. For the most part he had been very supportive during this difficult time in my life, and I appreciated that greatly.

I am truly thankful to Jay for having put Tony in my life. The thought occurred to me that perhaps this was all a part of Jay's mission on this earth. Christine said that Jay told her after we were all together at Christmas that he knew I was going to be all right now, and he wouldn't need to worry about me being taken care of.

It's funny how I recommended Russell to my mother twenty-six years ago, and my son arranged for me to meet Tony. "Are these what people call a match made in heaven?" I wondered.

I had another one of those songs playing in my mind before going to sleep. This one called "They Don't Make 'Em Like That Anymore." As I was nearly asleep, I saw a moving picture in my mind of a soaring eagle, flying over trees and land. It lasted only a brief second but was very clear and vivid in my mind.

Chapter Twenty-Nine

Tony and I had only been asleep for a few hours when I woke up realizing that we were getting into a most wonderful amorous situation. Both of us, elated from this awakening, commented and laughed together about how we woke up.

I remembered having a dream prior to waking. But it didn't seem to be the kind of dream that would have brought on something like this. At least I didn't think so.

I was seeing page after page of written papers. I remember thinking in the dream, "When I wake up I will remember to remember what was written on the pages." Also, I had the thought that I would have someone to translate or interpret the writings for me.

Before I went back to sleep, I realized another song in my head. A big smile came to my face as I remembered "Blues For Dixie," one of the songs on the tape I dedicated to Dad during the drive home. I felt it was a little gift to me from him. The thought also came that he may have had something to do with Tony and I waking up at the same time as we just did.

Just as I was about to drift off to sleep, I heard very plainly my name being spoken. "Judith Jane" was how I heard it, not Judy. My dad is the only one in my adult life that occasionally called me by my proper and second name. My mother would call me that sometimes as a child. But when she did, I knew I was in trouble. When I heard my name, at the same instant I knew it was my dad.

We continued to sleep for the duration of the night. In my sleep, I had a dream. When morning came, I wrote about it in my journal.

I dreamed of a large house that was all torn up. It had people venturing through it, working to straighten it up so someone else could have it. The road leading to the house had floodwater flowing across it toward the house. I saw an uncaring army doctor coldly working on an injured man. He quit working on him and began to make love to another man's pregnant wife.

What this dream meant seemed as only speculation to me. Somehow, I related the house to me. The people straightening it up are the loved ones who care enough about me to assist and encourage me to get my affairs in order within myself. After the floodwater comes it leaves new fertile soil to start new life. They were flowing toward the house—me. The uncaring army doctor was waging battle against the negative influence, waging war in my life, which is in fact very loving and nurturing of new life.

I made another appointment to see Sammye.[17] The day I made the trip to see her, July 12, 1994, something interesting happened as I was getting ready to leave her reading room. I saw something lying on a little table next to her couch. It looked like a little pressed flower on an index card with cellophane wrapped around it. I bent over to take a closer look. As I looked closer and picked it up to inspect it, I realized it looked like a four-leaf clover.

"Is this a four leaf clover?" I asked Sammye.

"Yes, I don't know why it's lying out. I've had it around here for years," she replied.

"You take it with you."

---

[17] See transcription of session with Sammye in Appendix C.

"Really? Thanks. It's funny. I kept noticing something lying there and was trying to figure out what it was. One of the songs that kept running through my head when I was away was 'I'm Looking Over a Four Leaf Clover,'" I told her.

"Well that must be why it was lying out here. It was for you" was Sammye's reply.

Over the next several days and weeks, I had other songs come into my mind.[18] I continued to hear that little still voice say things in my ear or in my mind.[19] The dreams came more frequently, and remembering the dreams came with greater ease.

One night in July, I heard a string of words that put a smile on my face as they entered my mind. "I can hardly keep the angels from lighting on my ear." I didn't know what it meant, but the words made me feel warm inside and gave me such a feeling of comfort.

I felt it was Jay saying this to me. "But what does it mean?" I said before I repeated the words to myself several times. My only understanding from this was that he was assuring me that he is all right where he is now, that the angels are taking care of him.

The following night I heard, "Let go of all animosity." It didn't take much thought to figure out what that meant. However, I did look up the definition in the dictionary just to confirm that I knew the true meaning of the word "animosity."[20]

The next message that I received was one day later at bedtime. I heard, "In gambling you play to win, but here in this game, loosing is winning!" Again, this message came to me so clearly as if someone next to me spoke, yet I knew I only heard it inside my head.

This is the understanding I got from this message: When a person dies, it appears they are dead and the life is lost. When in fact the true life beyond the deathbed is the prize. By giving up your life, you win it back.

An unusual idea popped in my mind during the day that I heard these previous messages. I had a picture in my mind that the earth's

---

[18] See list of songs heard on pages 177-180.

[19] See list of things heard on pages 181-185.

[20] Animosity: deep-seated hostility, enmity.

sphere is in reverse from that of the heavenly sphere. The example of a balloon with writing on the outside was shown to me as plain as if I already knew it.

When the balloon is blown up, the letters are read easily while viewing it from the outside, referring to the earth sphere. After deflating the balloon and turning it wrong side out and blowing it up again, the letters are backwards. Backwards now to the heavenly sphere but now in a form that the earthy sphere can see in it's proper perspective. Now reversed like a mirrored image.

Within two weeks from the time I took off for my hiatus in Hatteras Island, many things began to happen in my life. I made several decisions about changes I now felt I must make in my life too. One of the biggest decisions I made was to resign from my full-time position as general sales manager at the radio station.

I began to realize the importance of slowing my life down and beginning to enjoy it more. My fast-paced, intense life already seemed to have taken its toll on my stomach. What other things would go if I continued to live in that fashion? Right now, my mind seemed to behave differently from the stress of Jay's death. How could I possibly expect it to heal if I continue to put more pressure on myself?

The following is a list of the songs that would run through my mind at different times. Usually it would be a certain verse or phrase from the song that would appear to have a specific message for me. I included the date to show the relationship of the message as it came as an answer or as comforting words when I would be having a difficult time dealing with Jay's death.

7/2/94	– "Independence Day" by Martina McBride
7/3/94	– "Every Once in a While" by Black Hawk
	– "Pennies from Heaven"
7/4/94	– "I'm Looking Over a Four Leaf Clover"
7/6/94	– "They Don't Make 'Em Like That Anymore"
	– "Blues for Dixie"
7/7/94	– "Ruby Tuesday"
7/10/94	– "Take It on Down to My House Honey"
	– "I'm Standing in Clear Waters"

	– "Ida Red"
7/11/94	– "Yearning Just for You"
7/12/94	– "I'm a Girl Watcher"
7/13/94	– "Still Water Runs the Deepest"
7/14/94	– "Deep Water"
7/15/94	– "Red Wing"
	– "Gonna Have a Party"
	– "Billy Dale"
7/16/94	– "Yearning Just for You"
7/17/94	– "Yearning Just for You"
	– "Bring It On Down to My House Honey"
7/18/94	– "Misery"
7/19/94	– "Release Me"
7/21/94	– "Here Comes the Sun"
7/25/94	– "It Is No Secret"
7/26/94	– "Renegades, Rebels and Rogues"
7/28/94	– "Hangin' In, Hangin' Out, Hangin' On" by Tanya Tucker
7/29/94	– "Oh Happy Day" (Tony woke up singing the song, a rare occasion.)
7/30/94	– "Ruby Tuesday"
7/31/94	– "Gonna Have a Party All Night Long"
8/3/94	– "Hangin' In, Hangin' Out, Hangin' On" by Tanya Tucker
8/6/94	– "Standing Outside the Fire" by Garth Brooks

*Life is not tried, it is only survived
if you're standing outside the fire*

8/18/94	– "Here We Come to Save the Day"
8/31/94	– "She Loves You" by the Beatles
9/1/94	– "Spent My Whole Life Dreaming with My Eyes Wide Open"
9/2/94	– "I'm a Yankee Doodle Dandee"
9/4/94	– "Don't Let the Rain Come Down"
9/11/94	– "You're All I Think About These Days" by Patty Loveless

9/30/94   – "Onward Christian Soldier"
10/1/94   – "Everlasting Love," "Angel of the Morning"
10/5/94   – "Yankee Doodle Dandee"
10/8/94   – "Oh! Susanna"
10/30/94 – "If I Could Make a Living"
11/4/94   – "Jukebox Junkie"
11/5/94   – "Mr. Big Stuff"
11/6/94   – "I've Been Wondering If I Can Live Without You"
11/8/94   – "Elusive Dreams"

You know I'm tired of following my elusive dreams

11/9/94   – "Somewhere Written in My Mind" by Clint Black
11/11/94 – "Waterloo" by Stonewall Jackson
11/24/94 – "You Don't Have to Say You Love Me"

Just be close at hand
You don't have to stay forever
I will understand
Believe me, believe me

       – "I Never Promised You a Rose Garden"
12/10/94 – "Chim Chim Cher-ee"
1/17/95   – "Tonight"

Tonight, tonight
won't be just any night
Tonight there will be no morning star
Tonight, tonight, I'll see my love tonight…
Today the minutes seem like hours
The hours go so slowly
And still the sky is light

2/4/95   – "You're the One"

You're the one that I love to kiss
You're the one that I love to miss
We're still havin' fun
And you're still the one

4/3/95–4/5/95 – "That's Amore"
6/20/95   – "In the Misty Moonlight"
7/5/95   – "Crying Time"

Oh it's crying time again, you're gonna leave me…

7/22/95   – "Rawhide"
7/22/95   – "Have You Ever Really Loved a Woman?"

*So tell me have you ever really
Really, really ever loved a woman?*

8/12/95   – "Do You Know Where You're Going To?"
8/13/95   – "Hold Your Head Up"

*Hold your head up high
Hold your head up high
Hold your head high*

8/14/95   – "Across the Alley from the Alamo"

Looking back over the past several months I can see approximately the time that I began to hear certain things that would seem to come from different sources than others. Generally I would hear the soft gentle voice in my ear—sometimes the right ear and other times the left. At times it would seem to be heard outside, close to my ear with a feeling of a gentle touch.

Earlier I usually would hear words, but later, sentences. These are heard most often within the mind. They wouldn't be heard as we normally would think of hearing another person speaking, but as if a thought was simply placed within the mind, and simultaneously the awareness and understanding of the words would be there also.

The following are words, phrases, and sentences that I remembered to record in my journal from the time I began to keep one. Sometimes what I would hear would make sense to me when I heard it, and other times I wouldn't understand what I heard until later. A few things still don't make sense, but maybe someday they will.

Dates are being shown to correspond with the growth process I believe I have been going through with this.

4/3/94	– "Flat on the bottom."
7/2/94	– "I am not as one."
7/6/94	– "Judith Jane."
7/8/94	– "I can hardly keep the angels from lighting on my ear."
7/9/94	– "Let go of all animosity."
7/10/94	– "In gambling you play to win, but here in this game, loosing is winning."
7/18/94	– "I will escort you to…"
7/19/94	– "Electromagnetic field, electromagnetic energy."
7/21/94	– "For every year of age. Give yourself one month for every year to grieve and become full again. [Twenty-five years equals to twenty-five months: April/May 1996] Give yourself that much time."
7/22/94	– "Sixty-six twenty-seven." (66-27)
7/25/94	– "There's only one, Judy!"
7/27/94	– "Promise, Mom, it's just underneath the road." When I received this, I also saw it in my mind. It was written on a four-leaf clover made of construction paper. It was folded up in a square—yellow in color. As it was unfolded, it looked like a green four leaf clover. The top left leaf said "Promise." The top right leaf said "Mom." The bottom left leaf said "It's just underneath," and the lower left leaf said "the road."
8/3/94	– "Tony." (I heard in an echoey voice.)
8/4/94	– "Go to Skats. Billy Smithigus." (Or it could have been Smith.) Skats is an actual restaurant name my dad used to take me to.
8/7/94	– "James Christopher Lee, Elizabeth Marie Lee, Robert E. Lee." I saw something about brochures that had something to do with the boardwalk at Carolina Beach. You made a willful decision to be

quiet. Stop chattering—now stop the chatter. Just be still. "Know that, that which is in your mind is you." "These are meant to relax and settle down." "God is with thee!" "Love is a heavy attitude." "Judy, Judy, American spa- ghetti has a beginning and end. Like Spaghetti Os, the beginning and end meet together on this one." "Attention! Pay attention. Sammye sits up in a chair. It's easier to fall asleep when lying down."

"What shall I write about?" This was a question in my mind. Tony. "What do I write about Tony?" Another question in my mind.

"Minding the mooners!" "Mooners" or "manners?" This was how it sounded to me and I questioned it. "Showing your ass is a mooner." This definitely sounded like something Jay or my Dad would have said to me.

8/8/94	– "You need to clean your ears out!" Dad?
8/9/94	– "Anomaly"
8/17/94	– "Eight, twelve, twenty-four, twenty-eight, thirty." I woke up repeating these five numbers.
9/28/94	– "Wait a whale and then you'll see." "Drives me crazy." Seems like I heard the same thing a night or two before, but I didn't write it down.
8/6/94	– I heard a name but forgot it.
10/7/94	– "You are one spring of many, flowing from one well."
10/9/94	– "Jason." I heard this as it was long and stretched out in a male voice that echoed.
10/10/94	– Tinkling sounds, like distant, light, airy wind chimes. Very faint but clear sounding. The sound was a gentle message up close to my left ear.
10/17/94	– "Two forty" (240)
10/24/94	– "5323" (Could have been 5223)
11/3/94	– "David Slater"
11/6/94	– "Bye, Judy." It sounded like a child's voice.

11/12/94 – "You sound different." Then I heard something about grief, but I couldn't get it. Next I felt a tickle on my cheek.
11/13/94 – "I had my penis and my urethra removed."
12/1/94 – "Indigenous"—living or occurring naturally in an area: native (*Webster's II New Riverside Dictionary*)
12/10/94 – "You're six years old."
12/14/94 – "It's one billion, rather than sixteen million."
12/18/94 – "Hast now more colors."
12/18/94 – "It is not the amount of courage that is important, but the lack of fear that counts!"
12/25/94 – "Tone the book."
12/28/94 – "Wynon Mull"
1/4/95 – "Pictures taken without my permission will be charged to your heavenly account." And "Craig Thompson."
1/5/95 – "I'm going to contact the state legislature, Mrs. Miller—Killer Miller. No, don't call now." Sounds like how Jay would talk to me, referring to me as Killer Miller.
1/6/95 – "Hi—you a hold, you a hold."
1/7/95 – "Judy!" I heard it in my right ear as a feminine voice. Very clear and peaceful sounding.
1/8/95 – "Or has it occurred to you?" Next I saw a picture in mind of an armored car. "Two things—stick to story," and "It's the personal things that matter."
1/13/95 – "Hi, Judy!"
1/15/95 – "Judy—power. And the idea's result—it's learned."
1/17/95 – "Actually it's rough, Judy!"
1/23/95 – "Seventh and eighth floor."
1/27/95 – "What are you talking about, bird?" I heard this in Tony's voice. He always called me "Bird."
2/4/95 – "Listen in your ear."
5/5/95 – "Hi to Alice. Always love. It's important to you to love unconditionally. Love. Learn that now. Happiness is

just around the corner. Be there for me. Tell her." I felt certain that this was from my step-dad, Russell.

6/5/95 — "Jon Savogne Pepperidge"
6/6/95 — "Larry's Rose Scents," and "792-8844"
6/9/95 — "Think about baggies and Cootering also." This sounds like Jay. "Not many writing here in Bucharest," capital city of Romania. I felt this was from Dad.
6/12/95 — "What would you do for a Klondike bar?" Funny! Could be Jay, Dad, or Russell (also now passed over).
6/15/95 — "You can't snatch people and put them in your fantasies and expect them to respond."
6/23/95 — "Kim."
6/26/95 — "Robert Ketchum better go with the cameries." (Cameras?)
6/27/95 — "I'm not tired of this. I'm not sorry to bother you."
— "Cot."
— "It's shaky. It's meaningful to others."
6/28/95 — "A motherly revue."
6/30/95 — "Every four to five minutes."
— "From beginning to end and back again!"
7/3/95 — "New Jersey"
— "I've got to buy a little kid."
— "Nina" (Knee-na)
— "Hey Judy, Choo, Choo"
— "You got that right, John."
— "Didn't you want to see me?
— "To get on with it?"
7/4/95 — "Tell all your ex-husbands. Especially the ones that begin with *W* and *P*. As she looks at money with Jefferson, Lincoln or Washington, she is able to become like them."
7/7/95 — "You could look at the legs, but you would be inwardly looking at what is out. I'll go get Maggie."
7/14/95 — "Isabel sent me."
7/15/95 — "Sounds like he left Shallotte."

7/22/95 – "New Jersey. I know what they are. They are vinegar."

7/23/95 – "And Cat had a tough time too, didn't she? Yes. I was running around going crazy trying to get your attention. My plan now is up. It doesn't work—Shay-Y-D. Lunch today, peanut butter. Unless he is not ready, you two will hold the two gold keys."

7/26/95 – "Master point"

7/28/95 – "Better hurry!"

8/2/95 – "Fresh frosting—frozen icing" and "I believe it's *Arizona Highways*." (One of my dad's favorite magazines.)

8/4/95 – "Everybody wants to look at me and say something about something."

8/9/95 – "Bad bullets and beforehand."

8/12/95 – "Billy Hunter" (Billie?)

8/15/95 – "He's not asleep, he's just mad"; "How ya doin?"; "I think she came in here and stood"; and "And I don't think its going to get any better."

8/20/95 – "Donna Price—Donna Hill."

8/22/95 – "Meatballs"

8/23/95 – "Where is your imagination?"

8/30/95 – "I'll be right back!"

I have developed the belief that I have become and open channel to pick up on others who are trying to get a message to someone through me.

Chapter Thirty

Life for me seemed to have been turned upside down, shaken up and turned around. Suddenly it appeared that when the shaking was completed, all of my genes settled in a different position, giving rise to new feelings, attitudes and understanding. Unusual things began to happen in and around me.

Most days I would wake up feeling good and refreshed, but by midafternoon I would feel achy, feverish, and very tired. This would drive me to my bed for rest. After a period of doing this, I began to recognize that I could easily make myself relax and drift into that pre-sleep or alpha state.

While in this state I began to realize the things I would hear, know, or see. Sometimes I would drift into sleep and forget what I heard or seen.[21] When I woke up, I would remember that I had picked something up in the mind but I couldn't recall what it was.

After loosing several bits of information, I began to write everything down as it came. Keeping my journal on the bedside table makes

---

[21] See list of things seen on pages 189-192.

it easy to quickly write things down and then go back to the resting state.

I began to read and learn about meditation. The understanding of what meditation does to assist a person to know the inner self became apparent to me. I had used prayer in my life to talk to God, but I learned that in meditation God can talk to me.

The driving force within myself began to be more easily recognized. I began to be able to see the larger picture of the events in my life and the reason why certain things were happening to me.

One evening I felt drawn to look for something in my *Good News Bible*. I opened it and looked right at a scripture that seemed to be a direct answer to a question I kept asking myself. "Why do I long to leave this world? I love my husband, family, and friends; but still, why do I desire to leave knowing that I would be leaving them all behind?" The scripture—one I could not remember ever seeing before—simply jumped out at me.

2 Corinthians 5: 1–10

For we know that when this tent we live in—our body here on earth—is torn down, God will have a house in heaven for us to live in, a home he himself has made, which will last forever. And now we sigh, so great is our desire that our home which comes from heaven should be put on over us: by being clothed with it we shall not be without a body. While we live in this earthly tent, we groan with a feeling of oppression; it is not that we want to get rid of our earthly body, but that we want to have the heavenly one put on over us, so that what is mortal will be transformed by life. God is the one who has prepared us for this change, and he gave us his Spirit as the guarantee of all that he has in store for us.

So we are always full of courage. We know that as long as we are at home in the body we are away from the Lord's home. For our life is a matter of faith, not of sight. We are full of courage and would much prefer to leave our home in the body and be at home with the Lord. More than anything else, however, we want to please him, whether in our home here or there. For all of us must appear before Christ, to be judged by him. Each one will receive what he deserves, according to everything he has done, good or bad, in his bodily life.

After reading the scripture I felt better. My desire to leave had in fact seemed normal for me. However, when I had mentioned it to certain people, I would come away feeling confused. I was told that I had given up on life, or that I was being selfish by thinking only of myself and not how it would make those left behind feel. Needless to say, I had been feeling a little guilt for having this desire. But the guilt was relinquished with the revelation of the scripture.

The following pages will attempt to describe the things or types of things that I would see in my mind. Most of the time I would see these as quick flashes. Occasionally they would appear in my mind with movement, color, and clarity. Over a period the images would last longer and be more precise and detailed.

At first, when I began to see, I would feel stunned and would snap instantly back into a full waking condition. Later I learned to go with the flow of it and not allow myself to be as startled.

4/3/94	– Very peaceful, still, crystal clear water. On the floor, beneath the water in the vision, were tiny little coral colored pebbles. Above the water was a space of air, separating the water from a rock ceiling.
	– I saw Jay's face. He was looking at me from behind my closed eyes with his usual grin on his face.
7/6/94	– Eagle soaring over trees and land.
7/12/94	– §, (A legal symbol called a section sign.) a symbol that looked like two *S*'s.
7/13/94	– Caribou in a pond.
	– Wagons pulled by horses.
	– A cowboy leaning on a doorway.
	– A short hose with water spraying out.
7/30/94	– Signature of the artist who made Dad's turquoise bowline tie. The symbol used by this artist is a clover.
8/1/94	– Large white plastic pig.
8/3/94	– Gray, black, and white Chevrolet Blazer move quickly in front of me.
	– Saw my step-grandmother getting into a car.
	– An older blonde girl child was pushing a younger brunette girl child on a tricycle.
8/4/94	– Side view of a man wearing a burgundy golf shirt. He had dark hair with a touch of gray in it. He was wearing glasses with dark-colored frames and was looking down.
8/5/94	– A little light-colored mouse run from behind a box in to a hole in the corner.

8/8/94 — Road or path with ruts all the way through on its left side. Ruts were only partly through on the right side.

8/10/94 — Woman with long dark hair.
— Man standing out on the side of an extension of a stone (castle type) building overlooking a deep valley. The view from above. The picture below is what I was seeing from above.

8/12/94 — Saw what we would recognize as the face of Jesus as a man.
— Skies with clouds. A few of the clouds were close and were gray in color.
— Stacks and stacks of (silver-dollar-type) coins.
— The back side of a naked man from the mid-back down.

8/13/94 — Jay's face upside down.

8/20/94 — Jay wearing a bathing suit and sitting in a beach chair. His looks changed to the appearance of my brother (Alan). He was looking directly at me.
— Hands holding something dark.

8/21/94	– Sky with clouds parted. An object with colored lights moved across and between the clouds.
8/24/94	– Dark colored spider with legs all around it.
	– Book cover with a title on it. Parts of it were greenish colored.
8/29/94	– Bright yellow Caution sign with deer crossing on it. Another sign indicated curves ahead of the road.
	– I noticed a woman ahead leaning into the window of a dark colored car. She turned and ran away as she looked toward me.
	– The back of a woman with her arms around the backs of three girl children. They were wearing floor-length dresses made of a small floral-print design. They were skipping down the road.
	– The face of my friend, Cindy.
9 /3/94	– Burgundy-colored strawberries. Some were sliced and the others we whole.
9/14/94	– Man with a long-sleeved white shirt on. He had his arms raised and bent at the elbows. His hands were holding the back of his head.
9/30/94	– Darkened sky with about three unusual aircraft soaring around.
10/13/94	– The thunderbird symbol (phoenix).
12/1/94	– Woman wearing glasses. The lens over the left eye was tinted dark. The lens over the right eye was clear.
12/10/94	– Young girl with chin-length medium dark hair. She had a very sad look on her face.
12/29/94	– Blossoms or blooms in my body.
	– Symbol of a star: ✤
1/8/95	– Large (clipper-style) ship. I've seen several different times.
1/15/95	– Telephones.
	– The archetype or sound pattern of my soul, moving and changing.

1/17/95	– Young man standing next to me as I was lying on the bed. He was looking at me and was bending over toward me.
	– I saw three eyes looking at me.
1/23/95	– Lower part of a beautiful woman's face.
6/5/95	– Saw my husband, Tony, being handed two citations for our boat.
6/12/95	– Slim tanned woman slipping out of clothing. She was naked from the waist down.
6/27/95	– My hand running through words and definitions in a dictionary.
6/28/95	– Front page of a newspaper. In the lower left corner were ten little boxes with symbols in each one. A message was written next to the first eight boxes. The last two were not completed.
	– Saw the date "9/3" and the face of a black man.
7/4/95	– Two men fighting on the top edge of a boat.
	– I saw my hands reaching up and then felt myself being lifted up.
7/12/95	– My purple impatiens plant. It was full grown and bushy with long shoots spreading out from it.
7/26/95	– Girl riding a cycle was knocked over backwards, cycle and all.
8/15/95	– My name signed by my husband, Tony.
	– Motorcycle falling through the air.
8/28/95	– Two men each wearing red plaid flannel shirts and bright orange hard hats.
8/30/95	– Thunder (my childhood miniature horse) running toward me, carrying a rider.
	– Star sensor. A round donut shaped device that was mounted in the center of the chest, just over the heart. It was being saturated with a yellowish colored liquid.

Chapter Thirty-One

Many different things happened in and around me over the months since Jay's so-called death. I became convinced that "death" is a word that may be misleading. One definition in *Webster's II New Riverside Dictionary* describes death as "1. the cessation of life."

This definition is difficult for me to believe now because of the many experiences I have had. There is no doubt in my mind that life exists after the death of the body. The life of the person as we knew them in, the physical body, simply transforms back into life in the spirit—further advanced than before, hopefully.

I know without a doubt that Jay, in the manner that I knew him as my son, continues to live. Not in the form I remember him, but in spirit form, which is the true reality for all of us.

I was relieved to find out that I was not crazy after visiting the psychiatrist in which I was referred to. In fact, he suggested that I continue with what I was already doing, working through this difficult phase in my life. From that time forward I did what I felt led to do, listening to the directive of my own heart.

Along the way I have recognized signals of confirmation that I was on the right track. At other times I saw myself being blocked from doing what I wasn't supposed to be doing.

Many times at night, before going to sleep, I would quietly talk to Jay about writing the book and my love for him. On many occasions I would wake up in the night to find my bedside lamp on. At times Tony and I would be awakened to find both lamps on.

One particular afternoon I walked in the bedroom, and my lamp was on and my radio was playing. I would always have a comforting feeling that would accompany these times.

The first time this happened was almost four months from Jay's transition. I woke at my usual time to see the light flickering on and off. This was also the morning I woke with the song "Here Comes the Sun" running through my mind.

The next day was the second occurrence of the bedside lamps turning on. I woke up at 1:49 a.m. to find my lamp on and Tony turning his off. It was this morning that I woke up with the numbers *6627* or *66-27*.

The thought crossed my mind that by adding the two sets of numbers together, I would have the new spring rating for the radio station I worked for. The ratings were not due out for almost two weeks. When we received the advance ratings, we were told that we received 12.9 shares of the market (6+6=12 / 2+7=9). I began to realize the numbers confirmed this to be an authentic message sent to me from the otherside.

Later in the afternoon, I went into the bedroom to find my lamp on again. From there I went upstairs to my office to work on some things and ended up reorganizing my file cabinet. I ran across a box where I had saved some things. As I looked through these things to see what to keep and what to throw away, I found three items that Jay had given me.

Two pictures he had drawn and a written piece.[22] I felt a tingle go through my body as I looked at them. I decided to take them to a friend (LaVerne) and have her look at them the next day. She agreed

---

[22] See pictures and writing in Appendix A.

that they have great significance in this entire chain of events. By her suggestion, the two pictures were taken to Seaside Designs to be printed on T-shirts and sold to raise money for the Jay Hensley Endowment for Marine Studies at UNCW.

Three days after this experience, I sat at my computer and wrote the first paragraph of this book. At this point forward, there would be no more doubt about me writing the book. I simply knew that was to be my mission, and fulfilling that mission would be of utmost importance in the resolution of Jay's death experience.

A clear memory came to mind during this time. It was a memory of something that had happened exactly one year before. Jay had come to visit at the same time that Mother and Russell were visiting from Kansas. We went to dinner at an Oriental restaurant and received the complimentary fortune cookies. When Jay opened his, he said, "Mom, look at this! It is going to happen, Mom." As I read his fortune, I remember it saying, "You will soon find the treasure you've been looking for."

I told Jay, "It is true! You will find your treasure."

The memory brought the thought of how we are to store our treasures up in heaven. I knew that Jay had succeeded in finding his treasure. A feeling of happiness came over me for him as I remembered this, and I could no longer feel sad for him—only happiness for his discovery.

There would not always be happiness for myself. I continued to have sad days when I would miss hearing his voice. Especially in the earlier months. It never failed that something would happen that would make me feel better.

One month for several days in a row, I would enter one of our guest rooms and I would hear a frog croaking right outside the window. Each time I heard the frog, I remembered the frogs I heard singing in the cistern. This was on the second night in the Bahamas as I sat thinking about Jay and whether or not we would be able to find him.

Chapter Thirty-Two

*I*n September, Christine came to Wilmington for a visit and surprised me on the night of my birthday. I knew she would be coming; I just didn't know she would be a couple of days early. A nice young man had given her a ride, and she introduced him to me as her friend, Pat, who was going on to Michigan. He also had some friends in Wilmington that he wanted to see, so they came together. Somehow, I immediately knew that this would be the young man that Christine would be spending more time with.

About two months after I had returned from the Bahamas, I was talking to Christine on the phone. As we talked and shared what had been going on with each other, Christine's tone changed as she began to tell me that she was going over to some friends for dinner. She began to sound much happier as she told me about a family she had become close to and the things they had been doing together.

Just as her tone changed, static became so prevalent on the phone that it was somewhat difficult to hear her. I experienced such a strong feeling from it that I believed that Jay was the cause of it. I didn't say anything to Christine, but after we ended our conversation I told Tony how I felt that Jay was listening to the phone call. "Perhaps he was having some difficulty with what Christine was telling me about her friends," I explained.

In November, Christine came back to Wilmington for the endowment fundraiser. One afternoon during her visit, she said she needed to tell me something. She explained that she had been seeing a man for a couple of months and wanted to tell me about it because it bothered her to try to keep it from me. She explained that it was the young man (Pat) that had brought her to Wilmington in September.

I told her that I had a feeling that may be the case, and it was all right. Spending her life alone was not something that I would ever expect her to do. I said that I believe she has a good head on her shoulders and that I have confidence in her decisions for her own life of what would be right or wrong for her.

Christine and Pat are still seeing each other to this day. It wouldn't surprise me if they should decide to be married in the near future.

While Christine was visiting in September, Patte called from Hope Town to tell Christine of Number Nine's sudden illness. Patte was taking care of Number Nine while Christine had been away. This cat that I became attached to while I was there had been sick, and Patte had it flown to Nassau to have a veterinarian look at him. It turned out that Number Nine had developed a tumor, and the only thing that could be done was to have him flown to the States for radiation therapy or put him down.

My immediate thought was that the cat was to be released to join Jay. When I told Christine that Patte needed to know what to do about Number Nine, she felt it would be best to have the cat put to sleep. We both agreed that it would be torturous to the cat to have to go through such treatment.

Another thing that I experienced toward the end of September '94 was a very real dream of Jay. We were preparing to leave for a vacation in Florida the following morning. We would also be giving Christine a ride back to her parents' house in West Palm Beach.

The dream was of me walking into the bedroom and seeing Jay standing by the bed. As he turned to look at me, I noticed how he looked very mature, and his skin was very tan. I thought of how I shouldn't take my eyes off of him because if I did, he may disappear. Continuing to look at him, I walked toward him to give him a hug and kiss. He looked concerned at my approach to him as if he wasn't sure I should touch him. I hugged him, and it all seemed OK as he hugged me back.

Our trip to Florida began before sunrise. We picked up my husband's twin sister, Sis, and then went to Chris W's apartment to pick Christine up. Before we got very far out of town, Christine was fast asleep. Suddenly I remembered the dream and began to tell Sis about it. Tony listened as I told what I saw in my dream and how real it had seemed to me.

Tony said that I had been talking in my sleep as if I were talking to someone. I asked what I was saying, but he said he couldn't understand any of it. He described it as if I were talking to someone very fast. So fast that he couldn't make out any of the words. "This was around 3 a.m.," he said.

The following Thursday morning, I woke up and found a very unusual mark on my upper left arm. I could tell that it was not a scratch. As I looked at it closely, I saw that the lines were very precise and defined. I looked in the bed to see if I had been lying on something. There was nothing out of the ordinary that I could see.

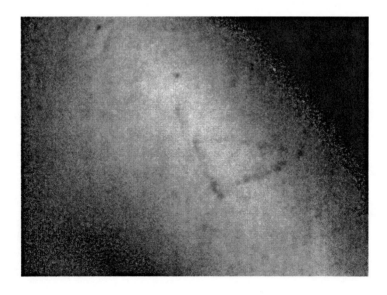

As soon as I saw it in the mirror, I felt sure that Jay had put it there; but I was still trying to find some rational explanation. I felt compelled to take a picture of it as proof that it was there.[23] I did show the mark to Sis and Tony, mainly because I wanted to see their reaction as they observed it. The mark was distinguishable for three days before it disappeared.

The same morning that I woke up with the mark on my arm, I heard in my mind, "Wait a whale and then you'll see." We had just been to Sea World the day before, and I could definitely see Jay's sense of humor coming out in this message. Rather than saying, "Wait a while," it would be his style to make it more entertaining to me by saying, "Wait a whale."

I did wait until we got home to speak with Sammye about the mark on my arm. It was at this time that I decided to have a past-life reading, and the explanation of the mark was given at the same time.[24]

---

[23] See picture taken of the mark on page 198.

[24] See transcription of past life reading in Appendix C.

Chapter Thirty-Three

Consistently I would see or hear people speak of clover, four-leaf clovers or shamrocks, everywhere. Each time I would have that comforting feeling as a reminder that Jay is all right.

It seemed that pennies would turn up everywhere too. This would also give me the feeling of comfort for Jay. Each time I would run into one of these things, I would remember the two songs. "I'm Looking Over a Four Leaf Clover" and "Pennies From Heaven" as I heard them while on my sabbatical.

My friend Cheryl called me one day in August '94 to tell me that her husband had been having a sore throat and that the doctor was running some tests. She said, "I just have a bad feeling about it."

It turned out that he was diagnosed with having squamous cell carcinoma of the trachea, and it was spreading out to his larynx and esophagus. This was the beginning of a very difficult time for them. Not much hope was being given for him and they said it was inoperable. Cheryl began searching high and low for a doctor that might know more about this type of cancer. She found a doctor in Boston, and they rushed off for weeks of treatment and surgery.

My close friend was now miles away with problems of her own to deal with. I tried to stay in touch with her as often as possible to help her as she had helped me.

One day, shortly before Cheryl had found out about her husband's cancer, a former employee (De Ana) of the station walked in and said, "I think I made a mistake by leaving. Is there any chance that I can come back to work here?"

This was the beginning of another close friendship that developed for me. Cheryl had been working on the fund raiser, and when De Ana came back to work, she also began to help out. She took over when Cheryl left to be with her husband in Boston.

Another friendship developed during this time as well. This being with Carolyn, my oldest stepson's wife. We began to spend more time together, talking and listening to each other's experiences. Her brother died a few years ago, and she had a very compassionate ear. We sometimes spent hours sitting out on the porch talking about the unusual developments and things that happened since Jay's death. Carolyn also worked diligently with the fundraiser at the station.

We saw everything come together so perfectly while planning and preparing for the fundraiser. People were most generous in their donations of auction items, money, and time. When it was all over, enough money was raised to have the named endowment in place. Gisella and Tom along with many friends and coworkers warmed my heart with caring support.

After the endowment fundraiser was all over, I resigned from the station to dedicate myself to the completion of the book that I was feeling driven to write. I discovered that writing this book would take my full attention. After trying to write periodically between work, the fundraiser, and home, I found that it would not be easy.

When I began to write about the actual death experience and the first few weeks following it, I would get physically ill. Maybe I would only write as much as one paragraph, and my entire body would begin to ache. Many times I would be filled with so much despair over what I was writing that I would have to stop because of my crying.

After getting through each phase of the experience, I would begin to feel relief. It was as if the chains that had me bound to it were undone, and I was free from the pain of that particular issue. Then each time I would begin to proceed I would again experience those feelings all over again.

At one point I couldn't write about the death experience phase at all. I wrote whatever would come to mind during times of rest and relaxation. Many pages of information poured out of me that I questioned where it was coming from. I even began to think that the direction of my original writing was wrong and that the book had taken on an entirely different direction.

Later I thought that this information was to follow the death experience in the book. Maybe the book would be in two parts. Part 1 based on the death experience, and part 2 relating the information that came from somewhere. (Where, I didn't know for sure.)

As I returned to the death experience and began getting this all out, I felt renewed. My son was still not here on Earth as I knew him before, but I felt his presence in different ways. Happiness was beginning to return to me as the pain was poured out into the computer for me to see and feel. The pain of thinking about the actual dying didn't feel the same way. Actually, the pain in the way I had known it before no longer existed.

My lifestyle changed from that of an overstressed business woman to that of a quiet writer. My time was now being spent enjoying the beauty of the earth around me. Seeking answers to my many questions through reading and meditation. Spending time with friends and simply taking life as it comes—day by day.

When writing, time became a breeze. It would start and end as if I had just begun. The words seem to fall into place without a lot of effort on my part. When I had experienced difficulty with writing, it was when I was attempting to force the words to come. I soon discovered for myself that this was not the time for me to be writing, but rather a time to be listening or resting.

The first time I sat for writing and learned I wasn't supposed to be writing at that particular time, was an afternoon when I began to feel drudgery for the writing. A negative state of mind crept up on me, and the writing reflected that. Stubbornly, I continued to write anyway. Then I noticed that what I was writing wasn't what was appearing on my screen. Words mingled with symbols were showing up. I tried to write some more, and the same thing continued to happen.

I decided to print it out and look it over. When I began to print this page to study it, it would not print. After attempting again and again, a quarter page of these words and symbols finally printed out on the paper. Feeling rather disgusted with all this and my computer for not working right, I decided to quit for the night. As I was saving what I had done during the past few hours, I had the feeling that something wasn't right. Just to double check myself, I reopened the document to see that one entire chapter and part of another had completely vanished.

I called the man who works on my computer and found that he was out of town. I remembered that a friend of mine had a brother in the computer business, so she got me in touch with him. He said he would stop by the next day and see if he could find my missing work.

The following morning I began to get the idea that what I had written was not the way it was meant to be written. I had forced the words to come out on the page. The computer expert worked and worked trying to find that portion of my lost document to no avail. This had definitely not been the right time for me to write, and I learned that quickly.

I had other holdups with the writing, especially when I would get away from the story and get sidetracked doing or thinking of something else. A double line of *K*s appeared on the screen one time. I caught myself beginning to dwell on the thought of the funeral service. It seemed that in my mind, I had drifted away from the writing. Suddenly I realized that I had just been sitting, thinking about how awful I felt that day, when I saw and thought about the ashes of my son in the gray canvas backpack. All the same sick feelings had recreated themselves in me.

I quickly reminded myself that my son was not in that backpack. Only the remains of what was formerly his body was in there. He himself, his soul, his spirit was no longer in that body. At this point the writing came back naturally.

When the writing takes place, it has been when I felt good about sitting. Once the portion of the death experience was all out, the writing became effortless. I wrote down lots of notes of things that had happened and when they happened, but I found that I really didn't have to refer to the notes very often. Even though I had experienced some problems with my memory during the earlier weeks, the memory of things that occurred and the sequence that they occurred seemed to flow as I would sit writing. At other times, when I wasn't writing, I would tend to have a little difficulty remembering these things.

At the end of the year I received my last paycheck, and the financial load shifted onto Tony. We had already noticed quite a difference in my income over the past nine months. I had given up my salary as general sales manager. Also at that time I was relieved of a lot of the advertising accounts I had worked with. My commissions began to get smaller as the year came to a close.

I was already prepared for the idea of us having to sell our house, but the idea of actually doing it wasn't an easy thing for me to accept. Our beautiful, comfortable home was not another thing I was ready to give up quite yet. However, I had made my decision to lighten my load, enjoy life more, allow myself time to heal, and most of all write the book that I came to believe was my mission to fulfill.

Our house was put on the market, and I told myself that if it is meant to be sold, it will sell—if not, it won't. After being on the market a couple of different times, it did not sell. Right before the last contract ran out, we had two offers on it in one night. We accepted the best offer, and we began to make arrangements to move to a condo. I had contacted movers, our insurance agent, and was waiting for word on which condo would be available for us to rent. Then the buyers changed their mind about buying our house, and it never happened.

It had been difficult for me at one time to think of leaving our home. Once the plans to move were started, the leaving and moving on seemed much easier. The porch that I became very acquainted with in the past months had less of a hold on me. I realized the reason I had become so attached to the porch. It was that I could sit there and visualize the last time that Jay and I sat there and had a person-to-person (in-depth) conversation.

I could see him walk around the back of the house, enter the porch, and sit down with me. This was the talk that revealed his memory of birth and the desire of a sea burial if anything ever were to happen to him. He also told me of seeing the ghost at the Cay during this talk.

We may still sell our home, but I see now that the time was not right yet. Only as time unfolds will I see the answer to this, I believe.

Chapter Thirty-Four

Earlier, I felt I had already lost so much—my dad and my only child. How could I also deal with losing my home? Now I see that it is the life that is of the utmost importance. The lives of my dad and my son continue to live in the spirit. The home has lots of spirit of its own and plenty of memories. What I had come to accept was that it can be replaced with something more suitable, another temporary home that will be designed to fit the situation that we live in at the time.

I have come to see our earthly existence as merely a temporary thing. We are here, we do what we came to do, and then we return to our home in the spiritual realm.

My step-dad has been another big influence in my life. Another one, like my dad and my son, of those important people I have and will always know and love. He passed over April 7, 1995 at the age of 62, six weeks after having a heart attack and going through major heart surgery. He and my mother had been home three weeks when an aneurysm, which was to be operated on in the following weeks, burst; and he departed quickly and quietly.

Earlier in the evening, he had been laughing and talking to my mother and some friends saying, "No one really ever knows exactly just how much time we actually have here." At bedtime, as they talked after the light had been turned out, "he made a sound and then he was gone," Mother explained.

When I went to Kansas to be with the family for his funeral, I woke up the first morning with a song that repeatedly ran over and over in my mind. "That's Amore" was the song that would not go away. I had the feeling that it was coming to me from more than one of our members on the other side.

I never met Tony's dad—he passed several years ago—but I had a strong notion that he was one of the source's bringing me this melody. Tony's mother told of how he had visited her in her bedroom one night and talked to her about Tony. "What are we going to do about Tony?" he said to her.

I don't understand what this meant. This was long before I met Tony. However, I'm certain that Tony's mom knows, but speaking about such things is not something that I hear her do very often.

One night while I was still staying with Mother after Russell's transition, I went into their bedroom to put Russell's reading glasses on the chest. While I was standing there looking at some of Russell's things and thinking about him, Mother walked in and began laying some clothes out on the end of the bed.

Over the bed is a ceiling fan with a light, and hanging down from it are two chains that turn the light and fan on. I had my back to Mother and the bed. I heard the chain snap, as if someone had yanked on it and let if fly loose. Suddenly the light went off, and Mother said, "Judy?" I turned around to see why she had turned the light out, and she said she thought I did it.

"I didn't do it." I said.

"Well, I didn't either. Judy, do you suppose?"

I knew what Mother was about to say, and I said, "See? These are the kinds of things that have been happening around my house. I've come to the place where I'm hesitant to tell anyone about it because they act as if they think I'm crazy."

I continued to describe our bedside lamps and the radio coming on at various times. In February the TV came on by itself. Two other people were in the room with me, and I thought one person had bumped the remote control. We both began looking for it and saw it had not been touched. I picked it up and turned the TV off.

When I told Carolyn about the TV incident, she too looked at me like I was a little touched. But a couple of months later while she was at the house with me, it happened again. It popped on the first time and I said, "See? This is what I told you happened before." When I turned it off, it came on again. So I turned it off another time. Still it came on again. By this timed Carolyn said, "Maybe there is something on that we are supposed to be watching." We watched for a while but didn't see anything that appeared to be meant for us to see. I simply left the TV on for the rest of the afternoon.

After returning home from Kansas, I called Mother often to see how she was doing. She gave me an update with each call of how she felt, how busy she had been, and who had come to visit. Around the third week after Russell's passing, Mother told me about her experience while cleaning up the garage.

She said she had been working away and was trying to figure out how to do something when she got directions in her mind of how to do it. "It was as if Russell was telling me—in the way he would have if he were standing right there—how to do it."

While resting one afternoon, I began to hear in my mind a message that I believe to have been from Russell for Mother. What I heard was "Hi to Alice. Always love. It's important to you to love unconditionally. Love. Learn that now. Happiness is just around the corner. Be there for me. Tell her."

Chapter Thirty-Five

As meditation became a bigger part of my life and the understanding of it's importance to me, I began to go to a weekly yoga class. I found this to be extremely helpful in preparing the body for meditation as well as giving the body better tone, agility, and strength.

Occasionally as I meditated, poetry would come to my mind.[25] Grabbing a pen and paper to jot down the words was the most difficult thing for me to do. Mainly because I was concerned that I would loose the meditative state that I was in as the words came to me.

I discovered that I could write while in that state as long as I continued to focus on the words and not other things. Just allowing the words to come to me while in that relaxed, peaceful state of mind seemed to be the answer.

The title of the book was something that I thought a lot about. I couldn't figure out what I would name it and finally resigned myself to the idea that it too would just come to me. When it did, it was an

---

[25] See poetry in Appendix B.

exciting revelation. It was not given to me in words as much as it was as an illustration in the mind.

One time while I was resting, I began to think about the book and how it would look if I printed it to read. I saw the first half printed out on one side of the paper. Then the second half printed on the reverse side of the page. The directions of how to read the book would be start at the beginning and read to the end of the first half; then turn the book over and read back to the beginning or end of second half. *From Beginning to End and Back Again!*

It did turn out that this book would be in two parts. The second part is material or writing I had a problem accepting for publication previously. Gradually, as I worked on the book it became easier for me to be willing to share this information.

The thoughts of how people would react when reading certain portions was difficult for me. I rationalized that I shouldn't print something that points out to others that I may be a person that has gone insane, especially admitting that I hear, see and come to know things that (normal) people generally would not.

Many wonderful things have come about in the past several months. I have come to see many gifts that I have received. The seeing, hearing, and knowing are samples of the many gifts that are ours simply by receiving them.

Jay now has a namesake. His friends Jim and Anita gave birth to a baby boy on May 12, 1995 at 4:55 p.m. Kagan Jay was Jim and Anita's second pregnancy. Anita miscarried the first child very shortly after Jay's transition. Kagan Jay came a year later.

When I talked to Jim after three months of having his new son, I asked him, "What do you call him the most? Kagan or Jay?"

"Well," Jim replied, "actually we call him…This may sound funny, but we call him Punky."

Laughing with excitement I said, "Punky? I used to call Jay 'Punky Doodle' when he was a little boy. Isn't that something? How did you happen to start calling him that?"

"Well, it sort of started with us calling him Pumkin, and then we just started calling him Punky for some reason," Jim explained.

Very, very few people knew or even remembered that I had ever called Jay "Punky Doodle." Mother could remember after thinking about it for a while, but I doubt that anyone else other than Jay would have remembered it. It was sort of a private little pet name I had for him when he was still quite small.

The second Mother's Day after Jay's transition was much easier for me. I got cards from caring friends and close family. The first Mother's Day had seemed confusing to me as to whether I was still even a mother. This one was different. I know I still am a mother and will be as long as I remain on this earth! More than that, I know that Jay and I are friends and will be forever.

Just as the ending to this book began to become clear in my mind, I walked out on my porch and sat watching the birds. To my amazement I saw the first and only hummingbird in my yard. It was hovering around a branch of a tree. At first I thought it was a rather large bumble bee. I got up and walked to the corner of the porch to look at this little creature as it rested itself on the branch. Then it hovered around the branch for a few seconds, sat again on the branch giving me a good look at it, and then darted away.

It looked very much like the hummingbird on the face of my watch. It was a gift from Jay. Just as he is now, free and mobile as the little hummingbird! This also feels right to be what Sammye had told me to watch for in my yard. My yard is filled with flowers and flowering bushes.

Appendix A

JUDITH MILLER

My Autobiography

by Jay Hensley
English III
Mr. Allford
Great Bend High School
Great Bend, Kansas
May 21, 1986

Table of Contents

Chapter I: The Wonderful Vacant Lot 1–2

Chapter II: Playing with Matches 3

Chapter III: The Meanest Thing I Ever Did 4

Chapter IV: A Painful Incident 5

The Wonderful Vacant Lot

An interesting thing happened to me once that I have never forgotten. You see I lived in a house at 1800 Park Street. It was directly across from St. Rose Church. I had made several friends there, and we always found ourselves playing some kind of sport or another. We always played in the huge field behind St. Rose, where the whole neighborhood met to choose teams and get on with the game.

Although that field never really belonged to anyone, it had each and every kid's name on it. I still remember its rightful owners today: Hammekes, Wheelers, Stephensons, Keenans, Karsts, and yes, me. It never failed that when something didn't go my way or theirs, it was time to kick everyone who crossed me off the land that I claimed. My favorite line was always stated plain and clear. "Well if you don't like my rules and can't play fair, you can get off my land." Of course they always came back with the reply, "This isn't your land. It's more mine than yours cause I go to church here."

Well, needless to say, the argument just got worse. It always got personal. "I go to church here too," I'd say even if it was untrue.

"But I sit closer to the father and I go four times a week. I pray morning, noon, and night," he'd say. Then I, struggling for something to say, would say, "So? That don't matter, my house is closer than yours to here. That's what counts." Then John Keenan would step in and say, "Well, my house is right there, and it's closer than any other, so my family owns it." That would pretty much do us in. We were out of tales to tell to get possession of that field.

John was always bigger than we were and looked mean, so he never got an argument from me or any of the other kids.

Playing with Matches

One hot summer day when I was about five years old, a new girl moved into the trailer park where I was living. Although I don't remember her name today, I learned early that impressing girls just isn't worth it.

It seemed that every boy who had an interest in girls was doin' somersaults and on and on. Well, I had a sudden brainstorm that was gonna get that girl. I remembered my father on a deer hunting trip saying to me as he was starting a camp fire, "You gotta be smart and good to light a good fire." Well, needless to say, I ran inside and robbed the matches my dad kept in his coat, then came back out. I told all the kids in the park to come. I said, "Now watch this. You gotta be good to do this." I struck a match. As it lit it fell onto all the others and started the whole pack. I dropped them, and the yard caught on fire. My father smelled the smoke and came out to put it out. After he was done, the whole yard had burned and part of the house's skirting. He looked at me like he would kill me, and I said to him, "That was a lot better fire than you did in the mountains, Dad." That was one night I didn't sit down. My rear was tanned good, and not from the fire.

JUDITH MILLER

The Meanest Thing I Ever Did

At the age of seven I found myself at the orneriest stage of my life, and I'm not foolin'. I never managed more than one day to be nice. At this time I had a buddy named Tracy Routin. We did nearly everything together, but he always liked to come out to the farm I lived on because he thought there was more to do. I felt just the opposite. I hated the farm. I wanted to go to town. But he always won. One day when he was to be coming out after he was out of summer school, I decided this would be a good time to fix him.

My father had just put up a rope from a limb so I could swing on it, and Tracy loved it. I knew it would be the first thing he got on when he got to my house. So I innocently moved the rope over about six feet so when he swung he would land in a different place. Sure enough, as soon as he got to my place he ran right to the rope. But the one thing I least expected was that he pulled his mom over to watch him swing. I was so scared. But then he swung, showing off, and went about thirty feet and hit smack into the big cottonwood tree, next to the tree with the swing. He wasn't hurt too badly, but I sure got yelled at by his mother. I've never seen Tracy since, and he probably wouldn't want to.

A Painful Incident

I think love is one of the greatest feelings there is in the world. But it can be turned in one moment to a pain you can hardly live with.

I know who I love the most. I always have and always will. My grandma Hensley, my father's mother. She was by far the greatest thing that ever happened to me. She showed a love to me I'll never forget. She was really a mother to me for the things she did for me. But on one night when she was in the hospital, God took her life so she wouldn't suffer the problems she was having. At the time she was fifty-six. It took a part of me that will never be replaced. I loved my grandma, and I'm not ashamed to say it.

JUDITH MILLER

Jay's art picture (Love Life)

FROM BEGINNING TO END AND BACK AGAIN

Jay's art picture (Peace)

JUDITH MILLER

When I draw a picture, I don't know why,
A sudden tear falls from my eye.
I draw what I feel, cuz then I know,
My feeling for life has begun to grow.

Why do people hate?
Is it jealousy of something they are not
Aware of?
Or is it cuz they are scared of the unknown?
Who knows—who cares?
Why do I worry about others when
I need help myself?

Why does a person kill?
To satisfy the aging beast or
The regressing angel?
Why does a person get greedy?
Cuz he thinks he earned it
And the others should too?

What would happen if every bit of money,
Every credit card was gone?
Would the savage human race survive?
No they need money to survive.

Will everyone die?
No, there would be ones who have foreseen
The miracle and prepared for
The greatest days of life.

Is there life after death?
There is no death only life.
You either pay for the ultimate sins or go free.
Where do you go when you go free?
Anywhere you want, it's your life!

—Jason "Jay" Hensley, 1991

Appendix B

JUDITH MILLER

A Precious Soul

By Judith Jane Miller

In the freezing rain, to me,
He came,
with gifts of joy and laughter.

A precious soul with love untold,
He lingers on with me,
Here after.

His smile,
His grace,
His loving face,
are but reminders of yesterday.

The hopes,
The dreams
of heavenly things
are sure to Lead the way.

I move along the path he made,
with desire to meet him there.

We'll meet beside the river wide,
no earthly reunion to compare.

Published by the National Library of Poetry|
The Garden of Life
1995

FROM BEGINNING TO END AND BACK AGAIN

Reluctant to Leave You

By Judith Jane Miller

It is because of the pain
I know you will feel,
That makes me reluctant
to leave you.

The pain you will feel
will seem to be real,
As to tear you in two
like a sole from it's shoe.
Just know there is strength
thru me, working for you.

I'm going on ahead
to prepare us the way,
To come together again
on a much brighter day.

Find courage and strength
in these words that I say.
I Love You, I Love You,
This is all I must say
'til we meet again,
Dear One, I Love You.

Published by the National Library of Poetry
Best Poems of 1996

Appendix C

Session One with Sammye

June 28, 1994

SAMMYE: The first thing I want to talk to you about is your spiritual self. You are a very, very spiritual person. Only in this last six to eight months, maybe more, maybe less, in that approximate time frame, you haven't really felt that. It's like you know it but you don't know it. Do you understand what I'm saying there?

JUDY: Yes.

SAMMYE: You will see within the coming three to four weeks that you will get centered back in, as far as the spiritual self is concerned. What I am seeing that is causing this unrest—"disease"—in relation to that is that you made some major, major, major changes, mental changes, and when we do make mental changes, mental changes within ourselves, within our consciousness and within our lives, it's kind of like the old fights with the new. Do you understand what I'm talking about there?

JUDY: Yes.

SAMMYE: And these changes that you have made are much, much, very much for the better. The only thing that I am seeing is, quit beating yourself up so bad. You have a tendency to really treat yourself bad. You don't need to do that. Just always remember that you are a spiritual person learning to be human, and that's the hard part. So, the thing that in this situation, where you are truly beating yourself up…what I'm seeing is that you have been a failure in some manner. And that is not true. It is just that we can't control another person's actions or reactions. And that is something that you're learning right now. But it is a very difficult lesson to learn. Also, on top of that you're having to learn what we call the lesson of receiving. Yours has always been the giving portion. And, OK, you have given and given and given, and given until there's nothing more to give. When we don't...haven't yet learned the lesson of receiving, then we get to that point where we have nothing else to give. And with that we have to learn to receive. You have a tendency to receive the bad stuff but reject the good stuff. It's time to turn that around. I feel like that's part of the decision you've made recently. That "I've had enough of this, I'm going to turn this sucker around to where I can deal with it. And where I'm willing to receive." It's going to take you another six to eight months to get yourself really...the word I'm getting is "free." I'm not sure why I'm getting the word "free," but really get yourself freed and when you are free, the lesson of receiving will no longer be a problem to you. OK, lets go for questions.

JUDY: Did Pat mention to you, she had asked a question about my son who died about three months ago in a diving accident?

SAMMYE: I don't remember, honey. The reason I don't remember is when I get through with your reading, when you walk out the door—

JUDY: You let it go?

SAMMYE: I have to.

JUDY: I was just wanting to know if my son's passing was...the experience...if it was pleasant for him?

SAMMYE: You want to do me a favor?

JUDY: Uh-huh.

SAMMYE: Let me find something that doesn't have any print on it. Write his name down on that for me, please. And fold it up and give it back. OK. Thank you. [*Long pause as she holds the paper with Jay's full name written on it.*]

SAMMYE: What I am seeing is that there was some...for a few seconds... and I'm not seeing any longer than seconds...there was some fear involved and then there was no longer fear. So the actual passing, when he left his body, was peaceful. And I'm seeing three people there…three people there to meet him. Ah…what I am hearing is two males and one female when he made his transition [*pauses, breathes deep, and sighs*].

Hum…hum…Yes, it was just that little bit, just a little bit of fear for two…approximately two seconds…a very short period of time, and then he was at peace. I don't—I'm not seeing a lot of struggle. None of that. It was like he was ready to go! I feel like he had attempted recently…I'm talking about in the last week 'cause it usually takes at least three to six months no matter how peaceful the transition was…but recently as well as right after he made his transition there. It's like he has been trying to get in touch with you to let you know that everything is all right and that he is all right, and I'm not sure…like what I'm looking…I'm looking at two different mediums. One is the dream state and one is when you're awake. It's like both times feeling the presence…but the dream…pay attention to your dreams. They now call it lucid dreaming, but it doesn't matter what they call it—the same stuff. But what you need… what I'm hearing [*sighs…breathes…hums*], I'm getting some nausea…Sometimes in these I pick up on part of the death experience…but I'm feeling some "nauseousness." It's stuck right here [*touches her throat*]. Ah…two factors, yeah OK… that he wants you to know that…and you already know this, but you don't know this…that doesn't make sense…that it had nothing to do with you. Of course you know that you were in no fault whatsoever. It's like he can feel or can perceive…knows that you're feeling…somewhat guilty? And he, I keep saying they want you to turn it loose and I know you just mentioned your son, but I'm feeling more than one. Is it they?

JUDY: Could be my dad.

SAMMYE: They…want you to turn it loose. Hum [*sighs…breathes*]? OK, I'm going to go ahead and lay that down for a little bit. Go ahead and ask me more questions [*breathes deep and sighs*].

JUDY: Well, a couple of them you have answered already.

SAMMYE: Thank you.

JUDY: I'm just wondering if he finished what he needed to do here?

SAMMYE: Yes! What I'm seeing is that he brought a tremendous amount of joy and understanding to…not only people in his own age group, but also older people. And that was the major purpose. A lot of happiness, a lot of joy, a lot of fun…to people who don't have enough of that. Yeah! But yes, he had fulfilled his purpose. Ah…didn't you know that there was something out of whack, say a week or week and a half before he died? The body died? A feeling, that sort of thing? That's what I'm hearing.

JUDY: Before he died?

SAMMYE: Um-huh…

JUDY: I felt an urgency in the way he called me and asked me…he had a couple of surfboards made and kind of an urgency in that he was wanting me to get them down there to him, to where he was, so he and his wife could enjoy them.

SAMMYE: Uh-huh….

JUDY: And he was wanting me to come down there sooner than my birthday.

SAMMYE: It wouldn't have mattered when you got there. You know that. We know it, but logic doesn't count [*laughs*] not now, logic doesn't count. But yes, he fulfilled his purpose. The other thing that I'm looking at is…and not sure why this is. Hopefully you will understand it. That his…in his coming to you it's apparent that there were not so many lessons to learn…It was just to be more fun than lessons. And that you were chosen as the parent because of your own goodness. And also one of his purposes for you was to teach you about freedom. Do you understand what I'm talking about there? Cause that's all I'm getting here, and I hope you understand it.

JUDY: The only other question I had was about the other two boys that died in the accident at the same time.

SAMMYE: What about them?

JUDY: If they passed OK.

SAMMYE: Hum...the one with the lighter hair...the one with the lighter hair had a...seemed to be a smaller frame too...had a little more difficulty because he didn't have the greater understanding. But the other one with the darker hair had no problems. But the one with the lighter hair seemed to be...What I'm hearing is that they fought life, so they fought everything. They're all right now [*sighs and pauses*]. Hum...that one was the one...the word I am getting is the radical of the group, very much the fighter. Not...not that the other boys weren't as assertive as far as their beliefs and all like that...but this one seemed to be fighting the world. But he's all right now. He's learning in a very...right now I feel with that one, there's still resting. More...take...when we're afraid of the world, and then we choose a different way to depart from the world, it takes us longer to acclimate. But he's still resting. But there were people that met him, but he just didn't want to believe that he had made his transition. So he's still resting. But the other one was fine. OK, as far as your son is concerned. There was something that you had begun, and I'm getting this in bits and pieces... so it will be in bits and pieces. There was something that you had begun to do that he was very, very encouraging of. There is something that he wants you to continue to finish. It has...it's like it has something to do with him, but it didn't have to do with him. It's not coming clear, but there's something that he wants you to continue to do. And I'm not getting it clear. I feel that if you don't know now—that if you pay attention to your dreams—he will show you in the dreams. And I keep...you know how it feels when the healing energy is going through your hands? That's what I'm feeling right now. Huh! See if I get anything else on that later. Go ahead.

JUDY: One of my questions was, when I feel that tingle go through my body, is that my son? Or what is that?

SAMMYE: That's what I was feeling.

JUDY: Is it like a healing energy?

SAMMYE: Uh-huh. The healing, assisting you to heal. Let me ask you a question now. Why aren't you working with some form of healing energy—laying on of hands, psychic healing, whatever they want to call it—more?

JUDY: Where would I find that?

SAMMYE: A Dr. Delores Kraeger has a book out called *The Therapeutic Touch*. She has a doctorate in nursing. And there are a number of other books out called *The Healing Touch* and different things like that. I would check with the Unity Church Bookstore, they have it, and Waldens and those bookstores have some books on that too. What I am seeing is that you would do very, very good in that area [*pauses*]. You have a very good healing ability, and I don't think I'm the first one that ever told you that. It could have been that people said to you, "Well I feel better when I'm around you. It feels good for you to touch me," things like that.

JUDY: I don't remember that I've heard that.

SAMMYE: I feel like you're...it'll come. But it will...that will help you to heal also. Dr. Kraeger is our foremost medical authority on that. Bernie Seagal, with *Love, Medicine and Miracles* and some of the other books. He works with cancer patients and other people that have debilitating disease to help them to feel better. He's a surgeon out of New York, I think, I'm not sure. But his books would be good for you to read too. He works with people with visualization, things like that also. Next question.

JUDY: I have one question that keeps coming back to me about the accident. That was, did the boys know that the parents had resurfaced? That they had gone up and that they weren't still down below in the water?

SAMMYE: No!

JUDY: They didn't know that?

SAMMYE: I don't feel that they did.

JUDY: I know I can't change what happened, but the mystery of why they didn't come back up and why the parents haven't talked to me. They didn't contact me. I've written to them, and I've wondered why they didn't get in touch with me.

SAMMYE: That's their guilt. Their feelings of guilt. Because they should have seen that the boys came up at the same time they did, and they didn't. I feel like they got tangled up in something. Tangled up…something…and one was trying to help the other, etc. I don't feel that there was any foul play or anything, but I feel that it's the other parents…it's their guilt because they feel extremely guilty, and they would have a hard time facing you.

JUDY: I felt like that may be it too. But I wasn't sure.

SAMMYE: Yeah, uh, because they feel…yes there are some things that they should have done differently. No doubt about that. But I don't feel…I don't know that it would have made any difference. But they are…their guilt is very, very strong. You will more than likely hear from them in the next…I'd say next two months. I hope they're getting some counseling.

JUDY: I do too.

SAMMYE: OK, OK.

JUDY: Also, I would like to know what it is that I need to do yet while I'm here.

SAMMYE: Well, part of it is the healing that we talked about. The other thing is, you have a tremendous or deity of—and it's still there and can't be expressed…but that will come later—amount of joy and the word "fun"…As the word came to me with your son, it comes to me with you. And you have an ability to create situations where people do have fun. And your son was the same way. You have a contagious energy, and part of it is the healing part and the other part is the joy of life. And I know right now that it's difficult to see that, but this comes. But we need more people…and there are more people coming in now, I feel…that are willing to be nonjudgmental as you are and to show…you have up until this time had the opportunity, and you have taken the opportunity to show other people that there is a lot of beauty in this life, and there is a lot of fun in this life. And that's the greatest gift we can give to another human being. And I think you need to write a book about it.

JUDY: I thought about writing a book, but I didn't know how I was going to write it [*both laugh*].

SAMMYE: Well, what I am hearing right now is to write a book and talk about your experience with your son. The legacy that your son gave you of the joy and the happiness and the fun…and because you gave him that too. Even though we know that our children choose us for the lessons they can learn from us…and part of his was to learn how to have fun and you gave him the opportunity to have fun. And in that opportunity, he passed it on to other people, and then it was his time to go. And now you don't have to. It would be advisable for you to pick it up and go further with it and let people know that life is to be enjoyed. Because most people do not know that.

JUDY: My thoughts have been going toward trying to simplify my life more and trying to get rid of some of the weights that have been holding me down and begin to enjoy life more, the way my son did.

SAMMYE: Uh-hum…See? Taught you a good lesson, didn't he? And to write about…simplification of life doesn't mean that you don't enjoy the beautiful things. It means you do enjoy the beautiful things. And to help people to understand their own divinity and the joy of being divine. It's not all hail, fire, and brimstone. But we tend to—a lot of people tend to feel that way. And I think you can—not think—know. You can write a book about that and write about it effectively. And also, you can help other parents to understand that their children—when the children come into life, they don't own the children. The children are a gift, and then they give us a gift and then they go on. Sometimes quicker than others. But the thing right now for you is to—it's going to take a little while, but you have this fantastic ability to say things in a manner that brings out the laughter and the joy in people, sense of humor, whatever. But you can do it, it's real easy. You're quick and you know. I would have to think about it for thirty days before I could come up with…but you're very easy and very quick, and that will be in the writing too. And one of the things your son did work with you very diligently on was helping you to laugh about mistakes.

JUDY: He was good at reminding me to lighten up at times.

SAMMYE: [*laughs*] And that's very important. And don't be surprised if you get some—say three months from now, four months from now—if you get some assistance from him. I mean, I'm looking at it on a mental level, where there is—through the dream state…I feel like it will go past the dream state. Possibly to impressions, things like that, that you'll want to get down on paper.

JUDY: I had one very vivid dream that stays in my mind, not long after the accident. I was at the boat at the docks. I looked across the waterway and saw tornados spinning over the bank. I thought I should warn the people in the boat and tell them we should leave. Gisella and her husband were on the boat, and I told Gisella we should leave. She acted if she agreed and went to tell her husband and the others as I stood out on the dock watching the tornados. They didn't come out, so I went back to get them again, and they were sitting with their backs to me. I knew that they were staying. Then back on the dock Jay met me, and he took me to the end of the dock to show me something in the water. A small boat was in the waterway, and bodies were being pulled from the water. I looked at Jay and he looked so peaceful and calm and glanced away toward the bank across the water where the tornados were. Only now lava and rocks were flowing down the side of the bank into the water. Jay looked as he did before, with an enjoyable look on his face. He had his cap on. I was at first shook up that I couldn't get the others to leave, and we were all in danger by staying there.

SAMMYE: Do you think that in that dream that he was showing you that everything was all right? Because he was calm.

JUDY: Possibly, and it was as if he was wanting to show me something in the water.

SAMMYE: Did you recognize any of the bodies?

JUDY: No.

SAMMYE: What was the overall feeling of the dream?

JUDY: That perhaps it was not the other people's time, but maybe closer to my time to leave, and Jay was there with me.

SAMMYE: Oh he will be, there's no doubt about that. I don't feel that it's your time now. What does lava mean to you? What does lava symbolize to you?

JUDY: I never really thought about it much. I don't really know.

SAMMYE: OK, look at the lava as coming from the center of the earth, and then the tornado as being on the earth. And you were looking at these across the way. And the lava was across the way also, is that right?

JUDY: Just right below the tornados. The tornados were above the lava flowing down the side of the bank.

SAMMYE: Wouldn't that be an indicator that it's all one? The lava representing the earth, and the tornados representing the air and the water? One above and one below? But yet they were all together, it was all one? And him being at peace was letting you know that it was all one? And the other people that you knew, the other people that were on the boat, that had their back to you, that they would not listen, they made a choice to stay? That we all make our choices as to when we get ready to go? I think the major thing in there is that he was letting you know that he is at peace, and that you are going to be all right, and he was saying, "Look, here's a different way to go." And as far as the other people that represented the bodies they were taking out of the water, it was OK, he was in the physical body. "Now I am no longer in the physical body but I still exist, whole heartedly and fully, and I am at peace." That's what I'm seeing from that. But he will…my suggestion is…you ask him to make himself very clear in the future.

JUDY: Speak my language.

SAMMYE: Yeah, because he can hear, and he does know. Usually within, after about two weeks of the transition, the first few days if they're calm—if we're calm when we make our transition—then they still try to contact people here in this level of existence. Because they know we get all worried and go crazy, you know? And then there's a period of time that is more—that there's less contact where they are making their peace with themselves and resting after the transition. And there comes another time, usually between three and six months, where they are very, very, communicative. But they talk a lot.

JUDY: Right after the accident, the night of the accident, it felt like I felt a touch on the end of the bed. And after we came back after we went down there, and after the service, this little crystal ship we have that is on a little solar stand, that I couldn't get to work, was turning...was working.

SAMMYE: That was him letting you know that everything was all right.

JUDY: Two weeks later it quit, and I felt kind of bad. But I looked it over and when I put it back up it started turning again. It quit again about a week or so ago.

SAMMYE: Yeah! Well that's about the time frame we're talking about. But you need to write your book. And let other people know that life is to be enjoyed. Sometimes it's tough. And that those who come to us as gifts, when they leave us they give another gift. And when they leave they give us the gift of freedom, ordinarily. And then we're free to go on and to pursue whatever we need to pursue. So he's giving you the gift of freedom. And I feel that it would be, as a friend of mine says, in your best interest to give that gift to other people. Because you have a good way of turning a phrase. I feel that you will write very, very well. What is the...there is some symbology here that... or something that has to do with your son, it has to do with the outside. Not boats, not ships, and not water, but it has to do with flowers, flowers...I keep feeling and hearing about flowers in the yard. Flowers, something...something there. So pay attention to your garden, your yard, when you get back home because there's something there that is going to be strong coming in there.

JUDY: He knew my fondness for hummingbirds, and as a birthday gift—that he kept calling me and telling me that if I wanted it I would have to come down there to get it—his wife and friend gave it to me the day that I left to come back home. It's a stained-glass piece with a hummingbird and a flower.

SAMMYE: OK...OK.

JUDY: Maybe the flowers will invite hummingbirds to come into my yard [*both laugh*].

SAMMYE: Yeah, could be, could be. But I kept seeing something to do with flowers in the yard, and it wasn't clear. Next question, go ahead.

JUDY: Is there anything I can do to help my daughter-in-law? She's been having a rather difficult time.

SAMMYE: OK...It's just letting her know that you care and helping her to understand that she—in no manner—there was nothing that she could have done. 'Cause I'm feeling...I know you have a lot of guilt going, but you're getting better with yours. But hers is much deeper than yours. Yeah, and talking with her... OK, OK, OK...and talking with her about the mourning process. She doesn't know that it's all right to be angry. You need to let her know that. She's very angry. More than you were. Very angry. And it's all right. God understands, that's no problem. That's no problem. And a way to approach it is...OK...talking with her about how you were angry. You still are a little bit, but you're a lot better than you were. But God understands your anger, and that's normal. If there's no anger, then there's something out of whack. It's called total denial. Somebody's crazy if there's no anger. But she doesn't know that. Yeah, talk with her about that.

JUDY: Now about my situation with my husband and his family, is there any guidance there?

SAMMYE: The thing that I am seeing is, that you have already done everything you can possibly do. Isn't that correct? Now you'll have to take care of yourself. You've got to. There is nothing more that you can do. Anything that you would attempt to do to alleviate the situation at this time would be like banging your head up against that wall, except it would be an outside wall, and that's brutal. You can't change that situation, they made their choices. So just bless them to their best and highest good whatever it may be. But you have to take care of yourself. That came up in the beginning if I remember correctly. You're going to have to take care of you. And your life cannot be governed by what they would either think or feel or do. If you allow that, then you will be destroyed, and you know that. I don't mean destroyed, as far as physically, but mentally and emotionally. I want to ask you another question. Why do you think that they are more important than you?

JUDY: I think maybe it comes from me always giving all the time. Like you said, I don't have anything more to give.

SAMMYE: It's very, very important that you begin to rejuvenate yourself. And you can say very honestly and very truthfully, "I care for you, but I refuse to accept this situation." Usually—would you be willing to take three weeks, and just do what you wanted to do, when you wanted to do it? Get up when you want to get up, go to sleep when you wanted to go to sleep? Eat when you want to go to eat? Because I'm seeing you are going around and around in circles…around and round in circles…and it's time that you took some time for yourself. Say, "Wait a minute, I can't deal with this right now. I'm not going to deal with this right now. I refuse to deal with it right now. I've got to take care of me." And take three weeks. Go anyplace you want to go. Ah, you may take a week but three weeks would be better. And just allow yourself to rejuvenate, and pamper yourself. Be good to you.

JUDY: I know I need to.

SAMMYE: What do you think would happen if you told everybody and their brother that you were going to do it? And you didn't put a question mark on the end of it? You know how when we speak, the way we put a question mark on the end of a sentence? Raise the voice a little bit, you know pitch it a little higher. If it just went down lower at the end with a period [*laughs*], what do you think would happen?

JUDY: I really don't know. Probably the biggest problem would be me. Do I go off from work? I already missed work after the accident. I guess I would just think that I would be letting everybody down.

SAMMYE: Well, could you take a week?

JUDY: I probably could.

SAMMYE: Take a week. You need three weeks. But the best we can do right now with your consciousness is take a week. So take a week. And you'll be able to get everything pretty well in a row before you take that week off. And don't feel guilty because you're taking it off.

JUDY: And go alone, by myself?

SAMMYE: Um-huh! That way the only person you have to pamper is you. And go someplace where they either have room service… and take your coffee pot or tea pot or whatever, you know, so you don't have to get out of the room early in the morning to get a cup of coffee.

JUDY: That sounds like a nice idea.

SAMMYE: And take some books with you, you know. Things that you want to read. You'll find that you'll be more at peace when you come back. But that time for rejuvenation is extremely important. Extremely important. My suggestion is that you do it as soon as possible. Yeah. Because you have attempted to carry the load for everybody, and it's not working, is it?

JUDY: No. I been turning into almost a basket case it seems lately.

SAMMYE: And if you want an excuse to do it without any problems, my suggestion is that you just find yourself a good therapist in Wilmington. Go to the therapist and say, "I need some time off. Tell me I need some time off." Then you get back to the family and say, "My therapist said." [*She laughs.*] But you do need it.

JUDY: My doctor already told me that if I needed anything to let him know.

SAMMYE: Call him. Call him. Because you do. You cannot continue to be strong. You need some time to allow yourself…you to scream and holler and rant and rave, you to be weak. And of course for you, it's best if you do it in private. And I would suggest the mountains.

JUDY: Sounds nice.

SAMMYE: Yeah. I suggest the mountains (*pauses*). Boone, Black Mountain, that area keeps coming to mind. And I don't suggest a bed and breakfast. You need more anonymity than that would give you. It's really not private. Blowing Rock, Boone, Black Mountain.

JUDY: I've never been there.

SAMMYE: It's a nice place. Of course, there's not a lot at Black Mountain, there's not a lot at Blowing Rock. There's some nice hotels at Blowing Rock, and there's some at Black Mountain. Also, another place to go that is very, very nice—no TVs, no telephones—is Little Switzerland, up near Spruce Pine. It's an old inn that's been there for years and years and years. Big rooms, and they have a TV out in the lounge. If you wanted a TV you could take a little one, but no telephones in the rooms, and no TVs. And you can get room service and all of those things. And there's another place in Virginia. It's called the Peaks of Otter. It's right outside of Roanoke, Virginia. It's on a lake, and you look out at the Peaks of Otter, and it's on the skyline or drive or whatever, and they have excellent food, as Little Switzerland does at Spruce Pine. And they have room service, but they don't have any telephones or TVs in the room either. There's one in the loft. And each room overlooks the lake there. Spruce Pine, you look out over the mountain. That's Little Switzerland.

JUDY: That's about all the questions I had written.

SAMMYE: OK. I'd like to come back to your spiritual self. This...there is going to be...as we mentioned earlier...I think, a major transition in this coming three months. As far as spirituality is concerned. It doesn't mean that you're going to go off the deep end or anything like that. But you'll be very, very at peace with it. And that will...that will help with the writing of this book. But I am concerned with you not getting enough rest, and it's important that you learn the lesson of receiving. Allow other people to give to you. It's the worst lesson we have to learn. It is extremely important that you do that. My concern is that if you do not get some rest and you do not relieve some of the tension that you've been walking around with—rejuvenate yourself—that there is a possibility...not a probability as yet... but a possibility that you will be in the hospital before the year is out. And you know if Jesus could take off for forty days and forty nights whenever he chooses, you ought to be able to take off a little time every now and then.

JUDY: That's true.

SAMMYE: Because your body can only stand so much stress before it reacts.

JUDY: I have been getting to the point where I really didn't want to be here anymore.

SAMMYE: Well leaving is not going to solve the problem for you. If you leave, you're just going to have to come back and do it again... So you might as well get it straight this time so it will be better next time.

JUDY: Yeah, I had already decided that was the way it was going to be all along after all the other problems I have had. This is just one of the most difficult challenges I've ever come up against.

SAMMYE: I feel like this…this one…if you learn the lesson of receiving in this one, as I feel that you will, you've already begun a little bit. But if you do go ahead and learn the lesson of receiving, there will be no more major challenges like this. No more. It's the challenge part, that's served its purpose.

JUDY: OK.

Session Two with Sammye

July 12, 1994

SAMMYE: OK, what I'm seeing is that, yes you did…you are still some, you are relaxed, but there's still a ways to go and I don't know. It's like when you took your vacation, other things came up. You understand what I'm talking about? Why are you—let me ask you this. Why are you still pushing yourself so hard?

JUDY: I have a tendency to…take any challenge that I find in front of me, and I want to go for it as hard as I can to reach my goal sooner.

SAMMYE: Well, I understand that part. I can understand that part. But you really, really, really—it's like…OK, OK, OK, there it is, OK. What I'm seeing is that…that…I'm not talking about work, that sort of thing. That's not where I'm coming from now. You're still pushing yourself very hard on a personal level, and that needs to ease off some, needs to ease off. Give yourself some space. Give yourself…ah…OK. If you found a kitten on the side of the road that was hurt, you would be extremely gentle with it, wouldn't you? Why don't you be as nice to yourself? That's what I'm looking at. I'm not talking about work. Cause that…we're looking at two different things here…I'm talking about personally. It's like you want everything clear, now. Not tomorrow, and everything is not going to come clear right now. You have a much clearer vision of yourself now, but you're still not—well I don't know that any of us are really ever satisfied in the visions we see of ourselves, but don't push yourself so hard. Allow yourself time to heal. Because it's important. OK, questions, lets get on with it.

JUDY: Some of the things that have happened in my life concern things I've seen in the sky, lights, and objects. I've always had a curiosity about them and what they are.

SAMMYE: Are you telling me in a roundabout way, that you have seen UFOs? Is that what you're—

JUDY: Yeah. [*Both laugh.*]

SAMMYE: Well, they're real. They're real. I don't expect you to be abducted or anything like that, but they are real. And because of your extreme intuitiveness, they will appear to you, rather than to somebody else. That's a mighty factor in that [*pause*]. Hum…I don't expect it to become less. I expect it to become more. That's what I'm seeing. More…seeing more rather than less. It would be interesting if you carried a camera around with you for a while. Very interesting. But yes, you are seeing UFOs. One of the ways you can work with that is, when you do see it, become calm and listen to what you are hearing inside yourself. That will help you to…become more confident? Because you…you just question yourself something terrible. On everything. But it will help you to become more confident. Because you will hear. There's no doubt in my mind that you won't hear. You will hear…and make notes of what you hear. If you have a tape recorder, use a tape recorder. Because that's handy, you can just repeat it. Yeah, you are seeing UFOs. You saw some on your vacation, didn't you?

JUDY: [*thinks*]

SAMMYE: Ah, you're not really sure about that [*laughs*]?

JUDY: Yeah!

SAMMYE: I feel like you did.

JUDY: I was sitting on the balcony, but I wasn't sure. One morning, as I woke up, I heard a little voice say, "I am not as one."

SAMMYE: Pardon? Say it again.

JUDY: I heard something, "I am not as one," just as I was waking.

SAMMYE: I am not as one [*pauses*] All right. Hum. All right, what you're looking at there is—I don't want to…all right I'll use the term "angels" and then I'll clarify that. There is a part of us, within us that some people call angels—I call our higher personality—that…and I'm not saying there are no angels…OK? To me there is some confusion as to what is an angel and what is that part of us that is in direct connection to God. And I feel it was your higher personality, and as you were coming out of the dream state…the dream sleep state…that we are in—scientifically we are in the alpha state, which is the meditative state… the most receptive state that we can possibly be in. And what I feel was…that was your higher self talking to you, helping you to see that your own individuality, that you are an individual expression of the indivisible whole. We are one, but we are not one. And because of your extreme intuitiveness, what you do… you absorb other people's stuff. Quite often, especially if they are in a bad space, and you attempt to make it yours. So seeing the oneness, yes, we are one. But you don't have to make that yours, you have to express your individuality, see your individuality. I feel that's what that was. If you will listen, that is going to increase. This has happened before, in some respects? Where you hear?

JUDY: Hear…like a voice?

SAMMYE: Um-huh.

JUDY: Yes.

SAMMYE: OK. Pay attention because that is very, very important that you do. When—I call it the higher self, the inner self. It depends on where I am…and in teaching, that's what I call it. If I'm teaching in the college system, I call it the inner assistant. If I'm teaching with the metaphysical group, I call it the higher personality. What we're looking at there is that you are coming more and more in tune with you. And as you become more and more relaxed and become more in tune with you, you're going to hear more. And my suggestion is that you make some notes about what you hear. And learning not to absorb other people's stuff. Because you can't do anything about it. But you do have a tendency to take it on and then blame yourself because they don't make the changes. Maybe you didn't do enough, maybe you should have said something, done something differently. That sort of thing. And I'm talking about more on a personal relationship. I'm not talking about work. Work, you have a tendency to separate yourself. But it's in the personal things that you don't.

JUDY: The other thing I heard was "In gambling you play to win, but in this game, losing is winning."

SAMMYE: I understand that part. In life—truthfully in life—we are always winners. We cannot lose. As human beings, we cannot lose. We're always in a win-win situation, we're taught to look at any situation as a win-lose situation. But as human beings, we always win. And sometimes when we—quote, unquote—lose, it seems we've lost…but what we end up with is gaining in the respect of understanding of ourselves. Understanding of the universe. Greater spiritual understanding of what God is and who we are and what we are. So we, in learning that when we lose that part of us—not the ego because I believe the ego is that divine spark that keeps us going. That is what makes us get up in the morning and brush our teeth and attempt to be the best manifestation of God that we are. But when we lose fear—the out-of-balance ego is created by fear, not by love—when we lose the out-of-balance ego, we lose the fear. And when you lose the fear, we win ultimately. We always win. So in understanding that life is a win-win situation, and what seems to be a loss is usually a gain, if we really look at it and we keep our egos in check and see that everything that occurs in life is part of God. I know there are a lot of books out that say—well, Eric Butterworth says it and some of the others say it—that this is God in action and this is not God in action. Well, it doesn't make sense to me. Because if we're a part of God and God's a part of us, then how can we not be God in action at one time and be God in action at another time? If God is all good, then everything that occurs—if we have something that occurs that seems to be not good, then what occurs with that…that gives us an opportunity to make a change that we need to change, so it is good. We can't be God one minute and not God the next. It just is not logical, and my understanding is that God is totally logical. So I hope that clears it up.

JUDY: Yes.

SAMMYE: A lot of times we think that when people go out of ours lives that they're lost, but what occurs to us is that we didn't lose. We gained two things: We gained them in the physical—we had them in the physical, we had that enjoyment. We gain them in the spiritual, where they are really closer to us when they go on the other side than they were when they were in the physical. So we've got the two deals going. We tend to believe that we can't converse and we can't feel them and we can't enjoy them. But the truth is that we can if we would allow ourselves. If you will remind me, I have an article out there. One of my students brought it to me, talking about this thing that we're talking about here. So I'll make you a copy of it.

JUDY: Something still along this line that came to me was about the premonition or the vision I had sometime before my son's accident about him dying…

SAMMYE: Um-huh.

JUDY: And how I felt about that. I think I tried to hide that from myself. I tried to hide that I had felt that, or had seen it.

SAMMYE: See again, what you're looking at there is your major intuition, and you know it. When you have a person that is as extremely spiritual as you are—now you know I'm not talking about religion and that, that's a whole different deal, but as your are extremely spiritual, always have been, even though you feel you've done some things that weren't quite spiritual… just join the human race, you know? Spiritual beings learning to be human. But you will have this type of thing. You knew, and that was your higher self, your angels, whichever you choose to call it, preparing you, that God-self within you, preparing you for what was to come. It was—even though it sounds awful—but your son's choice. You know, that's what he needed to do. For himself, for his own awareness and his own growth. And that's a hard row to hoe. We don't want to see that. So, just next time, write it down. I'm not saying that you're going to see death again, but when you get these feelings write it down. Keep a little diary of things that you see, hear, and feel.

JUDY: I've been doing that.

SAMMYE: Good, good.

JUDY: A couple of things from my childhood…I had convulsions when I was a child, and the doctors told my folks that it was because I was spoiled. And I was also in the hospital one time as a child, with what my mother had told me was some type of blood poisoning. When I have asked her as an adult what was wrong with me then, she now says she can't remember.

SAMMYE: They didn't really know. They really didn't know. I feel that the convulsions were related to previous incarnations somehow. It didn't have anything to do with you being spoiled. That's a— excuse me, I almost said that's a dumb-ass statement—but it was, you know [*laughs*].

    That was ridiculous. But I feel that…something must have occurred. What I am looking at is that something occurred that triggered a memory that created the convulsions. That's my feeling on it. Raymond Moody had a good book out on past life therapy, and I can't remember the name of it right now.

JUDY: *Life After Life?*

SAMMYE: No…but it may be in this article. But he's using past life therapy to help people overcome certain fears, phobias, and things like that—in this life. And it's surprising the heck out of him, the results he's getting.

JUDY: Sometime, around about that same time, there was a relative of ours, an older man that took me and abused me. I've often wondered if maybe that was what brought on the convulsions.

SAMMYE: That could have been the trick. That very well could have been the trigger. But the other time in the hospital, not the convulsions, but they really have…what I'm feeling is that the doctor wasn't sure what the deal was. You were sick, and they didn't know what it was. There wasn't a long time space between those two things, was there?

JUDY: I don't really remember, but I think it was pretty close to being around that same age.

SAMMYE: Um-hum. Yeah.

JUDY: I don't remember if I was around two or three years old.

SAMMYE: It, a…I think it was all interrelated.

JUDY: Because he came to see me in the hospital and brought me a bubble gum box full of bubble gum and candy.

SAMMYE: I think it was all interrelated and at that time the medical community was not real…real…they were not as knowledgeable as they are now. I think the major factor in there—not saying the abuse was not a major factor, but I think that was the trigger. That triggered this situation from a previous incarnation. Hum…Still don't trust older men, do you?

JUDY: Not completely.

[*Both laugh.*]

SAMMYE: That's understandable. That's understandable. But I think that has to do with the previous incarnation too. Yeah. I don't have the capacity to get what it was. I get bits and pieces, but not all of it in this state. In the trance state I can get more of it, but that's what I'm getting now.

JUDY: Sometimes I think I would like to delve a little deeper into the past.

SAMMYE: Well if you ever—if you want to do it, I can do hypnosis or I can do it through trance, whichever one you prefer.

JUDY: I don't know.

SAMMYE: OK.

JUDY: Another thing as a child…I can remember two specific dreams where I was floating through the air, and it was like I was…maybe out of my body?

SAMMYE: Um-huh.

JUDY: And it was just really smooth and calm, and when I came back it was like crashing.

SAMMYE: A lot of times what happens with that, 'cause we usually go out of our body every night, in our sleep anyway, even as adults. But if there's a sharp noise outside, a door slamming, a horn blows, something like that, it will jerk us right back. And it's like your whole body feels just like a tuning fork going like that [*moving hands in and out from each other*], you know? So that's what occurred, I have no doubt in my mind about that. There was a sharp noise outside, and you came back. You got a little bit afraid of it, didn't you?

JUDY: Yes, it frightened me as a child, and when I came back both times, I screamed and began to cry. I also wet the bed.

SAMMYE: That would be understandable as a child. A major impact, not only to your mind, but to your body. As an adult, you won't do that. You won't wet the bed.

JUDY: [*laughs*] No, I don't think I've done that in a long time. My son told me one time that he remembered as a child seeing an angel in his room.

SAMMYE: [*pauses*] Yes, he did. Yes. He had a…a special gift with people…of helping them to understand their own goodness. And a lot of times, angels come to people like that, to help them, to give them strength sometimes. Sometimes it's to give them strength, sometimes it's to give them encouragement. But his job was to help people to understand their own greatness, which he did.

JUDY: He also told me that he could remember when he was born?

SAMMYE: Um-Huh. Extremely intuitive. Extremely spiritual. Did he also talk to you about some memories that were not of this incarnation? In some manner?

JUDY: I don't know...

SAMMYE: He may have called them dreams, but I don't see them as dreams.

JUDY: I'm not sure, he may have. There are a lot of things that I can't seem to remember.

SAMMYE: Well, that's understandable right now.

JUDY: Some of the things that I have written down are about dreams that I've had. Especially the ones where I'm starting to wake up, and I'm reading lines and lines of a book or a newspaper or something. And I keep thinking that if I keep reading it over and over and over, then I'll remember it when I wake up. Then I wake up and it's all gone.

SAMMYE: OK, one of the things you can do to assist you to remember is as you—OK, there's two factors in here. One, you're becoming more calm with your own intuition and not doubting it as much as you do. Releasing as much of the doubt as possible, that's why you need to keep your dairy to give you confirmation. The other is, right before you go to sleep at night, put a glass of water beside your bed, and when you're in that alpha state—we go to sleep in the alpha state, and we come out in the alpha state, unless we have an alarm clock that jerks us. And some people hit the snooze button, and they'll go into the alpha state and then come back out. That makes it easier for them. But right before you go to sleep at night, when you're in that limbo state, you know, you're there—you know you're there and everything's all right—take a sip of that water and tell yourself that in the morning when you wake up, you will take another sip of your water, and you will remember your dreams in detail and then write it down. Because even if you remember it, if you don't write it down, you're going to forget it an hour later. And also put in there the details you want to remember. You want to remember what you're reading. What I think is occurring is that you're going to school at night, and that sounds silly to a degree, but what we do as human beings, when we get on our spiritual path, and realizing that we are human beings, you know…I mean spiritual beings learning to be human…It's like we go to school at night. And you want to remember what you learned in school. Some nights with me, I wake up every hour on the hour. It's like I've been changing classes all night long. So I know when I start doing that, I know that there are going to be things that I'm going to know that are very important. So I begin to pay attention to what I hear when I wake up. So I think you're taking a trip, an astral trip and going out of your body and going to another level of existence and going to school. Because this is not the only school right here. That's for sure.

JUDY: Yeah, I think I could appreciate a place that's a little more above the human level.

[*Both laugh.*]

SAMMYE: Well, its not that you're exactly tired of being human, but you're tired of being human in the shape that you're in right now. Ah…but…OK, OK, OK. The thing that—and it keeps coming, so I may as well go ahead and say it. But the thing that I'm concerned about—not as much as I did have, but the concern is still there—is that the pain that you're going through as far as your son is concerned, and it's like that pain has got to be [*sighs and pauses*]. I can still say that you're better than you were, but I can still see you blaming yourself in some respects, and the pain [*pause*], part of the pain deals with your not saying anything…or attempting to remember your vision, your knowledge? And you have got to turn loose of your guilt. I know I sound like a broken record when I talk to you about that.

Judy: Yeah, I think that when I started remembering that it happened to me, I started thinking that, or realizing what I had felt, or seen or whatever it was that I had...that I may have brought it on.

Sammye: No. We all create our own reality. You cannot manifest for another human being. It is physically, mentally, emotionally, and spiritually impossible. That information was given to you to prepare you. Even if you had told him and sat down and talked with him and explained everything that you saw, it would not have solved the problem. It would not have stopped it. It was a choice that he made. He figured his work was done. We do attempt to accept responsibility for other people's actions, but we can't. You had an obligation to your son. You were obligated to teach him the very best you could and do the best you could with him, and you did. You know that, in here [*points to the heart*], and you also know that up here [*points to the head*]. But as far as creating a situation for him, no. We can't do that—I mean, everybody has free will. You do, I do. I may take your suggestion, but it's ultimately me who made the choice. You gave me a suggestion. You told me, "Do this," and if I do it, it's not your fault if I do it. I chose to do it. That's where our free will comes, and it's important that you know that.

You couldn't have changed it, and I feel he'll let you know that you couldn't have changed it. Yeah. It's like you're walking around, and you have this big sieve around you, you know? Or colander or something. And it has a few little holes in it, you know, not a lot of holes, like most colander's do. This one just has a few. And that colander is to hold you in place. To keep you from just exploding, not imploding, but exploding. And every now and then, we can call it the colander, the guilt, the pain, all of that stuff.

Every now and then as you go through life with this big metal box with the holes around it, you'll come to a place where there's a hole. And you'll get some insight and you'll get some freedom for a while, but then in a little while you're back where there is nothing. I'm using a colander because it's the only thing I can think of, but that's the pain, all around you. But the holes, you're getting more holes in it, so it won't be long before you—I'm not saying that there will ever be a time that there won't be a little bit of pain, but I am saying that there will come a time where you will have the greater understanding, and there will be just that little bit of residual that's sticking back here because you loved him, and he's not right here where you can touch him. But no, not major pain. You're poking holes in that right now. But I would like to see it where there's only this much metal and this much freedom. And you're working towards it. Yeah. OK, go ahead.

JUDY: One of the other things I had written down pertained to the UFOs again, and that was that I had heard other reports of others seeing strange black helicopters. Maybe this doesn't pertain to them and maybe it does. But the time I saw these black helicopters was right after the time I saw this craft fly over. They weren't lit up or anything, but they took a dive over the highway as I was going down the highway. I was just wondering if that had anything to do with the UFOs.

SAMMYE: I think it's part of that. I don't think it has anything to do with the United States government. Let's put it that way. And I don't think it has anything to do with the privately owned helicopters. One thing, they move too fast for helicopters, but I feel it is a part of the UFO experience. What is going on there is that you, what you saw were like if there's a craft here, big, these are little one's that go out around that can check closer. That's what I feel it is.

JUDY: The one that I saw over the condo was rather low. It looked kind of like an airplane, but not like any airplane I've ever been able to find a picture of. And it had some kind of strange writing on the one side. The left underneath side, and I've never been able to remember. I kept thinking while I was looking at this thing, "I'll remember this perfectly, I've got to study it carefully so I can remember it." And again, like my dream, those things have seemed to have left my mind.

SAMMYE: Um-huh. That's because of the energy from the—there is, from these UFOs, there is an energy that comes out from them. When people do see them, it really gives you selective memory in relation to the situation. Some hypnosis would probably bring it back if it's that important to you. But it's like every report that you read, everything, there's like selective memory in there. Some things are just as clear as a bell, others are not. So I feel that there's an energy that goes out. We know that we have energy, and this energy has been defined, the electromagnetic energy of life has been defined in such a manner that it can be selective. And the next time you see it, or something similar, just ask them straight out, "What was on that other one? I want to know, I need to know." Most people get so excited, they forget things. But you've come to a point in your life that you won't get that excited anymore. So I would ask.

JUDY: When my son was on this little island in the Bahamas where he was working, and he was alone, he said he saw a ghost there. I think other people had seen the ghost there too, and I was curious to who or what the ghost was doing there or why.

SAMMYE: Well I'm seeing more than one. I feel that the one that he saw…OK…I feel like the one he saw was somebody that he knew. Somebody he had known. But there's more than one ghost in that area. I think what he called the ghost was really more apparition than ghost. Something appearing to him to give him some information. More than just a ghost. But the people that do see the ghost, the ghosts that are there—the one's that are there are what we would call earthbound spirits. A very traumatic experience occurred in that area where he's talking about. What I'm seeing is men, not necessarily women. Was there a battle there of some sort?

JUDY: A shipwreck.[26]

---

[26] When I told Chris W. about Sammye asking if there was a battle in this location, he said that he had been told that there actually had been a battle in this location.

SAMMYE: OK. But I see men, I don't see any women in the trauma. But they're earthbound. It would be neat if somebody would go down and talk to them and say, "Hey, how about moving on." Yeah, there's more than one.

JUDY: One came up to one guy's wife and wiggled her toes.

SAMMYE: (Giggling) Yeah. They're not vicious or anything like that, they're just there. Because they still think they're…they still think they are sailing. Maybe somebody will talk to them, tell them to look for the light, and they can go on.

JUDY: That's what occurred to me the night that my son died. I was praying for him, and for some reason it came to me to tell him to look for the light. Even though I didn't want to believe that he was gone and he might still be down there someplace and be waiting to be found.

SAMMYE: Yeah.

JUDY: When I went to see my doctor, he suggested that I go see another doctor. I don't know that I want to, he is a psychiatrist, and the doctor gave me a prescription for antidepressants. I only took one, and it made me feel numb, and I don't especially feel that I need to go see this doctor. Do you feel differently?

SAMMYE: I don't think it would hurt. I would talk to him about the grief and the pain. And because you can always not go the next time if you don't feel that you need to go. I really think it would do you some good right now…as far as the pain and the grief. You're much better than you were, but if we can speed this process along by talking to somebody who is more knowledgeable—the only thing I have a concern about is they're wanting you to get back on antidepressants, and I don't think you need to be.

JUDY: I don't like the way they make me feel.

SAMMYE: Well…and I'm not sure whether this is my personal prejudice or whether it's psychic. Because I have a strong prejudice against antidepressants and tranquilizers and all that. Because all it does is cover up the poop to keep it from stinkin'. And if you come off them, then you still got it. And I am deathly afraid of Prozac. I am literally just afraid of what that drug will do for people. And I think part of that is intuitive and part is reading. But as far as I'm concerned, you are entirely correct in not taking the antidepressants. And I would—when you go to the other doctor, if he says anything about it, you can tell him, "Now he gave me these pills, but I didn't take them. Because they make me feel numb and I've got to feel. I have had enough time in my life stifling my feelings." Which is true. So you need to feel now and allow yourself the freedom to feel. If you feel anger, feel anger. If you feel pain, feel pain. Say, "I am in pain!" and scream. It's not going to hurt anything and it will help. But yes, I think going to the other doctor, he'll give you a little bit more insight. I have no problems with that. If you don't like him, don't go back.

JUDY: When I talked to you last time, you mentioned that there was something that I had started that my son wanted me to continue, and I have not seemed to become clear on that.

SAMMYE: Hum. I feel that it has to do with…your ESP experiences. I feel that it has to do with what you have been experiencing as far as the grieving process. Because what I am looking at…OK, OK, OK…incorporating the two, the ESP experience and the experiences and the grieving processes together with very likely…a probability of a book about it. It's a lot of work, but you can do it if you choose to.

JUDY: I've been putting thoughts together in my mind about that. And I think some of the things I've been writing down can be stored up for that too.

SAMMYE: Um-huh. Yeah. Yes ma'am.

Session Three with Sammye
Past Life Reading

August 22, 1994

SAMMYE: As you have come to an understanding of both life and so-called death, know that this knowledge, this understanding gives you the freedom to fulfill that which is your chosen destiny. In this understanding, as you write your thoughts, know that your thoughts your feelings, are real. As you write these, you can assist others to come to the understanding of life and so-called death. Is it clear what we are saying here?

JUDY: Yes.

SAMMYE: It is suggested that you put forth great effort to write, put down on paper, those thoughts and feelings at this time. For this will give to others the gift of healing. Is this also clear?

JUDY: Yes, it is.

SAMMYE: Now, as to your purpose. You have known for a very long time that there was a different purpose for you in this incarnation, have you not?

JUDY: Yes, I have.

SAMMYE: Now, as you write you will fulfill the purpose. Many have a purpose, yet few choose to fulfill the purpose. For in the course of life, many incarnations, many changes, one life. Many choose not to fulfill the purpose for it seems out of reach. Beyond their capacity. Understanding that all of the information you need is within self, and that there will be many who will benefit from this information. Is it clear what we are saying here?

JUDY: Yes.

SAMMYE: Now, there is another who desires to speak to you at this time. Is that all right with you?

JUDY: Yes, it is.

SAMMYE: [*sighs*] You need to know that my love for you is greater now than it was. I will help you. Listen and you'll hear me. I'm stronger now. I can contact you, and don't be afraid cause there's nothing to fear. I know now that I have and can help others. You know how much that meant to me, don't you?

JUDY: Yes, I do.

SAMMYE: Don't think that you had anything to do with what I decided to do.

JUDY: OK.

SAMMYE: Just know that I love you, and I'll help you in anyway I can. I know I'm slow, but I'll get faster. You wanna ask me anything? If you do, go ahead.

JUDY: Have we lived together before?

SAMMYE: Yes, you knew that already, didn't you?

JUDY: I thought so, but I can't remember when.

SAMMYE: We were friends in many incarnations, and we were friends in this one, even if I didn't do the way you wanted me to. We're still friends, aren't we?

JUDY: We sure are.

SAMMYE: I want you to forgive me because I know that I hurt you, and I didn't want to do that. Please forgive me.

JUDY: I forgive you.

SAMMYE: I'm tired now. I'll come back and talk to you later [*pauses and sighs*].

Now, let us begin with your questions.

JUDY: I'm wondering what I had experienced in a past life that would have been the reason that I have married five times in this life?

SAMMYE: With each husband, there was the need to learn to release, for as you are now learning to release others and to be in charge of self, are you not?

JUDY: Yes.

SAMMYE: And with each husband there was the attempt to hold to you, was there not?

JUDY: Yes.

SAMMYE: So, within the previous incarnations with these you held to the thought of holding to them, and in each you died and made your transition holding to them. You see? As if they could make you live. Yet in this present time, you have come to an understanding that the life is not dependent on another. Is that not correct?

JUDY: That's correct.

SAMMYE: So you have learned a lesson. And realizing that with the present you are not holding on to them as the lesser personality would say, with the death grip, are you?

JUDY: Right.

SAMMYE: Even if you were to choose to depart from the present situation, you would be free of the karmic debt. For one of the things that you have truly learned is to forgive self, is it not?

JUDY: Yes.

SAMMYE: And that, my child, is the true manner in which you release karma. So be in joy with self in this respect. Yah, with the present there was an incarnation in Spain and in England with this one. And in the incarnation in Spain in the late 1500s there you were the male, this one was the female. And there you kept, how shall we say, an extremely tight reign on the female. And in that there was no freedom for either you or the other, and you died in that incarnation following the female… and the horse reared. When it did you were thrown. When it did both your neck and your back were broken, you see? Then you came together again, in the incarnation in England. In the middle sixteen hundreds. And there you were the female and the other was the male. There was what you would call instant attraction. Yet again it was the attraction of confinement, you see? As if to say, "This one is mine, no one else needs come close to this one." You see?

JUDY: Yes.

SAMMYE: And the other one felt the same in relation to you, in that particular incarnation. And you each confined the other, so that all of your time was spent, not productively, but in assuring self that the other one was confined. And there came an epidemic in which you both died. Now, you have come back together again to free self and each other of the pain of restriction. And knowing this that as you allow self to be free, then you allow others to be free. It is not that others must act as you would act. It is that they are free to do or be whatever they chose to do or be, you see?

JUDY: Yes.

SAMMYE: And in this you are free. And in forgiving self again, in this present incarnation, you have released the fear which releases the karma. You will no longer be circling on that particular wheel, you see? Now, as you see self as you are beginning to do, as who and what you are, that you are part of God and God is part of you, and that you have as a portion of the purpose, you see? Each individual expression of the indivisible whole has one major purpose that is the same. Few things are the same, many are similar. But each individual expression of the indivisible whole, their purpose is to heal themselves, you see? That is what the incarnations are for. And through the healing of self, of the pain of life. you see? And the first step in the healing is forgiving self, which you have come to. Then second purpose for you as we discussed earlier is to write of this recent experience. The feelings, the knowing, in order to assist others. For many have written of this experience, yet have not written from the heart. From the perspective of the healing. And when you write of this experience, it will not be all sweetness and light. It will be truth, you see? Now, to continue with your questions.

JUDY: In this incarnation I had convulsions as a child…Sammye suggested that perhaps it was triggered by something in a past life. I was abused as child here, and was there something from a past life that may still be causing me problems here?

SAMMYE: Yes. In a recent incarnation to this one, you were very, very ill with an extremely high temperature, which created the convulsions. And the reason for the illness was that you had contacted that which is now called syphilis, you see? And in that incarnation you were in the last stages, and you knew what had created the disease, you see?

JUDY: Um-huh.

SAMMYE: Therefore, there was the fear in this incarnation that the abuse, for there was much. Not only sexual abuse, but mental abuse, emotional abuse and physical abuse in that incarnation, you see? Because you had contacted the disease, you see? So when there came the abuse it was automatic to go in to that mental state which creates the convulsion in order to escape, you see? For in the previous incarnation, the escape was in the high temperature and the convulsion, you see? For the mind did not work on the conscious level at that time. So that was a means of escape and to move you out of that particular incarnation. So in this incarnation, there was the desire to escape, which has been there quite all the time, has it not?

JUDY: Yes.

SAMMYE: So due to what you call modern medicine and also due to your desire within self to know—for on the superconscious level you are knowledgeable, you were knowledgeable then, you are knowledgeable now, that you would not escape, you see? You would only come back to try it again.

Judy: Right.

Sammye: So that is the reason for that, and as you know you have been looking for the escape to make the other your life, you see? As in the husbands. And now you must live your life, must you not?

Judy: Yes.

Sammye: It will be easy. It will not be difficult. And this particular incarnation also took place in that which is now called England. It was then called Great Britain, you see? And it was in the early seventeen hundreds, and you died at an early age even at that time. You were only sixteen. So please do go on.

Judy: Is my smoking habit also a way of my trying to be escaping?

Sammye: No, that is not the reason to escape, that is called the pacifier that assists in trying to keep you here, you see?

Judy: All right…

Sammye: There will be no problems with that. But as you look about you, my child, realize that each individual expression of the indivisible whole has some pacifier they use. Be it food, be it any type of drug. Be it, what shall we say, running, exercise. All of those things, when they are…they…yes as you say the habit, they become the pacifier. So do not condemn self for that.

Judy: OK. I felt I needed permission for that one.

Sammye: Ah. The lesser personality refuses to accept permission, she just does it. Please do go on.

Judy: How is my dad in relation to me in my past lives?

Sammye: Firstly, let us say that you came back together in this incarnation again to understand each other. To see that which was and is good in each other. Is it clear what we are saying here?

Judy: Yes.

Sammye: And as you were together in an incarnation in this country, in that which you now call Boston, there you were brothers. You did not like each other—you loved each other, but you did not like each other. So you were constantly bickering, you see? Each attempting to tell the other what to do and how to do it. So you came back, both of you together to learn the lesson of compassion. For you see, many, many, many of the past incarnations for you have to deal with personal freedom, do they not?

JUDY: It seems that way.

SAMMYE: So remember what you're learning in this incarnation, the major learning. But yes, the lesson of compassion there. Please do go on.

JUDY: Also the connection between my mother and myself in this life and previous lives?

SAMMYE: Ah, yes, in this incarnation it is also to understand that which is the mother and which is the child. Is it clear what we are saying here?

JUDY: Yes.

SAMMYE: For in the incarnation in Boston, this one was also your mother. Yet that one desired that the sons be responsible for them. And that was impossible, you see? And now you come together in this incarnation to see that the mother is the mother, not the child. Even there is the attempt to be the child. Is it clear what we are saying here?

JUDY: Yes.

SAMMYE: For you are not the mother, are you?

JUDY: No.

SAMMYE: You cannot be the mother, can you?

JUDY: No.

SAMMYE: Remember this, my child, remember this. And also with that one there was the time prior to the incarnation in Boston, in the early eighteen hundreds you see, where you were sisters. There was rivalry between the two. So that led to the situation of the mother, son, and then to the situation of now. Realizing that the mother need accept responsibility for the actions. Is it clear what we are saying here?

JUDY: Yes.

SAMMYE: You cannot do that, you see?

JUDY: I see that.

SAMMYE: Please do go on.

JUDY: You say that I was reunited in this life with someone. Is that Tony?

SAMMYE: Yes, my child, yes. To learn to assist and to know what freedom is, you see?

JUDY: In my previous incarnation when I was thrown from the horse, is that why I have neck and back problems now?

SAMMYE: Yes, my child, yes. Now understanding—as you begin and have begun rather, and continue to begin the lesson of forgiving self—this will become increasingly better and better. There will be less and less pain. Is this clear?

JUDY: OK.

SAMMYE: For one carries from one incarnation to another, within the mind which becomes the body, the old resentments toward self and the pain that the resentments created. Do you see?

JUDY: Yes.

SAMMYE: And you are forgiving self.

JUDY: So also when I was in the hospital as a child and they didn't seem to know what was wrong with me, that came from the incarnation when I had the syphilis?

SAMMYE: Yes.

JUDY: And that also triggered the sores that got on my body?

SAMMYE: Yes, my child.

JUDY: And it didn't mean that I had the disease here...

SAMMYE: No.

JUDY: OK.

SAMMYE: No. It was the mental. Understanding that the mind creates. The mind is the builder, so the mental in the mind of the child created the symptomology, not the disease. Yes.

JUDY: Before Jay's death here, I was given a vision, and in time will I begin to remember those things?

SAMMYE: Yes. It is only that now when you attempt to remember, you become very agitated with self, do you not?

JUDY: [*laughs*] Yeah, that's right.

SAMMYE: So is it not wise just to ask the totality, what you call God, to present it and allow it to occur?

JUDY: Yes, that I'm learning.

SAMMYE: Are you willing my child, to write the story?

JUDY: Yes.

SAMMYE: That is good. Please do go on with your questions.

JUDY: I've had an attraction for the stories about Atlantis. Is there any connection with me and past incarnations with Atlantis?

SAMMYE: Yes, with most who have come in to this incarnation in the last seventy years, there is the resurgence of those who were knowledgeable in the Atlantean time. There you were not involved with the energy, you were involved with teaching the children love. For as you well know even though children are…how shall we say…innocent when they come into an incarnation, it is necessary that they are taught what love is rather than—as they come in you see, they are only mentally and physically concerned about their survival, you see? So it was your position to assist in teaching the children love. To not only love others, but to love self. So again, what have you been doing in this incarnation, my child?

JUDY: Going around in circles?

SAMMYE: Ah, no, no, no. In your marriages, did you not attempt to assist those to love self?

JUDY: I see what you mean.

SAMMYE: To teach them love? You see? With your physical walk, has it not been a major portion of your purpose? To assist those within your environment to love self? Has this not been your work, my child?

JUDY: Yes, I seemed especially determined with William Patrick and Paul.

SAMMYE: So you gave them all you could, did you not?

JUDY: Yes.

SAMMYE: Now it is up to them whether they choose to use it in this incarnation or not, you see?

JUDY: Yeah.

SAMMYE: And look at those who you come in contact with throughout each day of this incarnation as you have become an adult. Isn't there always the thought within the mind to assist them to love? Have you not always attempted to build others up rather than to tear them down?

JUDY: Yeah, I guess I have.

SAMMYE: With the exceptions of the time that you were totally and absolutely frustrated, you see? Now those we will not consider. So again, you know the principles within the mind of the Atlantean time. It is only that during that time, in the later years that some forgot what was the energy that kept everything together. It was the energy of love, you see? And they began to be self-centered, and in their self-centeredness they misused the energy, which created the breakup of the continent, which created the downfall, you see? And many, many, many eons have passed, and now again it is time, and as you see the learning of Atlantis is coming again to the fore, to know that each human being is an individual expression of life. They are an individual expression of the indivisible whole, you see? And coming to know this, that the mind controls. As many have said before, the mind is the builder. It can either construct or destruct. So you are knowledgeable in this area, are you not?

JUDY: Yes.

SAMMYE: Yes. This is good. Now, please do go on with your questions.

JUDY: Is there anything other than the book that I need to work on now?

SAMMYE: Not at this time, no.

JUDY: The cross that I wear was a gift from Jay. Is there any connection between this and the Spanish incarnation? The one in Spain?

SAMMYE: Yes, my child. For there—in another incarnation, after that one which was not particularly enhancing—you see there was an incarnation there, where you gave yourself a time of rest, a time to enjoy life. Only for twenty one years, yet you gave yourself the time to see the beauty of life, to enjoy life in all its glory in that which you call Madrid. There you were female. There you were quite wealthy. There you did not marry. Yet you were free to enjoy life. Now there will be two coming into your environment within the coming twelve months. One male, one the female from that particular incarnation. And these will be of assistance to you, to again enjoy life in this present incarnation. For you see, as you are forgiving self, you are again giving self the opportunity to enjoy. And always remembering that it is not all so-called bad karma. There is also the good karma. Which these who are coming into your life are the result of the gifts you have given. Is this clear?

JUDY: Will I just know when they come in to my life?

SAMMYE: Yes, my child. Yes. This you will. Now, are there any further questions?

JUDY: Is my dad there with you?

SAMMYE: Yes. Do you wish to speak to this one?

JUDY: May I?

SAMMYE: Yes.

JUDY: [*sighs*]

SAMMYE: You're much wiser now, and so am I. When it is time for you to come to this side, you will become even more wise. And you will look at your life as I have. And look at all who have been in your life, and look at the small sins and the large sins, and you learn to forgive. You are very wise, for you are forgiving self. But know this one thing; how much I love you and to forgive me for my sins. I love you. Can you forgive me?

JUDY: Yes, I can forgive you and I love you too.

SAMMYE: And also, anytime you want to talk to me, you can. Just talk and I will hear. Cause I'm getting better. Much better.

JUDY: I thought so.

SAMMYE: I'm learning that it is not wise to be a jackass.

JUDY: [*laughs*] You were a lot of fun.

SAMMYE: So well…that I like. And you are learning to have fun too, aren't you? 'Cause I want you—

JUDY: Yeah, did you meet Jay?

SAMMYE: Yes. When he came. He is well. A little tired but well.

JUDY: Who was with you?

SAMMYE: The angels came for me even thought to some degree I said I didn't believe in angels. They came. There was the archangel Michael and the angel Joseph. They came to teach me what love truly is. It's interesting when you get to where I am that all of the things that you laughed about, that you enjoyed, that sometimes you made fun of, you know, turn out to be rather real.

JUDY: I think I understand.

SAMMYE: So enjoy the laughter, please enjoy the laughter. For that is the gift of the spirit. For the spirit of the totality within you is the joy, the laughter.

JUDY: Well, if anybody could make me laugh, it was always you.

SAMMYE: Yes, thank you for that. For you gave me the gift of your laughter. Now, I'm gonna go. But remember, if you ever want to talk, just talk. I'll hear. And then, as I grow stronger, I'll do something to make you laugh.

JUDY: All right [*laughs*].

SAMMYE: I love you.

JUDY: I love you.

SAMMYE: Bless you.

Now, are there any further questions?

JUDY: I have just one more that I can think of, and that is how the connection in this incarnations is in this life with the UFOs as we call them.

SAMMYE: Those what you call the UFOs are people, shall we say, who have advanced tremendously physically and in science, you see? And they come to the environment of the Earth to learn to advance spiritually. Even if it seems rather ridiculous that the Earth has advanced spiritually, doesn't it?

JUDY: Um-huh.

SAMMYE: But that is the purpose. When they come here, and they observe, they are attempting to find out what is the spirit that makes those which inhabit this planet to continually attempt to find life. For within them, it is the science and it is the physical, you see?

JUDY: I see.

SAMMYE: They are not looking within themselves. And their desire is to find that one physical thing, the one gene, the one cell that makes mankind look continually and lust for life. That part within mankind of this planet that knows there is more to life than what they are experiencing, you see? So hopefully they will find it soon. That it is not within the physical. It is within the soul, within the energy, that is the totality that is God. They are looking for that which creates mankind's lust for the greater knowledge. Not of the physical but of self. That which says, "Who and what am I?" For you see with them, there is not that question. Their eye is evolving around the science and also the physical, which this planet came very close to that approximately sixty years ago, did it not? That everything needed to be science, you see?

JUDY: I see.

SAMMYE: And replicable. If those such as you came again to assist from the Atlantean time to know the lust for the life that is God, the soul. So that—and you would like to teach them too, would you not?

JUDY: [*laughs*] Yeah, I would.

SAMMYE: Yes. Now understanding that as you assist self, you assist others.

JUDY: That's what Jay meant when he said to continue with something that I had started before?

SAMMYE: Yes. For you see, my child, as you assist self, then you give to others your best self. Is this clear what we are saying here?

JUDY: Yes.

SAMMYE: And now we thank you for the opportunity to be of service. And we give you our blessings, and we give you God's blessings. Bless you.

Session Four with Sammye
Past Life Reading

October 10, 1994

SAMMYE: As you have come to see self as the divine you are, know that this will continue, and as to the peace that you desire within self, you will be at that place within the coming six months. Know that as you travel through this incarnations, there will be times where there is challenge again, yet there will remain, within the challenge, the peace that you seek. Is it clear what we are saying here?

JUDY: Yes…

SAMMYE: Now as you are more and more at peace with self, this peace you give to others. When you feel that you are not following your purpose, understand that in giving peace to self, then giving peace to others, you are giving the gift of love, of God, to others. Is this clear what we are saying here?

JUDY: Yes…

SAMMYE: Now, since you are prepared, let us begin with your questions.

JUDY: I have questions about my work and the career that I've held that I gradually seem to be getting away from. What direction do I seem to be going in that and in my financial situation, and does it have anything to do with my lesson in receiving?

SAMMYE: Let us first begin with the career. You will continue to change the career, for as you become more at peace with self, the career you had previously chosen is no longer necessary. Is it?

JUDY: Right!

SAMMYE: Now within the coming twelve months, you will begin a new career. In this new career you will also assist others to become more abundant. Yet it will not be as in the present capacity. You will still be working with advertising, yet it will not be vocal advertising. It will be written advertising. Not just as with what you would call a newspaper etc., but with the newspapers and also the magazines and other forms of advertising. Such as your putting together a newspaper which would bring to many information as to life. Is it clear what we are saying here?

JUDY: I think so…

SAMMYE: Now understanding that this will be to assist others to know peace within self. It will encompass both visual as to paper and visual as to television, video tape, etc. Is this clear? For you have knowledge in this, do you not?

JUDY: Yes…

SAMMYE: Think on this. Has there not been the thought of how you can assist others who have been through similar trauma?

JUDY: Yes…

SAMMYE: Now this will evolve. It is not necessary that you pursue this at this moment. Allow it to evolve. Is it clear what we are saying here?

JUDY: Yes…

SAMMYE: Others will come into your environment to assist in this publication. Yet, there needs be advertisers to defray cost and to produce profit. Is this clear?

JUDY: Yes…

SAMMYE: For without this the cost would be—both for you and for those who desire the information—prohibitive. So in this manner all will share in the production and all will share in the benefit, the profit. Do not allow self to become the sole provider of this. Is this clear what we are saying here?

JUDY: Yes…

FROM BEGINNING TO END AND BACK AGAIN

SAMMYE: Now, as to your other question, please do repeat.

JUDY: I guess the financial part basically. Between one career and working into the other career. And also, is this a part of me learning the lesson of receiving?

SAMMYE: You need not ask that question. You knew the answer already. Did you not?

JUDY: I thought I did…[*laughs*]

SAMMYE: And that is good. That is good. There will be funds coming to you from your own endeavors. Yet you will also have free time as you have begun to give self. To think, to plan, to know. Is this clear?

JUDY: Yes…

SAMMYE: Now, please do go on with your questions.

JUDY: I have started writing on this book, and I write and then I wonder if I'm writing in the right direction.

SAMMYE: Yes, my child, you are writing from the heart, are you not?

JUDY: Yes…

SAMMYE: Then that is the right direction. Yes.

JUDY: OK…

SAMMYE: In fact, you're doing quite well with it, are you not?

JUDY: I…think I'm doing all right. Sometimes I wonder with the amount of time I need to spend on it that is uninterrupted is sometimes scarce.

SAMMYE: Ah, this will improve, you see? This will improve, the time, the amount of time will improve, yes.

SAMMYE: Now…ah…yes…One moment…please…There is another who wishes to converse with you…

JUDY: [*sighs*]

SAMMYE: As you know there is no death, only change. As I was, as I Am, and as I ever will be, so are you. Be consciously aware of your divinity. Do not concern self with fear of becoming out of balance. Either mentally or egotistically. For you have asked of the Father that you remain in balance, knowing that, that which you ask for is given. Do not fear your job, my child. For you are not only capable, you are worthy. As you have chosen to align your personal plan with divine plan, know that all that you need, all that you desire, will be provided. Remembering always, as the Father and I are one, you and I are one. All you need do is ask. I am your servant. Many feel I am the dictator. Yet is the Father a dictator? NO! God the Father is the liberator. Know that as you are part of God, an individual expression of the indivisible whole, that you are also a liberator. See yourself as divine. Know that, that which you place upon the paper, for the inspiration, for the insistence of self can and will be of assistance to others. Remembering, I'm always there, for the Father and I are one, and you and I are One. Bless You!

JUDY: [*sighs*]

SAMMYE: [*sighs*] Now, let us continue with your questions.

JUDY: When I have thoughts or when I have intuition, is my way of knowing the difference between the two based within the emotions that I have with those? Or how do I know what is coming from my own mind is what I'm thinking? How do I tell the difference?

SAMMYE: Ah…when the thought, the intuition, for both the thought is the intuition, and the intuition is the thought. Is it not? There is the feeling. The difference between, shall we put it this way, the intuition and the imagination. When there is the feeling that this will not go away, this intuition thought keeps recurring, and then you know. If it is imagination, it comes…and it goes…Is it clear what we are saying here?

JUDY: Yes…

SAMMYE: That is the difference. And there is also in domain with the intuition, there is the feeling of calmness, is there not?

JUDY: Yes…

SAMMYE: That is good. Yes, please do go on.

JUDY: I've been having dreams lately about my granddaddy.

SAMMYE: About what?

JUDY: My granddaddy! And I don't recall until recently about having dreams about my granddaddy. And I'm still at times having a little difficulty understanding the dreams.

SAMMYE: Um…ah…this is to assist you in knowing that all life is well. This one will also be well. It is not necessary to, how shall we say, concern self, worry about this one. You see?

JUDY: Uh-huh.

SAMMYE: There is the strong karmic tie there with this one as you well know. And so in seeing the dream, the dream represents truth: one the concern, secondly the lack of need for concern. Is it clear what we are saying here?

JUDY: Yes.

SAMMYE: So release the concern.

Now as to the mark upon the body,[27] let it be understood that the son gave you this to assist you in gaining more peace. It was the sign of the *unity* of all. It was the sign of body, mind, and spirit. Also of mind, God, energy, with the further extension to understand the emotions. You see? For the emotions of life are the energy, the governing portion of the energy. You see? All energy is governed by emotion, and if you will look, is not the energy at the top?

JUDY: Yes.

SAMMYE: Then body, mind, spirit. You see?

JUDY: Yes.

SAMMYE: Mind, God, energy, and the emotion, the feeling of life. For this one always was emotional about life. Were they not?

---

[27] See picture of mark on my arm on page 198.

JUDY: Yes.

SAMMYE: And you see to some degree you had, how shall we say, stifled the emotion for a period of time. Had you not?

JUDY: Yes.

SAMMYE: And this was to assist you to know that, that time is past. It is time to live again. Is this clear?

JUDY: Yes.

SAMMYE: Now, would you like to speak to another?

JUDY: Yes, I would.

SAMMYE: Will you ask please?

JUDY: (To Jay…)

SAMMYE: One moment please…

[*She sighs and pauses and then sighs again.*]

Yes. This one is saying it is time to live again. That you know now what it is to be dead and to be alive. Is it clear what we are saying here?

JUDY: Yes.

SAMMYE: Now, please do begin with your questions for this one.

JUDY: I was wondering who the apparition was that Jay said he saw at the Cay.

SAMMYE: Ah…phew…that was, I know now, the Christ which embodies all life. Manifesting itself in a manner, in a way, that I could understand. There is so much I want to say. Yet "thank you" is the greatest of what I want to say. When you begin to see all… everything is one life, that's what I stood for. And the best word to describe the love—that's really life—is the Christ. Look now to your right…See what I saw. All you need do is look [*sigh*]. Look on your left…and you'll see me. You'll write. What you're writing is right. It's much clearer than I could do [*sigh*]. Go ahead and ask the other things now.

JUDY: I wanted to know how you've been trying to contact me so I'll know what to look for.

SAMMYE: When there is…just a minute, I'm getting tired. When I touch you on your cheek, that is one way. The other is when you hear me talk to you. Know what I'm talking about. Don't think it's your imagination. I won't put any more marks, that was only so you'd know it was me. And you did, didn't you?

JUDY: Yes, and I thank you for that.

SAMMYE: I had to let you know that I was all right.

JUDY: I liked that.

SAMMYE: When you feel me touch your cheek—because I know you have the need of the physical touch but listen with your heart, which you always do. Never did do very well listening with your mind, did you?

JUDY: You knew me quite well, you still know me very well [*laughs*].

SAMMYE: I love you.

JUDY: I love you.

SAMMYE: And thank you. Everything you're doing for me. Still it's nice knowing from my side that our love is still there and strong. I was a little concerned, I guess afraid, that I wouldn't be able to feel it here, but I can. And it's even greater. I just—can you feel mine?

JUDY: Yes.

SAMMYE: I want you to know, to feel the love I have for you. And I didn't say had. I said have.

JUDY: [*laughs*] I feel that too.

SAMMYE: I have to go now…but I'm…I'll kinda hang around along.

JUDY: Good. I like my stained glass hummingbird piece.

SAMMYE: Yeah…I'll touch you just a little bit…just to let you know I'm there. But listen with the heart, and remember what Jesus said to you. All you need do is ask. I found that one out for sure [*weak laugh*] I love you.

JUDY: I love you.

SAMMYE: [*sighs*] Please, do go on with your questions.

JUDY: Jason's doing quite well. I know that when he passed, made his transition, that my dad was there.

SAMMYE: Yes.

JUDY: Who…were the other two?

SAMMYE: One…was the Christ, and the other was the Buddha. For this one, it was important that all be represented. Not just one. Is it clear what we are saying here?

JUDY: Uh-huh.

SAMMYE: Yes…ah…One moment please…Ah…. The Father says to tell you that you are extremely inquisitive!

JUDY: [*laughs*]

SAMMYE: Yes…And that is good! Yes…

JUDY: I've really got a…a lot of things that I want to find out about. I can't seem to read fast enough and long enough to find out all the things I want to find out.

SAMMYE: Well, understanding that as you listen to the inner self, you will be guided to that which will give you the most information the quickest.

JUDY: So the inner self is my best teacher?

SAMMYE: Yes…always…*always*! For have you not begun to know when to look where?

JUDY: Yes…I'm beginning to start recognizing that more.

SAMMYE: Yes…and use this in the writing also. That will assist. You're using it somewhat…but more, you see? Allow the words to flow. Then once you have said all that you need to say, then you have the opportunity to place them in their proper position, you see?

FROM BEGINNING TO END AND BACK AGAIN

"You're thinking that this is funny, don't you?" This line was not in the taped session. This was a clear statement that I heard through my headphones as I transcribed the tape recording of the session. It was a male voice, loud and clear. The words came through at a time that I had the cassette player's pause button on. The tape was stopped and not playing at the time.

JUDY: Uh-huh.

SAMMYE: It is not now the time to concern self with what goes where. It is only to concern self with what.

JUDY: I see.

SAMMYE: What goes where will come later. You see?

JUDY: OK!

SAMMYE: Also, would it not do well for you to use the tape recorder?

JUDY: Yes.

SAMMYE: When you are in the automobile, and then this can be transcribed.

JUDY: Uh-huh.

SAMMYE: Would that not move things along quicker?

JUDY: That's true. I do have lots of thoughts when I'm not near the computer.

SAMMYE: Use this and see how it, how shall we say, yes, works for you. For we feel it will go very well. Ah…you have some questions for the father?

JUDY: Father in…?

SAMMYE: Your father!

JUDY: My dad?

SAMMYE: Ah!

JUDY: Yes.

SAMMYE: We have had some confusion here today...in relation to that one, have we not?

JUDY: [*laughs*]

SAMMYE: Yes, please do go on.

JUDY: For my dad, I have a turquoise piece that belonged to him when he was here. And I'm questioning what to do with it. I can't seem to find a value on it. I don't know whether to sell it or hang on to it or to go ahead and give it to someone or what to do with it.

SAMMYE: At this time, allow it to stay with you. You see? Then you will know at a later date what to do. At this time, it needs be with you.

JUDY: OK.

SAMMYE: Yes...and the value...yes there is large monetary value in relation to this, but there is also major, how shall we say, spiritual value in relation to this for you at this time. Is that clear?

JUDY: Yes.

SAMMYE: Yes.

JUDY: In what way could I use that to help me with the spiritual value of it?

SAMMYE: Understanding that from this: for it was very, very, important to the father. Was it not?

JUDY: Yes.

SAMMYE: There is the impartment of your father's energy within that piece.

JUDY: Uh-huh.

SAMMYE: So this one will help you with the writing and will also help you to gain peace within self. Greater peace within self.

JUDY: OK...Is my dad able to talk to me today?

SAMMYE: Yes. He says...don't get rid of anything [*laughs*] at this time... ah!

JUDY: OK.

SAMMYE: Ahhh…dah…see! Ahhhh…

    Now you need things around you that are peaceful, that give you security and give you serenity. Those things that represent me when I was on earth, do that to some degree? Don't they?

JUDY: Uh-huh.

SAMMYE: So later it'll be all right to either give away or to sell that which you don't need anymore. But as you gain strength within yourself, you will begin to share those things with others. Yet not right now. Ah… Umm…You're not really listening when I talk to you, are you?

JUDY: When you talk to me today? Now? Or at other times?

SAMMYE: At other times!

JUDY: How do I know, when you are talking to me?

SAMMYE: When I say things to you, you will have the thought in the mind that is said similar, or maybe exactly as I would have said before. That is when you pay attention. And then allow yourself to relax.

JUDY: OK.

SAMMYE: And then you'll hear. And I know its important for you not to delude yourself, so this is the criteria for all that comes to you. For you are very open now. First, let all information be logical. That's very important, isn't it?

JUDY: Yes, it makes more sense when I understand things. I'm working to try to understand more.

SAMMYE: Second, that the information is consistent…one piece with the other. Third, that the information is always uplifting. And fourth, that it carries with it the feeling and expression of love because that's what you are. Now understand that it's all right for you to get angry every now and then. Cause as you know now, and this is wonderful, you are a spiritual being learning to be human. It would have been nice had I known that before. Trust yourself. You will not delude yourself. Always trust yourself. You are not crazy. I love you.

JUDY: I love you! I have one question.

SAMMYE: All right.

JUDY: You had mentioned before that you would do something to make me laugh. Was that something that happened on the boat?

SAMMYE: Yes! And since then too!

JUDY: [*laughs*] Uh-huh!

SAMMYE: Yes! For you know, laughter is the gift to heal the soul.

JUDY: That was a good one [*laughs*].

SAMMYE: Pardon?

JUDY: The one on the boat was a good one!

SAMMYE: Yes, I love you!

JUDY: I love you too!

SAMMYE: Bye [*sighs*]. Ah…he says, "Wasn't the one at the house as good?"

JUDY: The one at the house [*laughs*]? I forgot which one that was!

SAMMYE: Well, he's gone. You'll have to think about that!

JUDY: [*laughs*] OK!

SAMMYE: Ah, please do go on with your questions.

JUDY: Um, I had a dream that I came into a room, and Jay was standing next to a bed, and he looked more mature, very tan, and that seemed more real than a dream. I'm wondering if that may have been me meeting him in the spirit.

SAMMYE: Yes, my child, yes! He came to you when you were in what your scientists call the alpha state. And you were awake. And you chatted. And the bed represented the rest, so understand that you have been resting and he has been resting and the dream was to let you know that it was not a dream. Yes!

JUDY: Was that more like an out-of-body?

SAMMYE: Yes. And this will occur again…Ah…Also, you will see…this one in the physical form again…soon!

JUDY: Consciously?

SAMMYE: Yes. Not in the out of body as you say, not in the dream. It will be only a glimpse, but it will further reinforce for you the love that you need reinforced right now.

JUDY: I will look forward to that!

SAMMYE: Now we have time for one more question, then we must go.

JUDY: In the first time that I talked to Sammye, she picked up something about flowers in the yard and something for me to watch for that has something to do with my yard.

SAMMYE: That is where you will see Jay. Free. As he chose to be free. It will not be on the water. Is this clear?

JUDY: Yes.

SAMMYE: We thank you for the opportunity to be of service, and we give you our blessings and we give you God's blessings. Bless you.

Session One with B.J. King

June 6, 1995

B.J. KING: As we prepare to enter the realm of spirit, we deliberately open our consciousness to the power of the Holy Spirit, and we ask to have communication with all levels of Judy's oversoul. And if it is appropriate, we also ask to have communication with Jason's consciousness. And we ask to have access to the akashic record.

JUDY: [*deep breath*]

B.J. KING: Have you had direct communication with him yourself?

JUDY: Things like the little crystal ship turning on a solar stand that wouldn't work until after he died, and it was turning when we came home. Lights next to the bed coming on in the night, and the radio starting to play, and things like that.

B.J. KING: Um-huh.

JUDY: As far as hearing from him, I'm not sure. I'm still kind of new at all this. I did talk to another lady who is psychic three or four times in the past year, and she's given me different messages.

B.J. KING: Talking to people who are fairly recently dead is not something that I normally do. Because the direction of the way that my work goes and what I do with people is I...I connect to your oversoul rather than to entities, so to speak. And there is some concern with the fact that he has still been staying in this dimension, instead of going on, beyond into doing the next level of incarnation. Which is interesting because he doesn't seem to be trapped in the astral plane as one might think of a person being who is fairly recently dead, but he does still seem to have some dedication to the idea of remaining in this dimension or remaining close around you. And apparently this has to do with being around until somehow the duration of getting the book written. The duration of the commitment is about the presentation of what all of this is about. What is your focus in terms of writing the book? From your personal experience?

JUDY: It started out telling about the accident itself, and then it got in to more of about messages that I seem to be receiving. And then now in the past two to three months, I've gone back to completing the accident portion of it. When I would start writing on that, it would seem like I would get kind of physically ill and reluctant to get back into it. So it's been kind of a slow process going through that and writing it. But since I've gotten through the accident part—and I'm writing about the first month right now is where I'm at, after it happened—it's getting better. I feel a lot better since I've been getting through that.

B.J. KING: Good. One of the things that we would want to advise about is that, don't hold off on completing it because of a concern that if you complete it, that he won't be around anymore for you to communicate with him. Because my perception is that what will actually take place is once he is released from his commitment of being here until this first edition is completed, that then he will very likely be released and be able to go all the way into the light, so to speak, and make his completion of that cycle. Complete that cycle! And then at that point it's very possible that you'll be able to hear him telepathically in a much clearer way than you've been able to hear him or perceive him while he's been staying in this dimension. Because when they stay over in this dimension, the vibration is not real strong. It can't get very strong because if it got very strong they wouldn't stay in this dimension. So they stay in a controlled energy vibration in order to—it's kind of like a balloon. If you filled it full of helium, it would automatically lift off and go into that other dimension. But if you were continually in a state of either tying it down to something, it would have to stay bobbing up and down in this dimension. But it would have to be very controlled or you would be constantly letting a little bit of the helium out of it in order for it to stay in this dimension. So that's what is going on with him energetically.

His energy is not very high a frequency at this point. But as soon as you would be able to complete the book, then his cycle of what he agreed to do for this particular incarnation, which included the accident and included the visitations… his contract read, he was supposed to be an example of expiration without complete detachment. Meaning expiring from the physical body, but not completely detaching from this dimension. Very much like the movie *Ghost*, would be like an absolute example of what we're talking about. And then the purpose of what that young man's incarnation being to prove that the other world does exist and is interactive with this dimension. So since that was the nature of his contract, that contract will be fulfilled when you complete the book. And then he will make the cycle, but I very strongly suspect that he is a part of a larger energy system that will then very possibly begin to telepathically communicate with you and give you a much broader spectrum of awareness of what all the levels of heaven or all the levels of afterlife are like and about. So short of having your own death experience and coming back—like a lot of people are having now and writing books about it—this would be like the next best way of finding out what that experience is like because you would have a communication like that.

There is another book that was written by a man who lives in South Africa, about his son's death, and his son was killed in an automobile accident in front of him. And then when he got there the son and the friend, you know, were dead. Very shortly thereafter, a psychic, even I think before the funeral, contacted the father and said, "Please call me at this number." Because the son had already contacted this psychic and said that he wanted to speak to his father. And so after a few days the father remembered it, and he went to this other town where the psychic lived. And each time he would go and visit her, the son would actually come through that woman and actually speak to his father in a way that was really obvious to him that it was his son.

So I think that he wants to speak to you but he doesn't have a strong-enough energy vibration with me. Our energy vibrations are not similar enough that I can perceive what he's trying to say, other than that there are other things that he wants to say. But the information that I'm getting is coming from your soul, which is saying that it is important for him to be released from the commitment, meaning completing your portion of the writing, then him released to go into the oversoul.

And it's very possible that the whole oversoul consciousness is then going to communicate with you and tell you a lot about the dimensions. So this will probably not be the only book you write in my opinion. Have you perceived this suspicion yourself in terms that you'll probably write other things?

Judy: The thought has been starting to come into my mind just recently. Especially since I've gotten closer to seeing the end of this one. And I've been thinking, "I wonder where this could be leading?"

B.J. King: Yeah, that's…My belief is it's going to lead…the whole thing has been set up to lead you into a deeper state in belief in what we call virtual reality. This is a form of reality that we think of as very real. But the virtual reality is what is beyond this in the other dimensions and in the life that is going on in the other dimensions. So that's why the terminology is just now coming in as being a household word. The word—terminology "virtual reality" and why there are virtual reality machines or whatever. Because its time for there to be a collapse between this reality and those realities. To prepare for the interaction of what we now think of as space beings with human beings. It's time for that to take place. But the only way that that can take place is for there to be a collapse between the two or the many realities.

Did you have an interest in metaphysics before this took place, before his death?

JUDY: Well, back in the later part of the seventies I had an interest in it. Then my life kind of took a Christian angle, and I kind of got to hearing these messages from ministers and preachers that it was Satan and all this. Jay and I even went to the park together to burn the books that I had, you know [*laughs*]? So your story relates a lot to the things I've been through. So I had kind of put it on the back burner, put it behind me, and then it really wasn't until about the first of last year I read *Embraced by the Light* and—

B.J. KING: Boy she's coming from a very Christian background too.

JUDY: And then I started getting more interested in it. I also had an... before Jay died I guess what you would describe...the only explanation I've come up with is just a knowing that something was going to happen to him.

B.J. KING: Right. Well, I would imagine because of the connectedness that you have with him, that he would have, or at least his oversoul consciousness would have given you some kind of...not warning, but knowingness that his life was not going to be long. Because—and you may have even had that sense his whole life—you know that there was a possibility that he would not live a long life like a lot of people do. Because your prior to...yours together...prior to incarnational agreement was to live out this experience, and it was all prearranged. Not the nature of the accident, but the timing of the accident was arranged. That he would not live to be twenty-six. And the purpose being for the explicit teaching or confirmation to come through, that life does exist beyond the physical body. So through whatever kinds of experiences that you can allow to happen for you, whether that's in telepathy or feeling, that is your mission. And ultimately, it's very possible that you will do some form of radio talk show. Obviously you didn't get this training by any kind of accident as being involved with radio, but there is a possibility that you will do some kind of a combined thing between writing, radio, and television. How does your husband feel about this?

JUDY: He's not too crazy about metaphysics and when ever he sees a New Life anything, he comments how it's kind of a cultish thing or something. I think a lot of people think that. I don't know what he's going to think when he reads the book.

B.J. KING: Right. So he hasn't read it yet?

JUDY: No.

B.J. KING: OK. I think that for you to deny the metaphysical aspect or the beyond-this-life aspect and to try to stay in any form of Christian doctrine about it—or any mainstream kind of doctrine about it—would be as difficult for you as it was for me. You know, to do that would have been death in terms with what my real mission was. And I perceive that, that would be true for you too. To stay in that kind of a structure and yet do what spirit is trying to get you to do, in terms of what you've agreed to and in terms of your bigger contract. I don't see any way that those two things can fit together.

So I think through a set of circumstances, you're being forced into direct communication with your soul. Which is why I would like to recommend to you the method where you anchor yourself in the energy of the earth. You open up the top of your head. You send a beam of energy into your oversoul into the cosmic Christ consciousness version of your oversoul, which is in fact the highest form of Christianity we could participate in. And then open your heart in love and in compassion to your oversoul, to Jason's oversoul, and to whatever the cosmic plan is for your life. And then I think as a result of that, whether you're sitting in front of your typewriter or your computer, or just with pencil and paper in your lap, and beginning to write out any thoughts that come into your mind at all while you are in that state of relaxation. And the way I do it, and the way I did it in the beginning was, I would sit in that position and I would take a deep breath and I would hold that breath to the count of three. Like three, three, three, and then I would release the breath. Then I would take another deep breath and count two, two, two, and release the breath. Take another deep breath and count one, one, one and release the breath. Then I would breath normally and count backward from ten to one. Ten, nine, eight, seven, six, five, four, three, two, one. And you start using that as a ritual of how to go into that state of consciousness, the alpha state of consciousness, and in doing that you train your body.

That, that's what you expect it to do when it goes through that signal, just like the prayer that I go through before I start doing the soul communication. It's just the signal to my oversoul that we're ready to make the connection with whatever, with whoever I need to speak with. So I would recommend this to you in terms of the way that you begin to train yourself to connect with him after he goes into the light and possibly even before then. He will try to communicate with you. But your energy level is high enough that it may not be easy for him to communicate in words. You may feel his presence, you may see something move, you may feel a shadow, you may feel a light, a flash-by, and you may sense something. But in terms of actually being able to telepathically transmit words, his energy level may be too low for that. Because the longer he stays in this dimension, the lower his frequency will get. So at the time that the book gets published or gets completed—I would even say when it gets completed, even before it's published—what I would do if I were you is to do the prayer and call for the angels to come and take him into the light so that he can continue to grow and prosper with full confidence that ultimately you will communicate with him again.

And I know that it's a difficult thing to do because we don't ever want to disconnect. But in order for the constant communication to get established, there's going to need to be a temporary disconnection period. Is this what has been suggested to you by other people? Or have you already perceived this yourself?

JUDY: I pretty much perceived that he needed to be released and able to go on so he can do what he needs to do, and I was feeling concerned that I might be the reason…that I might be holding him back, but I didn't know for sure that it might be because I wasn't getting the book done.

B.J. KING: I think that's what he's waiting for, and so that's why I think it would be important to focus as much time and attention on getting it completed. Especially in a total first draft stage as you can because I think that's what he's waiting for. Because there is some sense about it, that he is concerned that if he doesn't stay around and kind of keep kind of nagging about it [*laughs*] that you might have a tendency to put it in the cupboard and not get it out again, but because it might cause a complication in your life when it gets published. In terms of your relationships and so forth. And he knows that you would probably rather not disturb things to that extent. So he is concerned that it won't get accomplished if he doesn't stay around to kind of pester you about it in some ways.

JUDY: Well, I felt that when I really got the first message to write a book that it was a direct message from him because as soon as I heard, "You should write a book about this," I was thinking, "Me, write a book?" You know, I've written radio copy and song lyrics and poems, and things like that, but I've never written a book before."

B.J. KING: Right.

JUDY: So, I came to the conclusion that, that message came from him.

B.J. KING: Um-huh. That's very accurate as far as I can perceive. But these other books that you could write ultimately could be extremely helpful to people. Because there's so much need for people to understand, not only that we don't die…there's a whole lot of books being written about that now because so many people are having near-death experiences…but people need to be—there need to be more people writing the sort of thing that Ruth Montgomery wrote. Those kinds of books, with her guides that actually tell about the world before, the world beyond. Have you read her books?

Judy: I think those were some I had—

[*light begins to flicker*]

B.J. King: Don't do that to the light, that's not nice.

[*laughs*]

Judy: That I was previously reading.

B.J. King: Right. So you do know about that? But you know, hers are really not as extensive as the information that is available now. That could be given to somebody whose consciousness is like yours, who is very sane and very compassionate and very willing to know these things, even whether they would be willing to write them down and want to publish them or not is another thing. But you are willing to know about other levels of reality, and that's what's important to somebody to be able to write that down. Some of us don't have time to do it. I have the capacity to communicate and the capacity to sit down and write it down, but because of the nature of my mission…I don't right now at this period of my life…I don't have the time to take away from the traveling that I'm supposed to do because not everybody can do what I do yet. Because ultimately everybody would be able to do it. But not right now. Everybody can't do it, so there's a demand for people like me to show up in places where there is a group of people whose consciousness is raised to the point where they are ready to hear those things. And so that seems to be more of a priority cosmically right now than me sitting down and writing these things out. But the nature of your life at this point is that you have that time period where you could sit down and do that, and therefore, it is important to avail yourself for doing it, you know?

Judy: I notice that my husband tends to find different things for me to do to.

B.J. King: Fill up your time?

JUDY: Yeah.

B.J. KING: Um-huh.

JUDY: And get me sidetracked…yes. And I guess I spent two and a half months sidetracked from it because he got me involved in a business and that didn't work out. So just recently he's been trying to get me involved in his business, which I thought otherwise.

B.J. KING: What is that?

JUDY: His business? He has an excavation and demolition business. But I told him that I didn't think that would be a good idea for me to work for him in his business.

B.J. KING: Well it wouldn't be good for your relationship, and it certainly is not in alignment with what you agreed to in your contract, as far as I can determine. So I don't think you would be happy with it, and I think ultimately it would be…it would probably be the demise of your marriage. So it would just depend on what you want to have happen.

JUDY: Um-huh. I really want to get the book finished. I just didn't expect so many interruptions.

B.J. KING: Right. Well, in actuality, you've done pretty well for it to have been just a year. Just to do as well as you are emotionally is amazing. But then to be able to do that well emotionally and to be able to have written as much of it as you have written is really good. It seems important that I send you a copy of this book that the man wrote in Africa.

JUDY: I would like that.

B.J. KING: *From My World to Yours*. It's not in print anymore, but I'll send it to you. Because it's the kind of book that can save people's sanity, who have lost somebody. And particularly if the somebody they've lost is a child. Because they need reassurance that, that person still exists, and this is one of the few books that I've read that's extremely believable. And it's very clear and it's very…it's dramatic and it gives a great deal of depth about what that's like and how that operates and what people do… do after they've been here. You know, between lives. I think that, that if their not going to republish this one, then somebody needs to publish something that's a lot more what I consider authentic and beyond "Well you just go through a tunnel of light and there are these beings." That's what pretty much everybody writes about. They don't go beyond that, to what goes on then. What happens next after that. So I definitely think you have the capacity to do that.

JUDY: Well, I know I've had a lot of help because when I go back and read some of the things or see how it flows and everything falls into place, I don't think I could have done that with just my own power.

B.J. KING: Right. Right. Yeah, I'm sure it's assisted. I'm sure it's ordained to be done, and I'm sure that it's divinely inspired and that you are being assisted. Not only by his consciousness but by your own oversoul consciousness. And the more deliberately you do it, the more factual you'll be able to become in what the afterlife is like. Meaning in the books that come after this one.

JUDY: There's one thing this week that came up that—I always had an appointment book that I kept with me, through my business especially, but I would even write little personal notes. And I have every year for the past eight years, but I can't find last year's appointment book. I searched my house high and low since I've resigned from my job, and I can't find it anyplace. There are certain dates—maybe it won't make any difference—but there are certain dates and certain things that happened on certain days that seemed to be needed in the book. I've seemed a little scatter-brained since last year. I forget certain things.

B.J. KING: That's very normal. That's very normal. Very normal. I would just write the events and not be as concerned about the absolute date that it took place on. Even of the fabrication of a day, as in your own mind it took place. And it's not as absolutely important in terms of chronological order according to your soul the events as to the order they did take place. And apparently there is some reason why it's been taken away or why you left it somewhere. Because they haven't wanted you to deny what went on in between there, but they also haven't wanted you to…kind of like obsess about it, you know, like obsess about "This is when this took place and when this took place," and be reminded by it all energetically, which apparently would have been much stronger to interact with the date book itself. Then it is to just depend on your memory. I know this has happened to me, I keep a day-timer type of thing, and I don't try to keep up with the dates of all these different events that have happened in the last fifteen years since my friend's death, and I know that ultimately I will have to go back and write several things about all this and I will have to go through those day-timers and pick out the dates and so forth. But so far it's almost as if they are frozen. Have you reread any of Ruth Montgomery's books?

JUDY: No.

B.J. KING: Since you burned them all [*laughs*]?

JUDY: No [*laughs*].

B.J. KING: You might want to do that. There seems to be some interest from your oversoul in you connecting to the energies that she was bringing those books through from. Apparently there's some strong inference here that you and she are from the same oversoul family. And so a lot of the same guidance system that she was getting her information from would also be members of your own oversoul. So that might have been one reason that you even felt compelled to read them to begin with. It would be because of the same energy relationship.

JUDY: When I did read them, I was very intrigued.

B.J. KING: You apparently, because of the nature of your mission, being as important as it is to the collective, when the events took place that caused you to react in a way that was intense enough for you to go burn these books and go back into Christianity, it's like a dark kind of…or counterforce kind of energy trying to discourage you from doing your mission. Because they know how valuable the works will be of what you can write and how valuable the information is to the collective in terms of removing fear from people. Fear of death and fear of the afterlife and so forth. And the healing of grief for people. So it was an intentional kind of discouragement that was taking place. So being aware of that may be helpful to you 'cause you can also watch for that in the future to know that if that doubt starts creeping in again, or if you're concerned for your sanity or you're concerned that maybe you're believing something that you're not to be believing, then you won't go back into that same kind of doubt again.

Because one of the reasons someone like me would be brought to talk with you is to affirm the fact that what you are doing is correct. Affirm the fact that there is a bigger mission than even this one book. And to explain that it wasn't just about you, it's about Jason participating in it because he knows how important it is for this information to get out. So for him to go to the trouble to come in, to have such a short life just to prove that is a big job for someone to do, and the two of you to come in and do it together makes it even more important. And to recognize that it's a big thing, it's not just something that you yourself are expected to do, it's something that's a cooperative effort between yourself and your soul.

And your husband's primary mission is providing for you while this takes place. Now if he doesn't get it about that, you know, that is his mission. And if he in any ways, in any active way, tries to deter you from doing what you are supposed to be doing, it is very possible that he may have to be replaced. So I wouldn't be totally surprised if I were you if that does take place. Because if he is this disinterested, or you know, this unaware of what's going on with you, then it may be appropriate for the universe to bring somebody more supportive to you personally while this all takes place. But I do perceive that you will be provided for financially while you are doing the work. That you're not expected to go out and get a job, plus doing the writing. Because the nature of this kind of writing is very demanding energetically and demanding as far as focusing is concerned. So I wouldn't worry in terms as far as that part of it. But it is important that you accept…the importance of the mission is more important than the survival of your relationship, in my opinion and in the opinion of your soul. And there is someone else that can be sent who is willing to fulfill that mission if in fact he does not decide to do that.

JUDY: I've had thoughts about that.

B.J. KING: Um-huh. I'm sure you would because your intuition is very strong and the other reason we're sent to point it out is so that you believe yourself.

JUDY: I appreciate that because there's times when I wonder if I'm flipping my lid and people might think, "Oh, she's crazy…"

B.J. KING: Um-huh.

JUDY: "And that when her son died, she just absolutely lost her mind."

B.J. KING: But the truth is you probably became the sanest that you've ever been at that point. Because we get jerked into reality at that point. Even though as much as we would like to tune out and not face what's going on, we really get confronted with the multidimensional reality at that point. It sure is what happened to me when my fiancé died, and then the reaction of the church to that even more graphically proved to me that, that wasn't the direction. The direction was…is directly linking to God and those other levels of life—period.

B.J. KING: Can you think of any other questions that you think would be helpful to you?

JUDY: Not really. Nothing comes to mind.

B.J. KING: You should have twelve years within which to write the books. And so it's not like it's going to have to happen overnight, but it is quit a large volume of work to be expected even to be accomplished in that length of time. And that's just the time frame in which they feel that it can be the most benefit to humanity, would be for them to come out in the next… you know, during the next twelve-year period of time. You can probably even find…you know, Ruth Montgomery's books are very available now in used bookstores, so you can probably find some of the earlier versions of those if you choose to reread them. Apparently the ones that they would recommend are *The World Before* and *The World Beyond*.

JUDY: I know I had *The World Beyond*, and the others I'm not sure.

B.J. KING: Um-huh. It's interesting how many people that spirit…you know that was one of the very first series of books that they had me read. And I guess that those that are supposed to write things, you know, that will come through telepathically from spirit, that would probably be the best example of somebody that did that and was credible in doing it than anybody else. So I guess that's why they have us read those first. Because I had those on my night table even before I even really understood what I was doing.

I had not read them, but I had purchased them. So it was pretty strange, and then to start reading them and then realize that this woman was doing the same thing that I was doing. It was extremely comforting for me at that point because I had no one to talk to about it. No one I had ever heard of who had that experience. When you wrote the poetry and songs and so forth, were you conscious that they were coming through to you? That the information was coming through to you?

JUDY: No. Just recently I wrote a couple of other poems. I hadn't written poetry in a long time. But recently I wrote a couple that will be published by the Library of Poetry. One in the fall book called *The Garden of Life* and one in a book called *The Best Poems of 1996*. Coming out in the spring next year, I think. But there's only one poem I can remember writing, probably back in the mid-seventies, and that was when my life was…I was just having all kinds of problems with me. Now that I think of it, maybe I do recall maybe thinking that it was coming from someplace, but I didn't know where.

B.J. KING: Um-huh. Were you praying for clarity or guidance or anything during that period when things were seemingly so screwed up?

JUDY: I'm not sure whether I was praying or...

B.J. KING: Or just desperate [*laughs*]?

JUDY: Yeah, I think I was just desperate for help in my life. I was just to the point where I was all messed up. I didn't know where I belonged. I was with my first husband, and I knew that he had somebody else. And I was getting into that same situation of trying to find somebody else too and Jay was just a child and it just wasn't my kind of life. There were too many parties and just too much going on. It was just...

B.J. KING: Crazy making?

JUDY: It was messing up my entire peace, you know?

B.J. KING: Um-huh. Did you ever read Ruth Montgomery's books about walk-ins? Did you ever get that far in the series? *Strangers Among Us* and *Aliens Among Us* and *Threshold to Tomorrow*?

JUDY: I have had some unusual experiences with...and I really don't have all the answers on all this...but I've seen things. Lights and...there was a light hovering over the car one night when Jason's father and I had been in an accident, and even since I've been in North Carolina I've seen things. But as far as aliens, you know like they say, the little beings and that type of thing, I don't know that I've seen anything like that. But I have seen the lights and a craft.

B.J. KING: This is an interesting book. I was led to start reading it last night. Called *Preparing for Contact*. It's written by a woman, Lisa Royal, and Keith Priest, and they are people who live out in Sadona. And I met her several years ago and listened to her channel several years ago. She's talking about it in here, and the entities that are talking to her in this book are telling her that most of us have contact when we're not conscious. Being like when we're asleep or when we're...whatever. And therefore we don't remember any of it. And that the way to prepare for contact is not to sit and focus on it and demand it or whatever—you know pray for it or whatever—but to admit that it probably has happened already and to admit that we're not opposed to it happening in a way that would be more evidential. But just preparing our consciousness to accept it as a normal part of reality, and it's much more likely to cause a direct contact to take place than anything else that we can do.

Because sitting in meditation for it doesn't speed up the possibility for it happening or so forth. But my perception is that when you're out of your body, that you do have a lot of contact. Not only with extraterrestrials but what we would think of as other-dimensional beings. Beings that operate in other dimensions including the angelic realms. So I think it's just a matter that you're still keeping the veils intact. That kind of protects your third-dimensional consciousness from stimulus overload of taking all of that in all at one time as your reality. Because as I said last night, they have a tendency to all talk at one time once they've found somebody who's open to listening.

So I think getting into a state of willingness to perceive all that you are capable of perceiving might be a helpful thing to you. Cause in that way they can begin to start kind of dribbling the information down into your consciousness in a way that will be structured enough that you can take it down. But it won't be coming in such volumes that it will be overwhelming or fearful to you. And I think practicing this meditation or sitting in this meditation briefly whenever you have time to do that, or when you're alone and have the freedom to do that, could be very insightful for you.

And if you ever receive anything and you need, you know, want to discuss it with me or feel, you know, where it's coming from or can I trust this or whatever, you can either send it to me and I can write you back about it, or you can call and tell me what it is or whatever. Because what you're going to do is important to all of us. So I would want to be very supportive of what you're going to do.

JUDY: There's been times when I can tell…when I just start to wake up and I'm not completely awake yet, or I'll hear something come into my mind. Yesterday morning I woke up with a name: Jon Savogne Pepperidge.

B.J. KING: Wow. That's an interesting name, isn't it?

JUDY: And this morning I woke up with…this sounds funny but… Larry's Rose Scents.

B.J. KING: Rose? Larry's Rose Scents? Hum!

JUDY: And then I sometimes have pictures in my mind with things, like people.

B.J. KING: You might want to take notes on it. Like you say, just write down whatever is there because in my experience whenever the things first started coming through, that's what I did. I kept a journal beside my bed, and when I'd wake up in the morning or if I woke up in the middle of the night and had to go to the bathroom, sometimes there was something there in my head. You know that…or I was in a state of a dream that I knew that wasn't a dream, that was like a vision, or I'd been someplace or something. Then I would just take time to write it down.

A lot of times when they start giving information through, they do it in the middle of the night. Somewhere between one o'clock and five o'clock in the morning because the airwaves are clearer at that point, and the telepathy is easier. Because there's not so many energies bombarding the airwaves at that point. So should that begin to happen, it would be to your advantage to sit up or go in another room if it disturbs your husband, and to take down whatever the information is that comes into your mind. Particularly if you begin to be awakened at a specific time every night, that's usually a sign that, that's what is trying to happen.

Judy: I've written a lot of things down in my...I'm not too good at this but I do try to keep a little tape recorder somewhere too.

B.J. King: Um-huh. I've never been as good at recording it as I am about writing it down for some reason. I don't know why that is. I bought one and I keep it beside the bed, but I still haven't used it very much.

Judy: It's easier for me to recall things if I just write a couple of words to help me to remember it.

B.J. King: But that, but that may be important in the future if they're creating characters for a book that they want you to read—or write, I mean. They may be giving you names now that they intend for you to use in terms of the names for characters and so forth in the future. So could be that kind of a very unique kind of name that they want to use for someone.

So everything is important in terms of what comes through, and writing it all down in terms of keeping a...a sort of a dairy about it is important. Because then ultimately in my experience, it all began to fit together in a way that made sense to me. Because obviously it did not in the beginning. It would be just like one word or one sentence or one part of a sentence making it's way through at first before it got to be long paragraphs and things. And I can see now where even before that one day, when a book fell off the shelf and I sat for the deliberate meditation and received the seven pages, I can even look back now and realize that there were glimpses or blips of information coming through before then. But I never understood before that, that's what they were, and I didn't write them down.

Judy: Yes, some things that have happened before to me in the past have begun to clear up a little bit now too, as for the meaning.

B.J. King: Um-huh.

Judy: Why it's happened or why I couldn't remember it until now. Different things.

B.J. King: Right. And I perceive that, that is what has happened with your extraterrestrial contact too. You've had it, but there is some reason that you don't want to remember it yet. And then when it becomes more mainstream and when it becomes more normal for everybody, then the memories will probably begin to reveal themselves to you. Particularly the way your life was in Kansas.

Judy: Yeah. That was my first time that I can remember seeing them.

B.J. King: Uh-huh.

Judy: I guess I was either twelve or thirteen. At least that's the first time I can remember it.

B.J. King: Uh-huh. But I don't perceive that you're going to be expected to use your ability in terms of doing readings for people or in terms of doing counseling for people. I think almost all of it will be done in writing, on talk shows.

Judy: Well, the other lady, the other psychic lady that I had talked to before last year, she had also mentioned something about that. That I would be doing something different after the first of the year, involving video, print, and the audio type of communication.

B.J. King: Um-huh.

Judy: And recently I was introduced to a lady who has a TV program in Raleigh, similar to what we're talking about. Maybe I'm just now being put together with these different people.

B.J. King: I'm sure. Um-huh. Because particularly once the book is published, you know there will be more and more of that. Obviously people wanting to talk to you, people wanting to interview you about what your experience is. And the more public exposure that you can allow about that, then the more that you will be completing what you came to do. Because it's about speaking about it, and its about writing about it and making it believable to people. Looking credible when you're presenting the idea to people. Which is one reason that you would have been raised a certain way and gone into a professional life, where you developed a professional persona and a professional image that would ultimately be used in a way that is…that comes across as nice. You know, a nice kind of presentation for television and radio and so forth.

It's interesting how everything that we've done up to the point where we wake up is all used in…it's all part of the education to prepare for the way we do the mission. I think that it would be important for you to possibly reread the books about the walk-in experiences. Because that apparently will…you will apparently have some kind of powerful experience about that. That would be something that you would ultimately write about. So you might want to refresh your memory about the things she said about it too.

JUDY: OK. I really can't remember that when I read them. I know I read the books, but I can't remember about that.

B.J. KING: Right. If you don't have some belief in it already or some kind of personal experience about it, it's not a concept that's very easy to grasp, or one that a person would even want to retain probably. Unless they have a personal experience or know someone well who is having that experience. And then it's useful, the things that she says about it.

I don't agree about everything she says about it because from my perspective, I think that the person walking in, or the entity that's walking in, is from the same oversoul as the entity that's leaving. So it's the same soul energy but a different level of that same soul energy. And in the impression that she gives in the book, it's just an entity. It just comes into the body of the person that no longer wants their body. And I think that there are several different ways that, that agreement gets made. Some people a prior incarnational contract where one part of the soul will use the body for X number of years and then they are going to let another part of the soul come in and use it for the remainder of the time. And then some people get into an incarnation, and they get very tired. And they get very depressed, and they just want out. And so in that case, rather than letting them destroy the body, another part of the oversoul will come in and more or less rescue that person and let that person go back into the soul and rest.

So there are several different ways that it takes place. And then sometimes, nobody walks out. There is a second energy that comes in and braids itself in with the energy that's already there and just expands the consciousness, and then there's a composite energy there that finishes out the lifetime.

JUDY: When you were saying that, it made me think that…I wondered if finishing the book, this book…would be my chance to walk out and let someone else come in to finish the other books.

B.J. KING: Well, I think…I think there may be a possibility that when this part of it is finished, when this book is written, it may be that they choose to braid in. Not that you will get to leave, but they may choose to braid in another level of the consciousness of the oversoul in with your physical body so that the amount of energy capacity that's available to write the rest of the scenarios will be larger than what your capacity is, which is one soul's lessons here. And in preparing yourself for that emotionally and intellectually, then when the time comes where it might take place energetically, you would be more receptive to it, there would be less resistance and there would be less fear and you could walk through it much more gracefully. And it could be more to your advantage than it would be a detriment. But that's probably why they're suggesting that you read it. Not that you already are a walk-in, but that you have the capacity to become what we call a composite soul. And composite soul is not something that she references at all, which is why I'm telling you that my belief goes beyond what they told her at that point.

There's a conference going to be held in September in St. Paul, Minnesota, where I've been invited to come and speak, which is a walk-in conference where walk-ins from all over the world are being invited to come there together and meet and to be supportive of each other and help each other to understand what has happened with them and so forth. So it is a concept that's becoming more and more known all the time. But it's a concept that's in all actuality happening more and more with people now because there's more and more people who don't want to stay and don't want to finish out the incarnation.

First Group Session with Barbara Rollinson, MS

June 27, 1995

BARBARA: Dear Lord of the Universe, we ask for thy loving protection to be with us this evening. I ask to be a perfect and open channel and that all information received will come with clarity and from the highest sources. We give thanks for the great blessings and healing that is taking place upon our planet at this time. For all the opportunities that come to us, for the many challenges that are given to us, and for the great gifts that are bound all the time.

This is my channel's Oriental guide, and I bid you welcome. I am indeed most pleased to enjoin your energies with this channel. I wish to give you a bit of information first, and then we will deal with your inquiries. It is to understand that each individual have certain guides, masters, angels and so forth that are abound them. Meaning that oftentimes you will feel a certain energy that is there with you.

Sometimes it is most observable and sometimes it is very subtle. Sometimes you are not even aware that there is this energy that is around you. But each of you has been given this opportunity of experience, so you will find that there will be times when this guidance will be given to you. There will be times when you will receive certain feelings, certain information, and also certain protections. Each of you in your own particular way will be given an opportunity to perceive these. And in this evening you will find that there will be more than one opportunity to have this experience. So I simply give you this bit of information, and we will now deal with your inquiries [*pause*]. We will deal with questions.

MALE GROUP MEMBER 1: I have a question that concerns some research that is being conducted in Florida, with dolphins and people with physical disabilities. It's operated with a group out of Key Largo that's called Dolphins Plus. I read an article about it. It seems that the researchers there…and I talked with one of the doctors, one of the biologists there that the patients come, they go out into the water with the dolphins. The dolphins are semi-wild, and when the dolphins are with the patient, oftentimes the patient describes that all of their pain disappears. And they are not sure how that takes place. They think it's happening on some type of biochemical level. They are doing research by drawing blood out of the patient before the session with the dolphin and afterwards to study what changes in the blood chemistry are occurring. And I'm wondering if you can give us some insight on what you feel is happening there?

BARBARA: Well, it is a bit more than just chemical. Often times the chemistry of the physical body does not respond to the research as readily as do certain brain wave conditions and so forth. What is happening in these particular cases, particularly with conditions of pain? Pain is a messenger. Pain is a way the body responds. Not just to the physicality of it, but to the core issues of what is going on that is causing this particular disharmony within the physical body. So what happens when they are put into water? First of all they are allowing themselves to be in a very lighter gravitational condition, so it is helping to have the body be more buoyant, more supportive, and so forth.

Secondly, it is, whether they are aware of it or not, taking them back into a condition of when they were in the fluid of the womb. In other words, it is taking them back to a situation where there was not pain, there was not concern, and there was not a way of having to deal with the outward world.

Thirdly, the condition of bringing dolphins or the dolphins have the opportunity to send out certain signals that are not readily discernable by the humans. In other words, they are of such high frequency and so forth, and such low intensity so to speak, that the individuals just know that something is going on. What they are doing is changing the patterns of the brain, and they are bringing in a different...not only chemical reaction, but different patterning to the brain itself. To the condition of sending information to the body that says, "You are protected, you are supported, and you do not have to be in a state of pain."

Now often times what occurs is that the pain is gone for a period of time, but it returns because the core issues of the physicality of the body have not been completely eradicated, so they need to be back there again. This will be more understood as there is continuing communication, telepathic communication, between humans and dolphins. The individuals with these particular pain syndromes, when they are opened up to the telepathic communication, dolphins can then relate through. Well I will simply call it communication...because what it is, is transferring a concept, a thought to the human, and then the human can be able to understand...ah yes...what it is at the core issue of why this body is being given this particular lesson to learn, why the pain is being given as the messenger and so forth. So there is in the infancy of this particular exchange at this time, and there will be more that as individuals open up they will begin to respond and talk about, "Yes, this is what I received. This is the experience that I was having." And then this will be documented and so forth.

When individuals, meaning the scientists or the doctors or whomever, wish to duplicate these particular experiments, it doesn't work, and I will tell you why. These particular experimentations are not done on just the physical level. They are done on many different energetic levels. So that each one is individual unto itself. What will happen with one individual will not necessarily happen to the next. So simply saying "We will do this particular thing, and then all the people who have this particular kind of pain will receive this kind of treatment and so forth,"—it doesn't work that way. Dolphins understand this and give on an individual basis whatever is needed for that particular person. Do you understand?

MALE GROUP MEMBER 1: That's making it clear. Thank you.

BARBARA: So that is what is happening. It is in the beginning, as all things need to start, and there are many more who will realize that dolphins are not only healers, they are communicators, and they are here to be as teachers to the humans. And do we have further questions?

FEMALE GROUP MEMBER 1: I have a question. In the past year, I have had a lot of physical problems that were unexpected, and I wondered if there is anything that you can tell me that would shed some light on that.

BARBARA: What is the major concern of the physical body?

FEMALE GROUP MEMBER 1: Well, cancer. And that seems to be under control now. But there just seems to be a…I don't know if it's from age coming on or if there's something that I'm not doing right that's causing some of this or what.

BARBARA: Let me give you a little broad-based information first, and then we will deal with your specific inquiry. I wish to address the whole idea about age. Age upon the physical body, on your earth plane, has many different dimensions. It isn't just physical because there are many who are chronologically young but very mentally and emotionally old, so that the physical body deteriorates more quickly. What you think and feel affects the physical body.

Conversely, what you are doing to the physical body also has an effect upon the emotional and mental and even spiritual states. What is happening now is the opportunity for individuals to recognize their potential to be who they are.

When you have a potential that is recognized, an awareness of it, then there can be certain steps that can be changed to correct an old thinking pattern, to correct an old feeling pattern, and so forth and so forth. Do you understand?

What I'm saying is…what you think you are, not what you do to exercise the physical body. Not what you do to put into it. It is what you think and feel about it. If you think certain foods are beneficial, then they will be. If you think certain foods are detrimental, then they will be. It is letting go of the assumption that certain things are good, bad, or indifferent. What you need to recognize is that the body knows how to repair itself, how to take care of itself, what it needs to eat and how it needs to move and so forth. What is most important is to listen to the physical body, not what someone else tells you what to do. But listen to the physical body.

There are always health facilitators that you can get information from and so forth and then to say, "How do you want to use it for the physical body?" But if you only turn your physical body over to a health facilitator, then you don't have any input to it. And if you don't have any input to it…and if you don't have any input then you don't have any output either. In other words, what I'm saying is, if you don't listen to it, then you aren't going to know.

Many of the experimentation's that have been done by drug companies, for instance, have been very outmoded because they are done by very specific conditions and specific areas of population. Mainly male. Only now are they beginning to use some statistics about how do certain drugs and so forth affect the female. Then they will begin to understand, how it does directed to the individual because each individual has different needs, tolerances, and so forth. Instead of blanketly saying "Well you get this drug, you take it this many times, and you take it for this length of time" regardless of who the individual is. Do you understand?

FEMALE GROUP MEMBER 1: Yes.

BARBARA: What has happened with yourself is that you have opened up the possibilities of looking at yourself differently, of allowing yourself to be involved in the healing process. There have been times when you have been quite annoyed at some of your health practitioners. Do you understand?

FEMALE GROUP MEMBER 1: Yes [*laughs*].

BARBARA: And so there has come about this feeling, "Well, I want to do some investigation, I want to listen, I want to find out," and so forth. Because what you got was very conflicting opinions and so forth. And what you realized is that when you are in the process of allowing yourself to heal, of allowing yourself to release, then you are in the process of knowing who you are. One of the things that you have truly wanted to know is what is your connection to your spiritual? Your spiritual life. You have feelings about it, but when there were spiritual disharmonies in the body, you thought, "Uh-oh, what have I done? Something is wrong. I'm doing something wrong. And what you were doing is something very right. And the reason for this, in speaking in terms of right and wrong, is you allowed yourself to truly be in touch with yourself. Do you understand?

FEMALE GROUP MEMBER 1: Yes.

BARBARA: You would have not done that if these certain conditions did not apply. First of all it is to recognize that you are a giver. You know very well how to do that. Very easy. Done it all your life. Been told all your life that, that's what you're supposed to do. What has not been there is knowing how to receive. Do you understand?

FEMALE GROUP MEMBER 1: Yes.

BARBARA: And in this process, you learned now that you could receive information, energies, health practitioner help, and so forth. But you are the healer. Do you understand?

FEMALE GROUP MEMBER 1: Yes. Thank you.

BARBARA: So what you are doing at this particular time is allowing yourself to pay attention. It has nothing to do with age, dear lady. It has to do with perception. Has to do with what you are willing to give to yourself. What you are willing to say no to. That word hasn't always been very large in your vocabulary. You are learning to use it more frequently now. And as you learn to do this, so the body responds by saying, "Yes. I understand, I know what to do. She's allowing me to function. I don't have to give her another symptom. I don't have to give her another condition to deal with." Cancer is not coming back. Do you understand?

FEMALE GROUP MEMBER 1: Yes!

MALE GROUP MEMBER 2: I have a question.

BARBARA: Yes.

MALE GROUP MEMBER 2: As far as guides, the theory or concept—that's a better term I think, of having guides—I was wondering if there is anything within your mind, if there is anything that I need to hear. Because, you know, I want to ask you a million questions and none of them seem to be coming out right, so I figured if there is anything that I need to hear in particular, if you can keep from embarrassing me too bad, then just let it rip [*laughs*]. Without being too, pardon my language, I'm not sure…I'm sure you know what I'm talking about exactly, but no disrespect intended.

BARBARA: Well, we're not going to embarrass you. What is here for you is a recognition of an energy, and what I am being allowed to do is to step aside and have this energy come to you. So I will retreat and then I shall return.

My name is Mary. I was known as the mother of Jesus. I come to you so that you may feel my energy. That you may know that unconditional love surrounds you. You have this path of white to walk upon. It is to know that you do not walk it alone, that it is not in darkness. That you know your true purpose and to know that I am with you. This is a way for you to recognize that deep within you there is the experience of your own knowledge, your own wisdom, and the ability to discern all that you wish to do. I am here only as a reminder. Only as one who comes with light. Who comes with love. To bring you healing and to bring you comfort. Blessings to you.

MALE GROUP MEMBER 2: [*sigh*]

BARBARA: This is my channel's Oriental guide again, and we will go on with inquiries?

JUDY: I would like to ask about my step-father who has recently passed and how he is doing.

BARBARA: And what is his name, please?

JUDY: Russell...

BARBARA: This one is giving many thanks for those who helped release him. In other words, he was having some difficulty in allowing himself to be released. Do you understand?

JUDY: Yes.

BARBARA: And in this process, there were yourself and others who were able to say to him, whether you were aware of this or not, "It is all right, you can be released." And this energy gave him the opportunity to do that. What he is doing at this particular time is being in what I would call a quiet state. It is a little akin to your sleep state. Although the individual is not asleep, but just resting quietly. Being attended by those who are there to help, and when it is appropriate and when he asks for it, then he will be guided into other avenues of learning and so forth. But he wishes you to know that he gives much appreciation and sends much love to his family.

BARBARA: We have reluctant sitters here. Are there any other inquiries?

MALE GROUP MEMBER 3: Yes, I have one. Around 1974 I was out on the beach, and it was a full moon—not a full moon, but a new moon evening which was, which I'm sure you're aware was all black darkness—and me and my animal were walking up and down the beach and we sat upon this hill and we were there for a couple of hours, you know, just enjoying it. And over my head came seven stars came shooting over going towards the east. And I was facing east, and I was wondering what kind of meaning that would have or whether—or should this be a direction for something to search at?

BARBARA: Well this is all very interesting. I've been also told to move aside and allow someone to come through to you that will give an explanation for this. So I will return later.

MALE GROUP MEMBER 3: [*sigh*]

BARBARA: We are the sisters of Pleiades, and we have chosen to come to you not only for the explanation of what you have received that particular evening, but the continuation of what has happened. That was a visual introduction to those from our planetary galaxy. You have known our energy in another lifetime. And so it is in this lifetime, you come back to the earth to experience and understand the connectedness of other planetary conditions. Because of the knowledge that you had received in that lifetime, so you are able to communicate with that galaxy again. In that particular manner, you will have in your dream state, or quietude of state, visitations of our energy. It is not that you must do anything or even remember, but it is to know that the energy that emanates through you makes a constant circular connection between yourself and that galaxy. This time upon the earth plane you will know a greater appreciation of this interstellar communication. You have also been taken upon other vehicles so that you could be given remembrance instructions. Again, it is not that you have to know of what to do or how to do it. But it is opening that particular communication so that you will seek other ways to communicate upon your land. Ways through the animals, ways through the plants, and even the minerals. We cannot hold our energies any longer, but we wish to give you many blessings.

BARBARA: This is my channel's Oriental guide and I am again up to receptivity of your inquiries.

MALE GROUP MEMBER 4: I have a question that deals with the relationship and non-relationship between a person's mind and his memory in his emotional experiences. And what I would like to…for me, when I meditate or when I'm not meditating and I have an emotional experience of I guess a more refined quality of some type of feeling, why it is when I come out of that feeling that I cannot remember what it felt like? I know that I was there, when I'm in it I know exactly what I am feeling, and yet when I come out of it I can't intellectually remember it. And I'm wondering, is there a technique to bridge that gap between remembering it intellectually, thinking about it and actually being able to go there again?

BARBARA: Well actually, it isn't an intellectual exercise. So that when you come back, if you are trying to grasp it on an intellectual basis so that you can go back, so to speak, it doesn't work that way. What is occurring is that you are going into a different energy level, a different dimension. So that in that dimension all is clarity. Crystal clear, so to speak. And when you come back into a denser energy, you cannot bring that necessarily back with you. What is happening is that the opportunity to change the energetic level from the physical body to the mental and emotional and spiritual bodies are now upon your earth plane. So you are gradually changing the energetic level to be able to remain in that other dimension more and more frequently. Do you understand?

MALE GROUP MEMBER 4: Somewhat.

BARBARA: What I'm saying is that in order to be able to remain more constantly in that, you have to change the physicality of your body. That's one thing. You have to change the energetic level of the thinking process. You have to acknowledge that there is a feeling level that is also in it. Let me give you a little broad-based information. In the past, well quite a few centuries, the feeling body has not truly been acknowledged. In other words, it has only been acknowledged when there has been a vast dramatic condition of the emotionality of the physical. Do you understand what I mean?

MALE GROUP MEMBER 4: Not really.

BARBARA: Well, it is like, if there is anger, if there is jealousy, if there is pain, if there is hurt, that is what has been acknowledged. And it has been said, "We don't want to deal with that," so it has been pushed away. And what has happened is that there has been a suppression of the emotional body, so that it needs to be acknowledged, honored, and fed now. And going into these different dimensions is helping to feed that particular body. What is also needed is to change the denseness of the physicality of the body, and this is done on a very minute step by minute step. Because if you did it all at once, you disintegrate. Do you understand?

MALE GROUP MEMBER 4: Um-huh. Right, right.

BARBARA: So all of these things are working to preserve the consciousness of your earth and all it's inhabitants. As well as to change the density: the density of thinking, the density of feeling, even the density of some individual spirituality. So that eventually your earth and all that are upon it will not have to have the dense physical body to deal with. Now this is not going to happen for eons of time, but it is going to happen. That is the direction that these energies now are being given.

So that is why many times individuals will feel certain changes in the physical body for no apparent outward reason. For instance there may be sudden irony, a drain of the physical energy, you will feel very tired, and you will think, "Well I haven't done anything, why am I suddenly tired?" Because you are taking on these finer energies, and it is utilizing all of the energy systems in the physical body, so it is like you have done a hard day's work.

Also, there are times when you are sparked to have a greater burst of energy. These are coming in wavelike motions. It is not that you are bombarded constantly, but there is a wavelike motion that will come when you will feel more energized and sometimes when you will not feel as energized. It also gives you a time of adaptability, of taking in these energies so that the physical body, which is the one you are most conscious of, does not have to be battered around but can begin to change the DNA for instance—can begin to change the genetic coding, can begin to change the cellular memory, and so forth. And as that happens, so it is also taking on the changing of the thinking process, the intellectual processes, and so forth. The intellect has been stressed for many eons of time. As the way in which things need to be carried on. What you are finding is that the intellect which created much of the technology upon your land is just destroying it. So there is a coming to change these compatibilities. You don't have to throw the technology away, but there needs to be a compatibility to have a remembrance of the spirituality. A remembrance of the emotional body and then the physical body. To come into harmony for this.

That is why at this particular time, there is much talk in your media and so forth, about the pollution, about changing the way that people live their lives, and so forth so that they don't have to pollute their energy systems, and their land, and so forth. So all of this is part and parcel of that.

Now in speaking of the remembrance, because of these changes of energies, what you are going to find is the minutia, I will call it, of remembrance is not going to be supported as much as it has in the past. In other words, the intellect is not going to hold on to all the little bits and pieces that are not particularly necessary for your existence. But it is opening up more avenues to take in a greater picture to see what the bigger picture is and so forth. Now what causes consternation among your peoples is that they are used to being able to keep everything in nice neat little compartments as their thinking goes. And their compartments have all vanished, and it is like having this big soup that's there with many different ingredients. But you really don't know what everything is until you dig down and bring up maybe one or two different ingredients and so forth.

In this particular timing, there will be certain little tricks that individuals will rely upon. Like writing things down more often or checking back and so forth so that they will feel more comfortable in carrying the energy of these little bits and pieces of information. That is why there is a grand and glorious "upsurge" of all of your technology and computers. Because these wonderful little machines can hang on to all this minutia that you don't have to. So there is a reason for it to be upon your earth plane, and you can rely upon its systems and you don't have to overload your system. Do you understand?

MALE GROUP MEMBER 4: Um-huh. Right.

BARBARA: And are there further inquiries?

MALE GROUP MEMBER 3: I have another question.

BARBARA: Yes!

MALE GROUP MEMBER 3: Is there anything about that artifact I found on the beach that you can add that I need to know, or is there anything more specific that you can add to that?

BARBARA: Well, I'm going to give you a little bit of information around that. First of all, it is to recognize that you have an ability to tune into these artifacts that you call them. What you are not quite trusting is that when you get flashes of insight or using your intuition and so forth, you are now thinking, "Well, perhaps that is not correct." What she did was to simply confirm much of what you already know. Do you understand? Is that clear?

MALE GROUP MEMBER 3: Common sense wise, yeah. Is that what you're saying? The common sense part of it?

BARBARA: If you want to call it common sense, you can do that. I'm talking about specifics. When you gave her certain words or you gave her certain information, and she reiterated by giving you information back, you resonated to certain information. So what I'm saying is that you have an inner knowing that you are not utilizing to its fullest. So it isn't so much that someone else tells you about these things, what they are really doing is simply confirming. It is like if you want to find out how old something is, you go to a particular archeologist or someone who understands this or has the machinery in which to look at it, and it may or may not coincide with what you really feel about it. What I'm saying is it doesn't matter what others say. They can confirm or not confirm.

You are now being given the opportunity to open up all of the avenues to bring this information to you as specifically as you want it. What is not there just yet is the trust in that. Do you understand?

MALE GROUP MEMBER 3: I think so.

BARBARA: I know so. Now I'm going to give you some other little bits of information. It is to recognize that you have opened up a… well I will simply call it a doorway of opportunity. There has been specific reasons that you have been drawn to these series of artifacts and so forth. Because you are now allowing yourself to listen inwardly. You are allowing them to call to you, to speak to you. You are allowing yourself to push out all the boundaries that says, "I can only do things according to what I think or feel or see, taste, touch, and so forth." Because this is on a very different energetic level.

What you are doing is not only listening to the particulars of these different pieces. You are listening to the energetic level of the earth. And what I mean by that is that there are whole grid systems that circle your earth. Above it, below it, through it, in it, and so forth. And you are tuning in to these different vibrational conditions. That is why there will be a certain energy at different places that you will be drawn to. Now the hooker that they have for you—"they" meaning certain guidances that are here for you—is that you have an interest and an energetic drawing for coming together with these particular pieces. But you are also being in areas where there is high energetic earth energy that you are tapping into.

What you are going to find is that it is changing your lifestyle. It is changing the way you think. It is changing the way you believe. You may resist it, that is fine. You could deny it, that is fine. All of the things that go on with any kind of addictive behavior. What I am telling you is that you have opened this door for your soul's purpose. Do you understand?

MALE GROUP MEMBER 3: Yeah, I think so.

BARBARA: Well you will understand more as you allow yourself to participate in it.

MALE GROUP MEMBER 3: Is there a particular guide? Like maybe an native American guide or Indian guide? Or should I just keep going with the way it has been and listen to…since you're here at this time, this would be the opportunity I would think to talk to any guide. This kind of gets back to the first question doesn't it? Well, I just want to know.

BARBARA: Well, then you must listen inwardly. That is how you are going to know. And it is to release yourself from conditions that hold this back. You may do this in whatever form that you want to. But you are understanding this very clearly within yourself. That if you continue to live a lifestyle that does not permit this openness of communication, then you are going to shut down a wonderful opportunity, and it is going to affect your physical body. And any time things are shut down, whether it is a mental energy, an emotional energy, a spiritual energy, it eventually comes into the discomfort of the physical body. Do you understand?

MALE GROUP MEMBER 3: Yeah.

BARBARA: So, it is up to you. And as to guidance, you will recognize when this guidance is with you. You not only have American Indian guidance, you have angelic guidance, and you have a doctor that is with you. You have many who have been with you before. So it's like you come with a whole entourage, and they work in concert with each other. So it isn't that you simply have to know, "Well I have an American Indian guide, his name is such and such." That is not the point. The point is, it is that you allow yourself to tap into those energies. It isn't how you do it, it is that you do it. Do you understand?

MALE GROUP MEMBER 3: Yeah, I think so.

BARBARA: Good!

MALE GROUP MEMBER 3: Is there any particular reason why they would pick me to find certain objects? Or is that just the way it works with each individual's situation?

BARBARA: You have chosen to do this on a soul level. It isn't that they look down and they say, "Aha, this is the one. We're going to turn our attention on him." No, it is your energies that bring them. Do you understand?

MALE GROUP MEMBER 3: No. I don't.

BARBARA: What I am saying is that guides are not simply showing up because they pick you. Your energy connects with them, and they offer to be of service. That's how it works. You see, they never interfere with anyone's free will. But they are always on call, so to speak. So when a individual is ready. Whether they are consciously aware of this or not, they are there to help and be of service in whatever manner that, that can happen. Is that clear?

MALE GROUP MEMBER 3: Yes it is. Thanks.

BARBARA: Good!

JUDY: I would like to ask another question. I am writing a book. It was inspired through the death of my son, Jay. I would like to know at this time, where I need to go with the writing and—

BARBARA: Have you completed this project?

JUDY: No.

BARBARA: One of the reasons that you are feeling a bit stuck is that you have completed a certain part of this journey through grief and so forth. And it is like having to conjure up what that feeling was about. Do you understand?

JUDY: Um-huh.

BARBARA: And because of that, it feels almost like it is something of a… more mechanical rather than flowing. When you first started, you were very full of it. Full of the feelings, full of the remembrances, and so forth. And it was easier to put this down. Easier in the terms that it was flowing. Now because you have released a great deal through this process, through the writing process and so forth that you are feeling, "Well, where is this going to lead? What kind of an ending am I going to put on this and so forth? It isn't just for myself, this is for others. So how do I express that and so forth.?" Do you understand?

JUDY: Yes.

BARBARA: What I would suggest to you is that you allow yourself to quietly come into contact with the one who left. Just quietly. And allow that individual to help you culminate what is and so forth. That will be beneficial for others. This is not to feel that…well you really want to get on with it because you feel that you have finished this part of your life, this way in which you have allowed yourself to release things and so forth. So you just want to get on with it, you want to finish it. But this part is even as equally as important as the first part that you did.

JUDY: Right.

BARBARA: And so it is allowing yourself to now open up to a more universal way of expressing yourself, of saying to many who have gone before you and who will continue to have different kinds of experiences this way. What it is that you feel can be best helpful through your experiences, through your thoughts, through ways in which you have perceived things, and so forth. What this particular project has done for you, not only in releasing conditions, but it has brought about a broadening of your own spiritual and…I will simply call it intuitive development. You have found a way to keep your heart open. Do you understand?

JUDY: Yes, I do.

BARBARA: You thought at first, it would have to close forever. That it would not be able to bear if it was left open. You felt to vulnerable and so forth. This is part of what you can reiterate to others. Do you understand?

Judy: Yes.

Barbara: The importance of keeping the heart open.

Judy: Thank you.

Barbara: You're most welcome.

Female Group Member 1: I have a question.

Barbara: Yes.

Female Group Member 1: I've been doing some writing too, and I have the feeling, although it's something that I've always wanted to do and I sort of pushed it aside until I had the illness last year, and I feel that, that sort of gave me a new direction to my life, which has been very valuable. It might never have happened if I had not gone through that experience. I would like to know what I can do to continue in this direction and things that I can do to advance the work that I am doing now.

Barbara: What is the project that you are doing right now?

Female Group Member 1: Well, I'm finishing a project on a collection of ghost stories, and I want to continue writing, but not that particular thing. Just some more stories.

Barbara: What...well there are two things that this particular project helped you with. First of all, it let you know that you really have talent. You weren't too sure. And you looked at others and you read books and you thought, "Oh, I wish I could be like that" or "I wish I could write that well." And what this has done is to give you an appreciation that, yes indeed, you have a great deal of talent. It gives you a part of your own creativity and so forth. This is what you would call the fluff, the light stuff. Do you understand?

Female Group Member 1: Yes.

Barbara: This has been a fun project in looking at different things. What you are going to learn through this project are certain techniques of research, certain techniques of not only how to put the words together, but how to release any tension that is there. So that if you want to go back and change a little of this and do a little of that, you can do that without feeling "Oh dear, I'm not good enough." Do you understand?

FEMALE GROUP MEMBER 1: Yes.

BARBARA: So this is your introduction. This is a way in which you can fulfill a project. There are others who are depending on you for this. Do you understand?

FEMALE GROUP MEMBER 1: Yes.

BARBARA: And so you felt obligated in some form. That yes, you had to get your part of that out and so forth. Now you want to reach in on a deeper level and bring about stories that are quietly curled up in you. And that will open up avenues for you to research things, to find ways in which you want to express yourself, and to truly appreciate the gift that you have. So that is all part and parcel of this first project.

FEMALE GROUP MEMBER 1: Thank you.

BARBARA: It is not going to be so difficult as you thought is was.

MALE GROUP MEMBER 6: I have a question about symbols. We have, I think in our culture, a lot of different societies either present or in the past that have produced symbols and left symbols with us and we have pyramids in Egypt. We're still trying to figure out what they're doing there in the middle of the dessert, and we have the blocks in Stonehenge, we have the temple at the top of the mountain in Machu Picchu, and we have the monuments on Easter Island. We have all these things on this earth that are symbols that we don't understand, that came evidently from another era. We try to figure out how they were built and constructed. We create these elaborate theories that thousands and thousands of workers carrying blocks up hundreds and hundreds of feet, that weigh many tons, but really don't make a lot of sense but never the less that's all we have to work with.

BARBARA: Well, you have a great deal more than that to work with. I would just interject that.

Male Group Member 6: Yeah. But I have a question about symbols that have been with us in all cultures and in numbers. I want to know what significance is there tied in with numbers? In other words, the number one is always the number one. Whether you're here or in the past or whatever culture you're in. The number two is the number two. It might be called something different, and I'm wondering, do these numbers, which are symbols, represent a stability that is almost like a part of God that never changes?

Barbara: Well all symbols are a part of God. And let me tell you a little bit about symbols. The ones that you are speaking of have come later. So they have been created to have a certain energy. All symbols were that way. Whether it was in hieroglyphs, whether it was in nature, or whether it was in writing. Words are symbols also. So all of the symbology that has been used for humankind throughout all the eons of time have come not only because of regularity, but because there was a need.

The symbol of the letters have one sort of circumstance. The symbol for the mathematical symbols have another set of circumstance. They were created so that there would be, as you call, a regularity. Because you can put these symbols together, and sometimes they will make sense to individuals and sometimes they won't. Just the same way as the symbols of the different letters and so forth. It is the perception of how they are to be used that comes from the individual. There are now people who are studying the energy around particular letters and particular documentation of math symbols and so forth.

All of it, all of it, began in the mental processes. It was observed long ago through nature. How did nature receive it's symbolic way? And there were more and more ways that individuals wanted a consistency. Hence came letters in whatever form they are, and hence came the numbers, and so forth. It still depends on how they are used and the perception of the individual. There are ways in which there are very complex mathematical equations and so forth that your average person does not understand. But a mathematician or a scientist and so forth, that has to use them all the time. They are a part of his tools so to speak, or her tools.

That is the way that they are consistently then turned over and over and over again to have a way in which to communicate. That is all symbols ever have been, is to the art of communication. When you look at different number systems you will find that there are different energies perceived by how these numbers are to be used. If they are used by certain scientists, they are used in one way. If they are used by astronomers, they are used in a different way. If they are used by a numerologist, they are used in a different way. But the numbers are still there to provide a regularity in something that is recognized. Do you understand?

MALE GROUP MEMBER 6: I understand, but I still feel like these symbols have a certain attraction. People have a certain attraction to symbols. For instance if I say the word "Oreo," everybody in this room sees those two chocolate wafers with vanilla cream inside, and we have an affection for them. We have this symbol that reminds us of this delicious cookie. Now I know that I feel that way, but now I'm starting to see numbers. And I have a reoccurring thing where numbers come up, like I see the number seven and I go, "God, I love that number," and I'm thinking, "Why do I love that number? I shouldn't be in love with a number."

Although I know that the number is representing…it's a symbol of some type of energy, and I don't know what the energy is, but nevertheless I'm having a feeling. And even though I don't understand why I'm having the feeling, I'm having it. So I don't doubt that it has some significance in my life. And that's what I was trying to ask in terms of these symbols and these numbers. Who are they representing? What energy are they representing? That makes them manifest in everybody's life?

BARBARA: Well, again, look at where they came from. They came from an intellectual idea. There was some regularity that had to be used in a particular way so communication could be done. You are still speaking of communication of how you relate to the symbol. So it is on an individual basis even though there is a certain regularity, there are certain conditions that are taking place and so forth and of understanding why this regularity takes place. But that is above and beyond what you are talking about. What you are talking about is the actual energy of the symbol. I would suggest that you investigate numerology. You will find it most appealing to your intellect and to your visceral feelings about numbers. Do you understand?

MALE GROUP MEMBER 6: Well, I hope I will later. But for now I do, yes. Thank you.

BARBARA: Good. And I will answer one or two more questions.

MALE GROUP MEMBER 3: I have one for you. Earlier I was telling you about an experience that I had when I was a younger man. And something I kind of left out of the picture was, as I was sitting on the beach and these stars had gone over my shoulders and was heading towards the east, I noticed as they got out towards the end of the horizon, they kind of all split up. And the brightest star I can remember was one that was going toward the south.

And since that time, a lot of things in my life have brought kind of southern interests. Like I am really into the Aztec's and the Mayan ruins and the SECCA's and everything is far south. I'm just wondering if maybe that particular star was…I know you said the last time we talked that it was a overall type picture of where the Pleiades, and I didn't know if that played a major part of the deal or if it is just something calling me from the south to direct my energy towards the south. If that makes sense.

BARBARA: Well one of the things that you are very much directed to do is to investigate much of what has gone on in ancient civilizations. And this particular experience that you had was a remembrance. They were directing remembrances to you so that you would then go and investigate. Does that make sense to you?

MALE GROUP MEMBER 3: A little bit. It's kind of strange because as a kid I had a fascination for the civil war, and this has kind of shook everything up here in my life for a few years. And why I'd be attracted to the south after growing up in the west. But anyway, I guess the south wasn't this route is what I'm getting at. It's real south, like South America or Central America. If that makes sense.

BARBARA: Well again, it is that you are allowing yourself to pay attention, to have an awareness. That these are interests of yours and you do investigate and it is leading you. There is a purpose for it. If you look at the synchronicity of things, having this particular experience when you did and then the different experiences as you call them as being in southern places, is part of this synchronicity. What is also being directed to you is from the area of the Pleiades. North, south, east, or west excluded. Do you understand?

MALE GROUP MEMBER 3: Yes, but I also have another question as I asked you. One is…is the southern star at the Pleiades…is it one of the brighter stars or is it…I don't know…It's the attraction of the southern star, I'm assuming, that's pulling me towards that light.

BARBARA: Yes. You have been there before.

MALE GROUP MEMBER 3: I'm sure I have. I'm just wondering if it's time for me to go again? That sounds kind of far-fetched, but—

BARBARA: What you are doing in this incarnation is grounding that energy in to the earth itself. To have a place for that energy to expand. Meaning the energy from the Pleiades. There are many who are interested in that particular energy and so forth, and there are many who are also quite frightened of anything that sounds like it's coming from something that is not upon the earth. What you are doing is allowing that energy to come through you. In to the earth itself, then to spread out and make a welcoming energy that is there. Do you understand?

MALE GROUP MEMBER 3: Yes, sort of. I'm trying to balance it out, but yes to an extent.

BARBARA: So you have given yourself over to the experiences of things, whether they are in the south, whether they—if you look at what they are alluding to, they are alluding to different historical events that completely changed certain parts of the country, of the earth. Do you understand these?

MALE GROUP MEMBER 3: Yes.

BARBARA: And that then you have the opportunity to change the energetic level of what remained there. Whether is was of a negative or a dramatic or a war condition or whatever. Because many of these different civilizations did not thrive. Do you understand?

MALE GROUP MEMBER 3: Oh, yes.

BARBARA: And so you allowing yourself to be acquainted with it, bringing in the Pleiadean energy, putting it into those places, whether you visit them or not, you can mentally or through your quiet time bring that energy into those places. To again clear and cleanse that particular area. Do you understand?

MALE GROUP MEMBER 3: Yes, I do. Thanks.

BARBARA: You're welcome. And any last question that I might entertain?

JUDY: I would like to ask one last question.

BARBARA: Yes!

JUDY: Carolyn is married to my oldest stepson, and she and I seem to have a connection with each other. Is there anything in our past that you can tell us about?

BARBARA: You're speaking of past lives?

JUDY: Yes.

BARBARA: Well to see…what you have noted is that there is almost a stronger connection to her than to him even though he is your son, do you understand?

JUDY: My stepson, yes.

BARBARA: And this has come about because you have had...yes you have had a time with her before when she was a child of yours, and in that particular incarnation, she died in infancy, and you felt that there was something you should have done, could have done, would have done and so forth. The circumstances were that she was taken from you. This was a wartime condition, and she was literally taken out of your arms and destroyed, right before your eyes, and you lived and you felt that there was something you should have been able to correct or do or something.

And there was this feeling through several different lifetimes searching for her. In this lifetime, she has come back, and you will find that there will be an affinity of interest and affinity on certain emotional levels and so forth, to complete this particular cycle. Do you understand?

JUDY: Yes.

BARBARA: Thank your stepson for doing so well...

JUDY: Um-huh.

BARBARA: In bringing her back.

It is time for me to leave for there is one other who wishes to come. But I wish to tell you all, in allowing yourselves to open up to the opportunities that abound, whether you are aware of your abilities or not, does not matter. It is the awareness of the opportunity and then to allow yourself to push out the boundaries that you have felt in the past. Each of you will be given opportunities to allow yourself to do this. So I say congratulations to you, give you great blessings, and I leave you now.

[*Pause*]

BARBARA: I am Michael. I come from that realm known as the archangels. In this realm, we visit frequently those who call upon us from the earth. This is a time of the strengthening of these interactions. It is a time when the veil threatens to come down. It is a time to see beyond what you can see now. Know that we are with you. Know that we send much love, much light, and much protection at all times. We come as a group, we come as an understanding and a wisdom, and we will impart these, as you are willing to accept them. Know that our blessings are with you on a daily basis. I leave you.

[*Sighs*] I'm coming back now [*sigh*].

About the Author

Judith J. Miller does not have formal education in writing. There aren't any big titles accompanying her name. Her portfolio does not include a long list of published work.

Writing experience for Ms. Miller derives from the self satisfaction of putting feelings into words and placing them on paper in the form of song lyrics and poetry. Her career in radio allowed for the writing of hundreds of pieces of commercial copy—most heard and then forgotten.

The book written about the death experience of her only child did not come easy. At least not until the painful *event* was dealt with through writing. When presented with the original idea of writing the story of this experience, Ms. Miller thought to herself, "Me? Write a book? I don't know how to write a book. All I've ever written was song lyrics, poetry and radio copy. How could I ever write a book."

The suggestion was heard as a gentle voice speaking in her right ear one afternoon, shortly after the death of her only child, a son named Jay. Without a doubt, Ms. Miller believes this prompting came from her son. Soon after that, multiple people hearing about her son began to make the same suggestions.

In late November of 1994, Ms. Miller resigned from her radio career to pursue the challenge of facing the truth about life and death, by writing this book. Through this process, a second book has been evolving and a relationship with the other side of life—as we know it—has come into focus.

Ms. Miller credits assistance from the other side for the completion of this first book and the prompting of a second. She does not feel as if she could ever accept all the recognition for the writing.

CPSIA information can be obtained
at www.ICGtesting.com
Printed in the USA
FFOW04n1547161014
8036FF